ENHANCING EAST ASIAN SECURITY COORDINATION

East Asian Security

Series Editors: Fu-Kuo Liu
(National Chengchi University, Taiwan)
Dean Karalekas
(University of Central Lancashire, UK)
Masahiro Matsumura
(St. Andrew's University (Momoyama Gakuin Daigaku), Japan)

Published

Vol. 2 *Enhancing East Asian Security Coordination*
edited by Dean Karalekas, Fu-Kuo Liu and Masahiro Matsumura

Vol. 1 *Defense Policy and Strategic Development:*
Coordination between Japan and Taiwan
edited by Fu-Kuo Liu, Dean Karalekas and Masahiro Matsumura

East Asian Security – Volume 2

ENHANCING EAST ASIAN SECURITY COORDINATION

Editors

Dean Karalekas
University of Central Lancashire, UK

Fu-Kuo Liu
National Chengchi University, Taiwan

Masahiro Matsumura
St. Andrew's University, Japan

World Scientific

NEW JERSEY · LONDON · SINGAPORE · BEIJING · SHANGHAI · HONG KONG · TAIPEI · CHENNAI · TOKYO

Published by

World Scientific Publishing Co. Pte. Ltd.

5 Toh Tuck Link, Singapore 596224

USA office: 27 Warren Street, Suite 401-402, Hackensack, NJ 07601

UK office: 57 Shelton Street, Covent Garden, London WC2H 9HE

British Library Cataloguing-in-Publication Data
A catalogue record for this book is available from the British Library.

East Asian Security — Vol. 2
ENHANCING EAST ASIAN SECURITY COORDINATION

Copyright © 2025 by World Scientific Publishing Co. Pte. Ltd.

All rights reserved. This book, or parts thereof, may not be reproduced in any form or by any means, electronic or mechanical, including photocopying, recording or any information storage and retrieval system now known or to be invented, without written permission from the publisher.

For photocopying of material in this volume, please pay a copying fee through the Copyright Clearance Center, Inc., 222 Rosewood Drive, Danvers, MA 01923, USA. In this case permission to photocopy is not required from the publisher.

ISBN 978-981-12-9829-5 (hardcover)
ISBN 978-981-12-9830-1 (ebook for institutions)
ISBN 978-981-12-9831-8 (ebook for individuals)

For any available supplementary material, please visit
https://www.worldscientific.com/worldscibooks/10.1142/13987#t=suppl

Desk Editors: Soundararajan Raghuraman/Kura Sunaina

Typeset by Stallion Press
Email: enquiries@stallionpress.com

About the Editors

Fu-Kuo Liu is a research fellow at the Institute of International Relations and a Professor at the International Doctoral Program in Asia-Pacific Studies (IDAS), College of Social Science, National Chengchi University, Taiwan. He is also the Director of the Taiwan Center for Security Studies (TCSS). His research focuses on Asia-Pacific security, Asian regionalism, national security and the South China Sea, the peace process across the Taiwan Strait, US strategy in Asia, Asian maritime security, and Taiwan's foreign and security policies.

Dean Karalekas is a research fellow at the Centre of Austronesian Studies at the University of Central Lancashire. He earned his Ph.D. from the International Doctoral Program in Asia-Pacific Studies at Taiwan's National Chengchi University and serves as Editor-at-Large of the security journal *Strategic Vision*.

Masahiro Matsumura is a Professor of International Politics and National Security at Osaka's Momoyama Gakuin University, also known as Saint Andrew's University. He received his Ph.D. from the University of Maryland at College Park, USA, and has held various fellowships, including at Harvard, Brookings, and NCCU-IIR.

© 2025 World Scientific Publishing Company
https://doi.org/10.1142/9789811298301_fmatter

About the Contributors

Sadamasa Oue is a senior fellow at the Institute of Geoeconomics. A retired Lieutenant General of the Japan Air Self-Defense Force, Oue is a graduate of the National Defense Academy of Japan and received his Master's degrees from the Harvard Kennedy School and the National Defense University.

Kuo Tzu-Yung is a Strategic Analyst at the Taiwan Center for Security Studies. He received his Ph.D. from the Department of Diplomacy at National Chengchi University, in Taiwan. His research interests include international relations, international security, and China issues.

Michał Lubina is an Associate Professor of political science at Jagiellonian University, Krakow, Poland, and was previously a MoFA Taiwan Fellow researching Taiwan's female leadership in comparison to Myanmar's. In his research, he mostly focuses on contemporary Myanmar and on Russia–China relations as well as on other East and Southeast Asian issues.

Hon-min Yau is a Professor at the ROC National Defense University. He received his Ph.D. from the Department of International Politics, Aberystwyth University, UK. His research interests focus on global security and national security policies.

vii

Takeuchi Toshitaka is a Professor of the Department of Global Studies, Faculty of Global Engagement, at the Kyoto University of Foreign Studies, Japan. He is also a Professor Emeritus at Osaka University, Japan. He took part in the Comprehensive Test Ban Treaty (CTBT) negotiations as legal advisor to the Japanese Delegation at the Conference on Disarmament in Geneva, Switzerland.

Alexandre Calvo is a law graduate of School of Oriental and African Studies, University of London (SOAS) and a former Guest Professor at Japan's Nagoya University. His research focuses on military history, security and defense policy, and international law, and he has a strong interest in the Taiwan Strait.

Li-Chung Yuan currently teaches at the International Doctoral Program in Asia-Pacific Studies at Taiwan's National Chengchi University. He received his Ph.D. in War Studies from King's College London. Dr. Yuan's military career covers a wide spectrum of services including Air Force Academy, National Defense University, Combined Logistics Command, Intelligence Division of MND (J2), and Air Combat Command as Defence Attaché to the UK.

© 2025 World Scientific Publishing Company
https://doi.org/10.1142/9789811298301_fmatter

Contents

About the Editors	v
About the Contributors	vii
Introduction	xvii

**Chapter 1 Establishing Japan–Taiwan Military Ties: A Legal
Breakthrough**   1
Masahiro Matsumura

1.1	The Differences in Legal Benefits and Protection between the American and Japanese Cases	3
1.2	The US Case	4
1.3	The Japanese Case	7
1.4	Non-combatant Evacuation Operation (NEO) As the Key	9
1.5	Necessary Amendment of the Self-Defense Forces Law: A Lesson from the Kabul NEO	12
1.6	Conclusion	14
Acknowledgments		15
References		15

**Chapter 2 Changes in Japan's Strategic Views on the Taiwan
Emergency and Its Implications for Japan–Taiwan
Relations**   19
Sadamasa Oue

2.1	Basic Stance on the Taiwan Issue of China, Taiwan, US, and Japan	20

ix

x *Contents*

2.2	Changes in Japan's Strategic Views on the Taiwan Contingency	21
	2.2.1 Review of the National Security Strategy	21
	2.2.2 Changes in strategic views concerning the Taiwan Strait crisis	22
	2.2.3 Japan's vital national interests in the Taiwan Strait crisis	24
2.3	Japan's Strategic Approach to Taiwan Emergency	25
	2.3.1 Challenges to deter the Taiwan Strait crisis	25
	2.3.2 Credibility of US military intervention	27
	2.3.3 Window of opportunity for China's military invasion	29
2.4	Suggestions for Japan–Taiwan Relations to Prepare for the Taiwan Crisis	30
	2.4.1 Overcoming the "One China" policy constraint	30
	2.4.2 Importance of strategic communication with China and Taiwan	32
	2.4.3 Issues requiring coordination with Taiwan	33
2.5	Conclusion	35
Acknowledgments		35
References		35

Chapter 3	Establishing Military Cooperation Between Taiwan and Japan: Policy Suggestions and Problems	39
	Kuo Tzu-Yung	
3.1	To Promote the Exchange of Military Intelligence	41
3.2	The Exchange of Military Intelligence Between Taiwan and Japan	42
3.3	To Develop Exchanges of Military Personnel	43
3.4	To Build Military-Technical Cooperation	45
3.5	To Conduct Joint Military Exercises	46
3.6	To Enable Direct Talks Between the Militaries of Taiwan and Japan	47
3.7	The Problems of Military Cooperation Between Taiwan and Japan	48
	3.7.1 No diplomatic relations	48
	3.7.2 China's pressure	49
3.8	China's Huge Market	49
3.9	Conclusion	50
References		53

Contents xi

Chapter 4	Russia–China Entente and the Challenge to East Asian Security *Michał Lubina*	57

4.1	The Literature	58
4.2	The Burden	60
4.3	From Turned Backs to Back-to-Back	62
4.4	The Art of Ambivalent Support	66
4.5	The Sino-Russian Challenge to East Asian Security	68
4.6	Conclusion	71
References		72

Chapter 5	An Evolving Approach Toward Japan–Taiwan Security and Defense Coordination *Hon-min Yau*	77

5.1	The Challenges and Opportunities of Taiwan–Japan Cooperation	79
5.2	Intelligence Sharing: A First Step to Improving Understanding	81
5.3	Chartering Toward Defense Cooperation: A Needed but Challenging Step to Increase Interoperability	87
5.4	Reducing China's Ability to Exploit the Security Context Over the Taiwan Strait	88
5.5	Conclusion: From Risk Management to Conflict Management	90
References		90

Chapter 6	Is a Taiwan Crisis Also a Japan Crisis? Japan's Complicated Security Laws *Takeuchi Toshitaka*	95

6.1	The Pelosi Visit and Its Aftermath	96
	6.1.1 The Pelosi visit and China's missile launch	96
	6.1.2 Japan's concerns and reactions	97
6.2	Opinions in Taiwan, Japan, and the US	98
	6.2.1 Taiwan	98
	6.2.2 Japan	100
	6.2.3 The United States	102
6.3	The Taiwan Relations Act and Japan–US Security Treaty	104
	6.3.1 The Taiwan Relations Act	104
	6.3.2 Japan–US Security Treaty	105

xii *Contents*

6.4 Japan's Complicated Legal System and What Japan Can Do 107
    6.4.1 What has Japan been doing recently? 107
    6.4.2 Japan's official position and constitutional
        restrictions 108
    6.4.3 Japan's complicated security laws 110
    6.4.4 Possible scenarios and a hitch 111
    6.4.5 Time-consuming 113
6.5 Tabletop Exercises 114
    6.5.1 Explaining a tabletop exercise 114
    6.5.2 How it went 115
6.6 Concluding Remarks 116
Acknowledgments 117
References 117

Chapter 7 Placating China is a Losing Game: Regional Security
           at Risk Without Taiwan–Japan Mutual Defense 121
           Dean Karalekas

7.1 An Intertwined History 123
7.2 Taiwanese Ambivalence about Japan 125
7.3 Japanese Ambivalence about Taiwan 125
7.4 The Diaoyutai/Senkaku Impediment 127
7.5 Placating China: A Losing Game 131
7.6 Negotiating Security 133
7.7 Conclusion 134
References 135

Chapter 8 Unprecedented Danger: Japanese Visions of
           Taiwan's Ordeal and the Role of Deterrence 137
           Alexandre Calvo

8.1 Unprecedented Danger 137
8.2 The Japanese Constitution, Collective Self-Defense,
    and Taiwan 139
8.3 Japanese Capabilities, Morale, Public Finances, and
    Industrial Base 143
8.4 Japan and the Doctrinal Debate on Taiwan: Non-lethal
    Force at Sea, Unconventional Warfare, Porcupine Strategy,
    and Deterrence 147
8.5 Lessons from Ukraine: A Wakeup Call for Tokyo and Taipei? 148
8.6 Summing Up: The Fate of Taiwan and Japan are Intertwined 149
References 151

Contents xiii

Chapter 9   Air Superiority: The Critical Element for Denying
a PLA Invasion of Taiwan   153
Sadamasa Oue

9.1   The PLA's War Plan and Military Balance   155
   9.1.1   Joint Island Attack Campaign   155
   9.1.2   Military balance of air and missile power   156
9.2   Defense Strategy for Taiwan: Active Denial   159
   9.2.1   Options for deterrence and defense   159
   9.2.2   Implementing an active denial strategy   160
9.3   Active Denial Strategy and Air Superiority   162
   9.3.1   A prerequisite to other operations   162
   9.3.2   Force protection and counter air operations   163
   9.3.3   Securing air superiority   165
   9.3.4   Force posture for active denial strategy   166
9.4   Policy Implications of the Overall Defense Concept   167
   9.4.1   Insufficient force protection measures   167
   9.4.2   Forward defense vs. active denial in coastal
campaign   168
   9.4.3   Tenacious resistance necessary   168
9.5   Conclusion   169
Acknowledgments   169
References   169

Chapter 10 Prescribing Taiwan's Submarine and Mine
Acquisition Policy: A Japanese Perspective   173
Masahiro Matsumura

10.1 The Strategic Context   174
10.2 Political Obstacles   175
10.3 Policy Alternatives   177
   10.3.1 Little operational need   177
   10.3.2 Inadequate technological capabilities   178
   10.3.3 Fiscal constraints and low cost-effectiveness   180
10.4 Weapons Systems Alternatives   181
   10.4.1 Small submarines   181
   10.4.2 Minelaying subs and AUV/UUV   183
Acknowledgments   184
References   185

xiv *Contents*

Chapter 11 Evaluating Taiwan's Defense Strategy in a Time of
Uncertainty: Diversified Challenges and Dilemma
of Responses   189
Hon-min Yau

11.1 A Recess of Liberal Order and Looming Military Threat   190
11.2 From Security Dilemma to Security Challenge   192
11.3 A Porcupine Strategy   194
11.4 Reflections on the Porcupine Strategy   196
11.5 Misconception of Taiwan Strait Contingencies   199
11.6 From Preventing War to Deterring Invasion   201
11.7 Enhancing Asymmetric Capabilities Over the Taiwan Strait   202
11.8 Policy Implications   203
11.9 Conclusion   205
References   206

Chapter 12 Unmanned Aerial Vehicles: The Answer for
Taiwan's Defense Capability Build-up   211
Takeuchi Toshitaka

12.1 General Defense Postures Compared   212
    12.1.1 Taiwan's defense posture   212
    12.1.2 Defense budgets compared   213
12.2 Addressing the Widening Gap   214
12.3 Review of Taiwan's Defense Concept   216
    12.3.1 The overall defense concept   216
    12.3.2 ODC's interest in drones   217
    12.3.3 The Washington factor   219
12.4 Unmanned Combat Aerial Vehicles   220
    12.4.1 Merits and utility of drones   220
    12.4.2 Swarming is key   222
    12.4.3 Proliferation of UAVs   223
12.5 Recommendations for Taiwan's Approach to UAVs   225
    12.5.1 China's interest in UAVs   225
    12.5.2 Taiwan's interest in UAVs   226
12.6 Recommendations   228
12.7 Concluding Remarks   230
Acknowledgments   230
References   230

Chapter 13 Taiwan's All-Out Defense and Enhancement
of Reserve Capability   235
Li-Chung Yuan

13.1 Taiwan's All-Out Defense   236
    13.1.1 Defense mobilization system   236
    13.1.2 All-out defense education   237
    13.1.3 Efforts for enhancing the capability of all-out defense 238
    13.1.4 Efforts to enhance all-out defense education
         and exercises   240
    13.1.5 Reserve force: Major pillar of all-out defense   241
    13.1.6 Gaps and shortfalls of the ROC reserve force   242
13.2 Reforming Mobilization of Reservists   245
    13.2.1 Revamping the reservist recall system   245
    13.2.2 Restructuring the reserve force   247
    13.2.3 Establishing the all-out defense mobilization agency 249
    13.2.4 Synchronizing weapons for active duty and
         reserve units   250
13.3 Recommendations   251
    13.3.1 Creating a territorial defense force   251
    13.3.2 Integrating reserve force into the overall
         defense concept   253
    13.3.3 Recruiting part-time volunteer reservists   254
13.4 Conclusion   255
References   256

Index   259

© 2025 World Scientific Publishing Company
https://doi.org/10.1142/9789811298301_fmatter

Introduction

Dean Karalekas, Fu-Kuo Liu and Masahiro Matsumura

The war in Ukraine, now well into its second year at the time of writing, continues to rage on in Europe, causing political leaders and defense planners in East Asia to re-evaluate many of the assumptions that have guided policy in this region. While the threat of armed attack by the People's Republic of China (PRC) has long been a vague and distant possibility, many thinkers largely believed that in this postmodern era, the sort of armed territorial aggression on one country by another, of the sort ordered by Russian President Vladimir Putin, was an anachronism: a holdover from mankind's less-enlightened past. Geopolitical disputes, it was believed, were now to be solved by dialogue and diplomacy, and naked aggression was confined to the dustbin of history. Alas, Putin showed the world the fallacy of this thinking, and since his invasion of Ukraine, plans and preparations for a similar attack on Taiwan, by a similar leader — China's Xi Jinping — have had to be taken off the proverbial backburner and addressed with a renewed sense of urgency.

Japan in particular — second only to Taiwan itself — is at risk of having what degree of geopolitical stability that exists in the region shattered by such an eventuality. Indeed, even the language that is commonly used to describe a potential Taiwan War highlights the difficulty of coming to terms with such a radical departure from what has largely been a trendline away from political violence and toward peaceful resolution of disputes between nations. "Taiwan contingency," for example, or "Taiwan crisis," the latter encapsulating slightly more urgency than the former, fails to convey the full weight of the threat should the events that have been playing out in Ukraine be even partially replicated in Taiwan. Putin's alleged Mariupol Massacre stands as a war crime, the city reduced to rubble with barely a fifth of its pre-war population remaining. Likewise, the brutality on display during the alleged Bucha Massacre, visited upon women and children, proved that no one was safe from this type of warfare — at once new and yet very, very old — that is quickly becoming the new norm.

The history of the People's Liberation Army (PLA) shows ample precedent for how the lessons of military engagement in faraway lands are swiftly learned and adopted by PLA commanders and strategists. Will the widely reported Russian brutality be an inspiration for what is increasingly being considered a likely kinetic action to forcefully annex Taiwan to the PRC? And if so, are American and Japanese defense planners prepared for news footage of blood in the streets of Taipei, women and children slaughtered in Kaohsiung, and Taichung reduced to rubble? These are the stakes for the people of Taiwan, and yet the euphemism "Taiwan contingency" somehow fails to reflect this level of threat, serving instead to sanitize and obfuscate its true magnitude.

The stakes being now so high, it is imperative that analysts and planners in East Asia take a sober look at the situation in the region and develop creative ways to overcome the challenges that stand in the way of providing an effective defense — for only an effective defense can serve as an effective deterrent — to any Taiwan contingencies that may arise. To that end, this book examines the issue from a variety of perspectives. It is the product of cooperation between the Taiwan Center for Security Studies of National Chengchi University and St. Andrew's University in Osaka, Japan, bringing together research and analysis from a number of experts in the field to examine the unique geopolitical circumstances described above. The collaborative research project of the Research Institute at St. Andrews University is titled "An Interdisciplinary Approach to Contemporary East Asian Studies" (21REN283). The six chapters by Matsumura, Oue, and Takeuchi are a result of the project, while the rest are those of the TCSS.

The stakes for the Chinese Communist Party (CCP) go much farther than merely expanding their territorial holdings by taking Taiwan and thereby also finally defeating the party's erstwhile enemy — the Kuomintang (KMT) — in the Chinese Civil War. The PRC is currently also engaged in a competition for regional hegemony against the United States, and this rivalry is heating up. Masahiro Matsumura, Professor of international politics and national security at Osaka's Momoyama Gakuin

University, examines a recent legal opportunity that may well greenlight the development of what has so far been an elusive military-to-military relationship between Tokyo and Taipei, and doing so in such a way that could sidestep legal warfare by the PRC aimed at stopping any such actions. The move confronts legal and political impediments because Japan and Taiwan lack any formal diplomatic relations. Tokyo, as a power that was defeated in WWII and was forced to surrender sovereignty over Taiwan, is constrained by a stringent "One China" policy. While America hews to its own "One China" policy while simultaneously continuing to support Taiwan's defense through the legal mechanism of the Taiwan Relations Act (TRA), this analysis suggests an alternative route for Japan, arguing that any attempt by the Japanese Diet to pass a Japanese equivalent of the TRA would be used by Beijing as a pretext for armed aggression against Taiwan. Rather, an amendment to Japan's Self-Defense Force Law is proposed, one that would open the door to military-to-military contact with an "unrecognized authority" for the purposes of non-combatant evacuation operations (NEO). Inspired by the lessons learned from the Japanese government's failed NEO, conducted in conjunction with the poorly executed US military withdrawal from Afghanistan in 2021, this amendment would not be specifically targeted at Taiwan *per se* but rather at any hypothetical unrecognized authority. This legalistic legerdemain would give Beijing no pretext for ire, neatly sidestepping any armed aggression against Taiwan in retaliation.

Using NEO to crack the door open to establishing a mechanism for strategic communication for Japan and other states to consult with Taiwan is likewise suggested in our second chapter, by retired Japan Air Self-Defense Force Lieutenant General Sadamasa Oue, a fellow at the Harvard University Asia Center and graduate of the National Defense Academy of Japan. General Oue points out that while the notion of a Taiwan emergency being just as much a Japanese emergency is an idea that is rapidly gaining currency, the Japanese government must do more to develop a strategy to deter a Taiwan crisis while making it clear that Japan's vital national interests are at stake in such a conflict. Japan has been reviewing its National Security Strategy given the worsening security environment in East Asia. Up to now, the strategic approach has been to focus on ways to deter China from a potential Chinese attack while enhancing the credibility of US military intervention, particularly through the framework of the Japan-US security alliance. This strategy is dependent, however, on Tokyo finding a way to overcome the dilemma posed by Japan's "One

China" policy. One of the central issues in such a perspective is the need to recognize the PRC as a threat to Japan's security. If China enters into bilateral negotiations with Taiwan, Japan would not have any need to intervene in the Taiwan Strait issue, provided such talks between Taipei and Beijing are conducted in good faith. If, however, the PRC were to make any attempt to unify Taiwan by force, the situation would be fundamentally different, and Japan should respond. What form would such a response take? It is only now that Japanese leaders are having to seriously consider how to answer that question.

Kuo Tzu-Yung, author of a number of books on such topics as international relations, China studies, and the Russia-Ukraine War, agrees that Taiwan and Japan are in the same boat. In his chapter, he highlights the urgent need for bilateral military coordination between the two neighbors and offers a series of policy suggestions for how this might be accomplished. Areas of potential military cooperation between Taiwan and Japan include intelligence collection and analysis, military personnel exchanges, technical coordination, and even joint military exercises. Rather than being triggers of a Chinese invasion of Taiwan, he argues that these measures would serve as a deterrent to such an eventuality. Problems remain, however, including the current lack of diplomatic relations, the ever-present Chinese pressure, and the leverage of China's huge market, all of which stand in the way of instantiating any form of military cooperation between Taiwan and Japan.

While legislative and diplomatic impediments bar the amelioration of relations between Taiwan and Japan, no such obstacles stand in the way of the deepening relations seen recently between China and Russia. As pointed out by Michał Lubina of Jagiellonian University in Krakow, Poland, Sino-Russian ties are evolving from being a mere axis of convenience to relations shared by "fellow travelers." This entente — which some have described as a "quasi-alliance" — is predicated upon three pillars: "strategic rears," global revisionism, and economic cooperation. The first refers to how each of these aspiring superpowers has the other's back, allowing both Moscow and Beijing to concentrate their efforts on a single front — one more immediate and urgent to their geopolitical goals. Though tacit, this relationship operates in much the same way that the Molotov–Ribbentrop Pact was intended to ensure non-aggression between Nazi Germany and the Soviet Union, in this case, allowing China to focus on establishing hegemony in the Asia-Pacific, and Russia free to deal with its near abroad, with neither having to worry about the other opening a distracting second front. Until the Russian invasion of Ukraine in 2022, both were seen as soft revisionists; mounting occasional and tentative challenges to the current rules-based international order. After the invasion, however, this soft revisionism got hard fast, Lubina points out. Moreover, the economic cooperation between the two has intensified, particularly since Western-led sanctions have denied access to Russian industry and oligarchs, opening the door to an expansion of economic relations and trade with China. What was once mostly trade in military technologies has flowered into a robust trade in raw materials, oil, gas, coal, wood, and more, benefiting both sides tremendously. Both Moscow and Beijing are keen to undermine the current international order and change the current architecture of East Asian security, though they remain too weak to do so, at least for the time being.

An example of Beijing's unconstrained actions aimed at undermining the rules-based international order, as well as the regional *status quo*, is the steep increase in incursions into Taiwanese airspace and waters, and the normalization of such revisionist behavior. This uptick began in earnest after the August 2022 visit to Taiwan of then US House Speaker Nancy Pelosi, and it has prompted security scholars from Taiwan and Japan to evaluate as far more plausible the threat of Taiwan's annexation — either by force or coercion — by the CCP, especially under Xi Jinping's leadership. Hon-min Yau, director of the Graduate Institute of International Security at the ROC National Defense University's College of International & National Defense Affairs, calls on regional security actors to do more to stabilize the region — to act with a sense of urgency. Yau's chapter highlights how the need to deepen coordination between Taiwan and Japan is becoming critical, and the rationale for such coordination is evolving. He proposes new initiatives that could be pursued gradually to enhance deterrence and increase interoperability in terms of the defense capabilities of Taiwan and Japan, the ultimate goal being to deliver critical deliberations as a timely response to the changing security dynamics in the Indo-Pacific region.

These changing security dynamics are all the more difficult for Japan to respond to due to the nature of its complicated security laws. The aggressive actions taken by the PRC following the aforementioned visit by then US House Speaker Nancy Pelosi included the intentional firing of five missiles directly into Japan's exclusive economic zone. This provocation has led to a heightened awareness about the risk of war in the Taiwan Strait, which would likely spread to Japan's Nansei Islands, situated very near to Taiwan, if not Japan proper itself. In his chapter, Takeuchi xxii *Introduction*

Toshitaka, dean of the Faculty of Global Engagement and a professor emeritus at Osaka University, offers an analysis of what Japan can do to prepare for such an eventuality given the general legal and political environment. He examines public opinion in Taiwan, Japan, and the United States, focusing mainly on Japan, and offers an explanation of Japan's legal complications that would make it difficult for the Japanese government to make straightforward decisions.

These legal complications are an impediment to any possibility for Japan to react swiftly and decisively to a PLA attack on Taiwan — an attack that would inevitably engulf Japan and threaten that country's territorial integrity. Indeed, the writing is on the wall: Chinese scholars are already laying the historical groundwork for a Chinese claim over the Ryukyu Islands, urging the CCP to address what they characterize as an "unresolved historical issue." Whatever the legal and procedural roadblocks to a closer defense relationship with Taiwan, it behooves Tokyo to overcome these, as Taiwan is, and has long been, a close historical and ideological friend to Japan. Dean Karalekas, editor-at-large of the English-language security journal *Strategic Vision*, investigates why amenable relations between the two neighbors seem so elusive, especially given the long history of close ties between the peoples of Taiwan and Japan — a relationship that goes back to prehistoric times. Despite this long history of a shared cultural inheritance, there is an ambivalence in each culture about the other, largely due to fear, on both sides, of displeasing a Beijing leadership class that is thin-skinned and spoiling for a fight. He argues that leaders in Taiwan and Japan must accept the fact China cannot be placated and stop trying. Only then can they set aside their differences — differences which include competing claims over the Diaoyutai/Senkaku Islands — and work together to safeguard not only their respective territorial integrity in the face of the growing PRC threat but also peace and continued prosperity in the region.

No discussion of Taiwan's defense is complete without factoring in Tokyo's policies, morale, and capabilities. Any hostile presence on Taiwan such as a PLA occupation of the island would pose a very serious threat to Japan's national security. This includes, but is not limited to, maritime security, where the security of Formosa and the Japanese archipelago have historically been strongly intertwined. Alex Calvo, a former guest professor at Nagoya University who specializes in defense policy, international law, and military history, examines Japanese policy toward

Introduction xxiii

Taiwan and its constitutional, legal, and treaty framework to ascertain the likelihood that Japanese planners would consider an attack, blockade, or attempted landing on Taiwan as a trigger for removing the many legal and political impediments standing in the way of collective self-defense. Japanese military capability is factored in, though this is only as important as Japanese morale: a concept that is difficult to quantify. Given the US policy of not fighting an enemy on its own soil, any US military engagement with the PLA would be prolonged open warfare in Japan's backyard. Morale and willingness to defend themselves are important factors, as are issues of Japan's public finances and industrial base and their ability to sustain the levels of production that are needed to fight such a war. Calvo looks at unconventional warfare, the porcupine strategy, and deterrence, and how these concepts are perceived in Japan within the context of the PRC's designs on Taiwan.

The following chapter examines the increase in PLAAF incursions into Taiwan's ADIZ and the importance of denying the Chinese air superiority. The author, Sadamasa Oue, traces the structural reforms undertaken by Xi to reshape the PLA in order to construct a military capable of complex joint operations and projecting power. The degree to which this goal has been achieved is as yet unknown, but the CCP's recent belligerence demonstrates a level of confidence that suggests it may be close. The PLA is making great strides in its anti-access/area-denial (A2/AD) capabilities within the First Island Chain and seeks to employ these further into the Pacific. This stands in stark contrast to the capabilities revealed by recent US wargames, jointly conducted by the Pentagon and RAND Corporation, that prefigure a US defeat in any such contest. Thus, it is incumbent upon Taipei to adopt a robust military strategy that would raise the costs of a PLA invasion, changing the calculus behind the PRC's decision as to whether or not to engage in any form of forceful annexation of the island. Attaining air superiority is a key element for Taipei's implementation of any such strategy.

Masahiro Matsumura offers a Japanese perspective on how best to aid Taiwan in its defense needs, specifically with respect to its submarine and mine acquisition policy. In his second chapter, Professor Matsumura examines the political obstacles to Japan's adoption of such a role and offers policy proposals with respect to naval armaments, with a focus on feasible, cost-effective acquisitions. This means that rather than seeking the acquisition and deployment of large-displacement submarines, Taipei planners would be well positioned instead to examine the purchase of smaller boats, even midget submarines that, together with the judicious deployment of mines, would serve as a deterrent strategy that punches above its budgetary weight.

Since ROC President Tsai Ing-wen was first elected in 2016, PLA activity designed to intimidate the island's inhabitants has seen a distinct uptick, serving as a clear warning against thoughts of independence or moving too closely into America's orbit. Given this activity, analysts perceive a security dilemma developing in the region, and Taipei policymakers cognizant of the military imbalance in the Taiwan Strait have begun re-examining the notion of adopting a "porcupine strategy." In his next chapter, Hon-min Yau argues that China's recent military intimidation does not constitute a security dilemma *per se* but is rather a security challenge for Taiwan. He suggests that a porcupine strategy would be better employed as a complement to, rather than a replacement for, Taiwan's existing offensive fighting capability.

The increase in Gray Zone intimidation tactics and ADIZ incursions by the PLA reflect Beijing's displeasure with Taiwan's improving image in the international community at a time when China is flagging. In solidarity with Taiwan's plight, there have been several pseudo-State visits to the island nation by high-ranking officials from abroad, including most notably the August 2022 visit of then US House Speaker Nancy Pelosi, which precipitated such a vociferous response from the PLA. For the first time in many years, Beijing is experiencing pushback against its diplomatic bullying of nations seeking closer overt ties with Taiwan, and it has fallen back on old intimidation tactics to express its displeasure. Add to this the need for the CCP to shore up its legitimacy in the eyes of the Chinese people and hence the increased rhetorical and military bellicosity. In this time of uncertainty, the challenges faced by defense planners in Taipei are diverse, and choosing the best way to move forward in response presents the nation with a dilemma.

As the gap in economic and military might across the Taiwan Strait grows, Taiwan is increasingly taking center stage as the potential flashpoint that threatens to embroil the region in conflict. Through little choice of its own, Taipei has responded by relying more heavily on its sole security guarantor, the United States. This, of course, only garners more pushback from the PRC, forming a self-reinforcing feedback loop. As American power, and the nation's commitment to the region, both appear to be waning, hope is high that Japan might choose to step up to the plate and serve as a supplement and/or complement to the deterrent effect heretofore provided solely by Washington. Unfortunately, Japan lacks sufficient power-projection capabilities required for that role and remains constrained by unique constitutional limits to the overseas deployment of its military forces.

Staying on the topic of creative, cost-effective defense measures, Takeuchi Toshitaka examines the potential of unmanned aerial vehicles (UAVs) as a means to build up the defense capacities of the ROC Armed Forces. If money were no object, it would be ideal for the ROC Armed Forces to be equipped with all sorts of armaments, but as there are limits to what is feasible, policymakers in Taipei would do well to take a "selection and concentration" approach to arms acquisition and focus on a larger number of cheaper-per-unit drones, for example, rather than the traditional big-ticket items, such as high-performance fighter jets. Professor Takeuchi provides an overview of Taiwan's current defense posture, followed by an examination of the Overall Defense Concept employed by the ROC, and how this concept factors into arms procurement decisions. This lays the foundation for a discussion of the utility of UAVs and the importance for the ROC of paying close attention to the potential that Unmanned Combat Aerial Vehicles (UCAVs) represent. In sum, the gap in equipment and resources between the ROC Armed Forces and the PLA is unlikely to close and indeed is getting very much wider. It is therefore imperative that Taipei take a hard look at investing in UAVs, especially UCAVs. The reality is there is little likelihood that Taiwan will emerge victorious in a conventional-weapons arms race against Beijing, and therefore it is imperative to find a way to overcome the PLA's overwhelming advantage in military resources. Fielding a fleet of UAVs will allow the ROC Armed Forces to saturate the skies and the waters of the Taiwan Strait to disrupt China's goal of military annexation.

In addition to its active-duty military servicemen and women, the ROC Armed Forces maintain — on paper, at least — a large number of reservists subject to mobilization in the event of a Chinese invasion. This reserve force represents a key component of Taiwan's all-out defense concept, which also incorporates mobilization and all-out defense education. In his chapter, Li-Chung Yuan investigates the current status of Taiwan's all-out defense and mobilization system, and surveys publicly available research and expert discussions to examine how Taiwan can enhance its reserve capabilities in terms of force structure, roles, and tasks. His findings reveal much work to be done in getting the ROC reserve force fighting fit and ready to respond in the event of a PLA attack. Reservists are largely seen as a symbolic backup force, with on-paper competence. Until recently, only about 300,000 of the listed 2.2 million ROC reservists were required to participate in regular refresher training under current regulations, and most of these are called up for a few days of annual training, mostly for classroom briefings and adminis-trative work — training that experts have adjudged as insufficient. A new program of call-up training was recently introduced that gives reservists more robust training. While this is undoubtedly an improvement over the previous system, what is required is the building of a capable territorial defense force manned and operated by well-trained and well-equipped "weekend warriors" who can supplement regular force units in resisting an enemy invasion and protect the homeland by waging a protracted insurgency using guerrilla tactics in urban, jungle, and mountain environments.

Budget constraints have forced military planners in Taipei to seek creative ways to meet the growing threat from China at an affordable cost. The reserve force represents a vast untapped source of expertise and man-power, and if used properly, it might just fit the bill. Fortunately, more attention is being paid in recent years to enhancing Taiwan's all-out defense capabilities and boosting reserve force readiness and effective-ness through an overhaul of the reserve system.

The theme that runs throughout this volume, and which has been embraced and expanded upon by each author, is doing more with less. Whether that be using the reserve force more effectively, purchasing more and smaller submarines, or deploying a fleet of UAVs in place of more expensive manned aircraft, it is incumbent upon ROC defense planners to think out-of-the-box and seek creative solutions to the security situation across the strait. It has been said that generals always fight the last war. This proverb serves as a warning to defense planners, especially those in Taipei, to make a sober assessment of the facts on the ground and let go of old paradigms that may have served them in the past, to instead prepare for the next war. The contributors, each in his own way, are adding to that effort by highlighting how Taiwan can best be equipped, trained, and made ready to defend the island against an adversary that has spared no expense to gear up for what Beijing considers to be its manifest destiny: to unify the great Chinese nation. While it is always difficult to attain vic-tory over a larger, better-equipped foe, it is even harder to emerge

Introduction xxvii

victorious against a foe with a fanatical sense of destiny. To do that, Taipei must think creatively and realistically about how to achieve its mission of repelling a Chinese onslaught, so that the future of Taiwan is not decided by force, but by the will of its 24 million people. This book, and the analysis contained herein, is therefore timely and important as the devastation occurring in Ukraine threatens to be visited upon this region.

© 2025 World Scientific Publishing Company
https://doi.org/10.1142/9789811298301_0001

Chapter 1

Establishing Japan–Taiwan Military Ties: A Legal Breakthrough

Masahiro Matsumura

The intensifying US–China hegemonic rivalry has highlighted the geo-strategic importance of Taiwan as an unsinkable aircraft carrier to block Beijing from projecting military power into the Western Pacific, as well as a crucial foothold to secure the security of the sea lines of communication (SLOC). There is growing concern about a power shift from the declining US hegemon to the rising hegemonic aspirant, China, in the foreseeable future, precipitating a full-scale Chinese invasion of the island. The communist regime in Beijing is facing a serious legitimacy deficit, providing its population with neither liberal democratic elections nor the once-high economic growth they previously enjoyed, and instead stirring hyper-nationalism in which the "unification" of Taiwan with China is considered as a core interest. With its accelerated arms buildup, China will catch up with the United States in terms of military power, at least quantitatively, and possibly surpass it in around 2050. In fact, in March 2021, Admiral Phillip Davidson, Commander of the US Indo-Pacific Command, stated before the Senate Committee on Armed Services that China could invade Taiwan in the following six years (Davidson, 2021). Deep concerns have been raised by China's unprecedented large-scale military drills against Taiwan in response to the official visit of then US House of Representatives Speaker Nancy Pelosi to Taiwan in August 2022, offering a solid base on which to infer the magnitude of China's invasion of the island (Matsumura, 2022a, 2022b).

To deter Chinese aggression, the United States can combine internal and external balancing against it: That is, with its own arms buildup, as well as through aggregating the military power of individual allies by strengthening alliances. But the United States is unable to build up overwhelming military power due to the growing constraints of fiscal resources under the accumulating federal debt and the growing economic vulnerabilities of the national economy. Naturally, in addition to its arms buildup efforts, the United States also has to enhance the warfighting capabilities of its qualitatively superior forces against China by working with allies. More specifically, this requires not only an effective operational division of roles and missions between US and allied forces but also their coordination and, most desirably, integration in command, control, communications, computers, cyberspace, intelligence, surveillance, and reconnaissance (C5ISR).

Among US allies and friendly nations, Taiwan and Japan will play most crucial roles to facilitate the maneuvering of US forces in the Taiwan theater of operations. Of course, the defense forces of the Republic of China (ROC) on Taiwan will have to defend the island against an overwhelming Chinese invasion force that would surely dwarf them, while coordinating their operations with US intervention forces that would countervail and plausibly repel the invasion forces. Japan is expected to provide US forces with rear-area support and, if deemed necessary and legal, exercise the right of collective self-defense to defend those forces. The treaty-based Japan–US alliance enables politico-strategic communication and operational coordination between Washington and Tokyo, while the semi-alliance relationship based on the US's Taiwan Relations Act (TRA) only allows for awkward interactions between Washington and Taipei. Yet, given the lack of formal diplomatic recognition between Japan and the ROC in Taiwan, there is no formal mechanism for such communication and coordination between Tokyo and Taipei, with little prospects for fundamental change on this front. Such a mechanism is a prerequisite for the two governments to set up formal and frequent contacts for dialogue, consultation, policy coordination, and planning in military security, as well as for attaining high efficiency in employing warfighting capabilities, munitions, and logistics resources, including preventing friendly fire incidents and collateral damage.

To fill in the blanks in the trilateral Washington–Tokyo–Taipei security ties, the Taiwan lobby in Japan, and pro-Taiwan ideological conservatives, are calling for the enactment of a TRA equivalent, emulating the US precedent. At a casual glance, such a law would render a US military defense of Taiwan more feasible through the support of the US–Japan alliance, at least from a legal perspective. Naturally, this begs the question of whether it makes politico-strategic sense.

This chapter will analyze the differences in legal benefits and protection between the US and Japanese cases that affect the politico-strategic stability of cross-strait relations. Then the chapter will argue against a Japanese TRA as this would exert destabilization, rather than stabilization, by giving Beijing a pretext for armed invasion of Taiwan. Instead, the study will propose amending Japan's Self-Defense Law in a way to enable military-to-military contacts with an unrecognized state or government for non-combatant evacuation of Japanese residents and travelers within the territory in question, which can be applied to the Japan–Taiwan relations. This inquiry is intended to provide US, Japanese, and ROC leaders with an innovative legal instrument to counter Beijing's legal warfare in enabling Tokyo to have semi-regular military-to-military contacts with Taipei, if not regular formal military-to-military relations, as a quintessential form of interstate relations.

1.1 The Differences in Legal Benefits and Protection Between the American and Japanese Cases

The contemporary Chinese security strategy can be highlighted by three non-military forms of warfare, which are political, informational, and pre-kinetic in nature: public opinion warfare, legal warfare, and psychological warfare. Known collectively as the "three warfares," their combined use is aimed at transforming the prevailing discourse and perceptions to China's advantage, placing heavy constraints on an opponent's policy choices and the use of armed force against the country (Kania, 2016).

Given the controversy surrounding the island's international legal status under the protracted US–China rivalry, the Taiwan issue can be an easy target for the "three warfares," through which to attain a pretext for armed unification of Taiwan and to deprive the United States, Japan, and other allies of a pretext for sending intervention forces to assist in the island's defense. Thus, Washington, Tokyo, and Taipei together have to match Beijing in legal warfare regarding how not to give it any *casus belli*.

Conversely, the United States, Japan, and Taiwan have faced a growing need to have regular military-to-military contacts for communication, coordination, and planning across the strategic, operational, and tactical levels. Japan and the United States have a fully developed bilateral alliance built over 70 years that is based on the mutual security treaty, with an established institutionalized mechanism that enables their continuous and substantial contacts. Moreover, the United States is equipped with the TRA, a domestic legal instrument that enables significant (albeit non-interstate) contacts with Taiwan, especially at the annual Monterey Talks, held since 1997 as bilateral institutional innovation (Matsumura, 2017, pp. 35–46). More recently, this collaboration has been bolstered by the Taiwan Travel Act of 2018. Yet, there remains no effective military-to-military contact between Japan and Taiwan. Given the absence of mutual state recognition between the two, this naturally begs the question of whether Japan can emulate the United States by enacting a TRA equivalent.

Tokyo faces a stark dilemma between the politico-military need for a TRA and the politico-legal constraints against one. Particular caution must be exercised, as Beijing would probably view the move toward a Japanese TRA as a serious challenge to its ambitions of annexing Taiwan. Then, Tokyo's security-seeking move might counterintuitively provoke Beijing to destabilize cross-strait relations, and possibly even give it a pretext for armed aggression against Taiwan, especially as China is now more confident than ever in its military power and coercive diplomacy. Thus, it is essential to grasp why the United States, in contrast to Japan, was able to evade the legal constraints, and why Japan is not, with a focus on the legal benefit and protection in legislating the TRA.

1.2 The US Case

The Republic of China under the Chinese Nationalist Party (Kuomintang, or KMT) was an American World War II ally. Upon Imperial Japan's surrender on September 2, 1945, General of the US Army Douglas MacArthur, who was General Headquarters Supreme Commander for the Allied Powers, appointed the ROC armed forces under Chiang Kai-shek to implement disarmament of the Japanese forces in Taiwan and the subsequent military occupation of the island (General Order No. 1 (1)a, 1945). In other words, the United States was the principal occupying power, with the ROC government as its agent up to the official end of the war — as a result of a peace treaty between the Allied powers and Japan — not as the newly designated holder of the sovereign title of Taiwan.

A few years later, the ROC government and military fled to Taiwan after it underwent a crushing defeat in the Chinese Civil War against the armed forces of the Chinese Communist Party (CCP), transferring its temporary seat of government to Taipei. The People's Republic of China (PRC) was established in 1949 under the CCP regime, while the ROC only retained its effective control over Taiwan, the Pescadores, the various other outlying islands, including Jinmen and Matsu, as well as some uninhabited inlets in the South China Sea (the Pratas Island and Itu Aba), while initially retaining its nominal jurisdictional claims over the vast mainland area. Due to the politico-diplomatic inertia of the Second World War, the United States as well as many of its allies and friendly nations continued to fictitiously recognize the ROC, not the PRC, as the sole legitimate government of China. Yet, the legal status of Taiwan remained undetermined, because Japan concluded the San Francisco Peace Treaty in 1952, in which Tokyo renounced its claims to the island without reassigning it to any particular state and because the United Nations Security Council had not made any decision regarding its status according to Article 22 of the Treaty.[1] Since then, the ROC government has exercised uninterrupted effective control over Taiwan without any formal international legal arrangements. The United States had been the ROC's sole security guarantor *vis-à-vis* the PRC through the mutual security treaty of 1955.[2]

In 1979, the administration of then-US President Jimmy Carter switched recognition from the ROC to the PRC. Consequently, the US Congress passed the Taiwan Relations Act of 1979, institutionalizing officially substantial, albeit non-diplomatic, relations between the two.[3] (Meanwhile, the bilateral security treaty terminated at the very beginning of 1980). In the US–PRC Joint Communiqués of 1972, 1979, and 1982, the United States officially acknowledged that "all Chinese on either side

---

[1] The Potsdam Declaration of 1945, an integral part of the Japanese Instrument of Surrender, refers to the Cairo Declaration of 1943, which states that Taiwan shall be returned to the ROC. Yet, the Instrument is merely effective as a ceasefire agreement, not as a peace treaty.

[2] The treaty did not apply to Jinmen and Matsu Islands, Pratas Island, or Itu Aba.

[3] The Act does not apply to the Jinmen and Matsu Islands, Pratas Island, or Itu Aba.

of the Taiwan Strait maintain there is but one China and that Taiwan is part of China." Washington pledged not to challenge this position. This presupposes that Taiwan's status remains undetermined. Washington reaffirmed its "interest in the peaceful settlement of the Taiwan question" by the Chinese people from the PRC and in Taiwan. Evidently, the United States does not recognize Taiwan as part of the PRC, but merely acknowledges that the PRC holds the position that Taiwan is part of the PRC. Moreover, the United States opposes either side unilaterally changing the *status quo*, seeing its interests in the peaceful resolution of the Taiwan question with the consent of the Taiwanese people. This phrasing has the dual aim of deterring Beijing from unilaterally attacking Taiwan and concurrently disincentivizing Taipei from unilaterally declaring de jure independence (Bush, 2017).

Due to the undetermined status of Taiwan, therefore, the United States arguably possesses legal benefit and protection as the client state that has relegated the island's occupation to the ROC as an agent. Hence, the United States retains the potential grounds of claim to preserve the territorial *status quo*.[4] Upon derecognition of the ROC, however, the United States ceased interstate relations with Taiwan in accordance with international law, necessitating a domestic legal basis upon which to build nondiplomatic but official bilateral relations. Thus, the United States needed to enact a domestic legal instrument designed not to provoke Beijing into an armed aggression against Taiwan, or to give it a pretext for doing so. In this light, the TRA is a highly effective instrument for such a purpose, particularly because any US re-recognition of the ROC, or of any such *de facto* Taiwanese state, would only be feasible if it were to declare de jure independence in response to Beijing's unprovoked armed aggression. Similarly, when Beijing first extends implicit recognition of a belligerent Taiwanese community through an act of war, such as a naval blockade or designation of a war zone in a Taiwan theater of operations, this act would permit the United States to open relations with the island according to international law.

The TRA does not guarantee that the United States will rush to Taiwan's defense in the event of an attack by the People's Liberation Army (PLA).

---

[4]Due to the client–agent relationship, it may be possible to argue that Taiwan remains under US military occupation (Hartzell, 2004).

The act provides that "the United States will make available to Taiwan such defense articles and defense services in such quantity as may be necessary to enable Taiwan to maintain a sufficient self-defense capability," and shall "maintain the capacity of the United States to resist any resort to force or other forms of coercion that would jeopardize the security, or the social or economic system, of the people on Taiwan." It simply ensures that the sitting US president will follow the set Taiwan policy and secure consent of the Congress in making any decision to defend Taiwan. In this particular sense, the TRA essentially established America's unilateral and limited commitment to a semi-alliance relationship with Taiwan.

The TRA, then, effectively enables military-to-military contacts between the United States and Taiwan as this relates to arms transfers and to the extent deemed necessary by the US President.[5] It is no wonder that, taking advantage of this flexibility in interpreting the TRA, the United States has increasingly expanded military-to-military contacts with Taiwan, not just for arms transfers but also for information-sharing and policy coordination to cope with China's unprecedented arms buildup.

1.3 The Japanese Case

In sharp contrast to the US case described earlier, Tokyo has strictly avoided direct state-to-state interaction with Taipei ever since Japan switched recognition from the ROC to the PRC in 1972, adhering to a non-governmental framework for unofficial ties with the island. This policy line is a logical progression from the 1952 San Francisco Peace Treaty, in which Japan abandoned its territorial sovereignty over Taiwan without assigning it to any country. No wonder Tokyo's official position is that the international legal status of Taiwan remains undetermined, despite Beijing's and Taipei's claims otherwise. With the growing need for military information-sharing with Taipei, in 2003 Tokyo created a new post at the Japan–Taiwan Exchange Association — the *de facto* embassy

---

[5] Such contacts include standing military officers in active service at field ranks as *de facto* military attachés, who work on secondment at the Taipei Main Office of the American Institute (AIT) in Taiwan, the *de facto* US Embassy. The AIT was officially created as a US government-sponsored non-profit, private corporation established under the auspices of the US government to serve its interests in Taiwan. The instrumentality is also a wholly owned subsidiary of the federal government of the United States under Congressional oversight.

in Taipei — for a "chief director of national security." The post, which is equivalent to the position of defense attaché at Japan's other embassies around the world, is routinely staffed by a retired military officer with the rank of major general. Tokyo adheres to the non-government framework but is currently planning to post a second Ministry of Defense official (but not a general nor field officer in active service) to the Taipei Office (Taiwan ni Gen'eki Boueishou, 2022). An additional civil defense servant in Taipei will be instrumental for further information-sharing and possible policy coordination in broader security policy affairs, not in specific military policy involving operational roles and missions, together with important tactical details.

Given that military-to-military contacts are a quintessential form of interstate relations, a Japanese TRA would constitute an about-face of the longtime policy that requires Tokyo to refrain from making direct interstate contact with Taipei. It would be in marked contrast to the TRA that the US Congress enacted in 1979 amid the normalization of US–China relations. The legislative move involved ending recognition of the ROC on Taiwan. The act was designed to preserve the *status quo* across the Taiwan Strait, which was then acceptable for Beijing, given its priority on swiftly normalizing relations with Washington. It bears reiterating that the TRA does not directly authorize US–Taiwan military-to-military contact: It simply stipulates that the United States shall provide Taiwan with defensive weapons and services, involving related military-to-military contacts.

Accordingly, Japan lacks legal benefit and protection on which to legislate a TRA equivalent that would enable military-to-military contacts with Taipei. Moreover, US and Japanese legal circumstances are greatly different in that the United States has made its ambiguous, but *de facto*, commitment under the TRA to the defense of Taiwan, while Japan has no such commitment at all because it renounced its claim to Taiwan through the San Francisco Peace Treaty. The contrast between the two cases makes it irrelevant for Japan to simply emulate the TRA as a precedent.

Without such necessary legal benefit and protection, Japan's defense policymakers and military leaders cannot have official policy talks and exchanges with their ROC counterparts, but only informal Japan–Taiwan defense interactions through low-profile, non-governmental, unofficial, and informal contacts and channels.

Thus, it is evident that proponents of a Japanese TRA either do not know, or choose to disregard, these critical details, instead placing priority on their ideological preferences or sympathy with Taiwan. Without adequate legal benefit and protection, such an instrument would only destabilize cross-strait relations, or even give Beijing a plausible pretext for armed aggression against Taiwan. These proponents are taking significant risks in prescribing such a counterproductive policy recommendation against their own goals. They have to give up the idea of a Japanese TRA.

Hence, there is a growing need for domestic legal innovation to authorize regular peacetime contact between the Japanese Self-Defense Forces (SDF) and the ROC military without incurring such risks.

1.4 Non-combatant Evacuation Operation (NEO) As the Key

To effectively deter China's aggression against Taiwan, the United States, Japan, and the ROC, as well as other major allies, all have to work together to significantly enhance their collective warfighting capabilities, particularly because China has made such a rapid arms buildup. This means that the US-led qualitative efforts in warfighting capability enhancement need to overtake China's quantitative drive to build up its arms, requiring substantial improvements in military information-sharing and policy coordination. Beijing will most probably strive to weaken its opponents' unity by applying not only strong military pressure but also employing the aforementioned "three warfares," of which legal warfare is a central component, given the complex and complicated controversy regarding the undetermined legal status of Taiwan outlined above. To effectively counter Beijing's legal warfare, Tokyo has to deprive Beijing of a pretext for armed annexation of Taiwan.

In this context, military operations other than war (MOOTW) are a legitimate peacetime form of military activity, such as counterinsurgency and law enforcement (civil affairs, counterterrorism, counterguerrilla, counterdrug, and maritime security operations), peacetime emergency (non-combatant nationals evacuation, humanitarian assistance, and disaster relief), and international peace operations (peacekeeping, disarmament, demobilization, and reintegration; and disbandment of illegal armed groups operations). Those of a humanitarian nature are also highly instrumental in being able to dodge the "three warfares," particularly because Beijing itself has taken full advantage of them (Siebens and Lucas, 2022).

Among MOOTW, the NEO is perhaps the most relevant in the event of a full-scale PLA invasion of Taiwan. According to official figures, there are some 24,000 Japanese residents in Taiwan as well as travelers, in addition to a considerable number of foreign residents and expatriates living there, plus a substantial number of nationals from the United States, its major Western allies, and friendly nations that would most probably request that Japan help evacuate them due to its geographic proximity and its comparatively large transport capacity.[6] Beijing will hardly be able to wage effective legal warfare against Tokyo's information-sharing, planning, and preparation for such an NEO, in general, because Beijing itself also has frequently used NEO over the last decade (Siebens and Lucas, 2022, pp. 47–49), and in particular because Beijing has made it clear that it would resort to the use of armed force against Taiwan only when it judges Taipei to have declared de jure independence, or if external powers attempt to intervene in its independence (TAO and SCIO, 2022; Tiezzi, 2022).

At the pre-combat stage, when a sense of crisis is heightened, and once an armed conflict starts, Tokyo will explore its options to dispatch military transports for evacuation of non-combatants.[7] To carry out swift and safe NEOs under such conditions, Tokyo will need to secure not only Taipei's but also Beijing's consent, as operations will surely be accompanied by security units on military aircraft and vessels to be temporarily deployed to airports and seaports in Taiwan, possibly with the use of weapons for self-defense. If this happens without its consent, Beijing would surely regard any such NEO as an infringement of its sovereignty and territorial integrity, given its claim that Taiwan is part of the PRC. More specifically, such an NEO would constitute military-to-military contact between Japan and Taiwan, involving their interstate relations that

---

[6]Articles 84-3 and 84-4 of the Self-Defense Law put the primary focus of an NEO on Japanese nationals, while attaching an auxiliary priority to that of foreign nationals to be implemented on the basis of a humanitarian consideration. The concept of "Japanese nationals" is expanded to some extent but would hardly accommodate massive needs of foreign nationals for an NEO in the event of a Taiwan crisis and a war. For the limited analytical purpose of this inquiry, this problem with the planning, preparation, and implementation of an NEO can be set aside (Nakamura, 2022).

[7]Prior to a combat situation in a full-blown Taiwan crisis, non-military evacuation operations for non-combatant nationals will be quite feasible when Taipei consents to receiving Japanese civil transports at major airports and seaports in Taiwan.

entail Tokyo's implicit recognition of the ROC. Thus, forced execution of such an NEO without Beijing's consent would incur significant risks by giving Beijing a pretext to attack not just Taiwan, but also Japan, and, possibly, the United States as well.

In general, a state can only invoke the right of individual self-defense to evacuate non-combatant nationals in another state under stringent conditions, which would otherwise be unlawful under international law as an unprovoked armed aggression to the political independence and territorial integrity of the targeted state. An act of anticipatory self-defense has to satisfy the Caroline test, or a 19th-century formulation of customary international law: namely, that such anticipatory self-defense be "instant, overwhelming, and leaving no choice of means, and no moment for deliberation" (Jennings, 1938; Rogoff and Collins, 1990). This requires conditions in which the state concerned does not have its own will or capability within the territory, or neither of the two, to rescue overseas nationals in the victimized country. In reality, an NEO in the event of a Taiwan crisis or war resembles a case in which a victimized state invokes the right of individual self-defense to rescue its nationals within the territory of another state concerned, but under the effective control of insurgents. It is hardly lawful to do so unless PLA forces attack Japanese nationals in Taiwan. Thus, it is very difficult for Tokyo to satisfy these conditions in the event of a Taiwan war, with substantial risks of committing a serious abuse of the controversial right of anticipatory self-defense.[8] An NEO without a cause of self-defense would surely turn Japan into a warring party.

In addition to the international legal constraints, the pacifist Japanese Constitution of 1947 that was imposed under the US-led occupation puts severe legal constraints on the use of armed force, or the threat of the same. More specifically, Article 9-2 prohibits the Japanese state from possessing "land, sea, air forces, as well as other war potential," and does not recognize the state's right of belligerency.[9] Thus, it is unconstitutional in

---

[8] A highly controversial classic case is Operation Entebbe, or a counterterrorist hostage-rescue mission carried out by commandos of the Israel Defense Forces (IDF) at Entebbe Airport in Uganda on July 4, 1976 (Gordon, 1977; Mayama, 2021).

[9] For several decades, Japanese political circles and the public have vainly engaged in intense debates on a constitutional amendment to transform the current pacifist Japanese state to a normal state. Yet, the amendment is extremely difficult to achieve given that the constitution is a *de facto* part of the integral legal arrangement for Japan's

principle for Tokyo to carry out an anticipatory self-defensive NEO, unless the government of the target state consents to it in advance. This means that such a military NEO will be practically infeasible, as Beijing can hardly be expected to consent.

Most importantly, however, it is adequate for the purpose of this inquiry to identify a necessary domestic legal instrument that enables Tokyo to engage in military-to-military contacts, if not regular military-to-military relations, for information-sharing to an extent necessary for an NEO with the unrecognized ROC authorities. In fact, even under the aforementioned international legal and constitutional constraints, Tokyo faces an increasing need to deal with the expected complexities of exceptionally large-scale NEOs in the event of a Taiwan crisis and war (Sekiguchi, 2021). Now it is necessary to understand the constraints on NEOs under the current Japanese defense laws and then explore the necessary amendments such an NEO would require.

1.5 Necessary Amendment of the Self-Defense Forces Law: A Lesson from the Kabul NEO

Japan's Kabul NEO for its nationals and Afghan citizens who worked closely with them ended in failure amid the withdrawal of US and NATO forces during the final days of the war in Afghanistan and the Taliban offensive there in 2021. The operation was expected to evacuate some 500 Japanese officials, local aid staffers, and their family members, but only ended up with the air transport of one Japanese field aid official and 14 Afghans. This is a far poorer performance than the Danish, Dutch, and even South Korean cases (Tanida, 2021; Jieitai Afugan-Haken, 2021).

For the purposes of this study, there is a great lesson to be learned from the failed NEO, because the Japan Air SDF could not dispatch its military transport aircraft to Kabul International Airport in a timely manner. The failure is ascribed in significant part to the legal constraints under SDF Law. More specifically, Article 84-3 stipulates not only that consent must be obtained from the recognized government of the country concerned before such an operation can be executed but also that there must

---

re-independence, together with the San Francisco Peace Treaty and the US-Japan Mutual Security Agreement, in addition to the entrenched pacifism among the public (Matsumura, 2023).

be high prospects for operational coordination and cooperation with that government regarding the smooth and safe execution of the operation. In planning and preparing for the Kabul NEO, however, the Japanese government could not communicate effectively with the then-Afghan president Ashraf Ghani's collapsing government, nor with the Taliban authorities that it did not yet recognize as the legal government of the country.

To ensure that this does not happen again, Article 84-3 of the SDF Law should be amended to expand the scope of its application to include the unrecognized authorities of the country concerned, or of a local area. By doing so, the SDF will be authorized to have necessary military-to-military contacts for NEO with unrecognized authorities, in addition to military-to-military relations with a recognized government. The Article, if so amended, would be applicable to any NEO, not just one specifically designed to apply to a Taiwan crisis or war. Thus, Beijing is simply not in a position to protest against such an amendment, because Japan has adequate legal benefit and protection regarding NEOs on which to legislate a domestic legal instrument. In other words, the amendment will be in marked contrast to a Japanese TRA, because it will fall within the sovereign purview of the Japanese state, against which Beijing would hardly be able to wage effective legal warfare nor obtain any meaningful pretext to destabilize cross-strait relations.

Tokyo would surely be able to invoke Article 84-3, so amended, to have necessary contacts between the SDF and the ROC military for NEO-related information-sharing.[10] Given the expected complexities of exceptionally large-scale NEOs in the event of a Taiwan crisis or war, an extensive range and scope of information-sharing is essential for Tokyo now rather than later to plan, prepare, and execute those NEOs while exploring operational coordination and cooperation with Taipei. Notably, Tokyo needs to obtain detailed operational and tactical information from Taipei as would be deemed necessary to carry out an NEO safely, particularly for the prevention of friendly fire incidents between Japanese and Taiwanese military aircraft and vessels, while securing military-to-military electronic communication channels.[11]

---

[10] To cope well with international legal constraints, Japan–Taipei contacts could be made, for example, on board either a Japanese or a Taiwanese naval vessel on the high seas.

[11] As reflective interests of such contacts, Tokyo may utilize information shared by Taipei to enhance its individual self-defense, especially in the areas close to Taiwan, and to

1.6 Conclusion

Hitherto, this study has explored an effective legal instrument to fill in the missing Tokyo–Taipei links in the US–Japan–Taiwan triangle by enabling military-to-military contacts between the SDF and the ROC military. Such an instrument is more important than ever because the three have to enhance their collective warfighting capabilities through military coordination in order to outperform China, which has made a significantly faster arms buildup than them. Under the intensified US–China rivalry, the instrument also would have to be effective in countering Beijing's legal warfare aimed at constraining US, Japanese, and ROC military power and in exerting their full collective military power potential.

In search of such an instrument, the Taiwan lobby in Japan and pro-Taiwan ideological conservatives are calling for the enactment of a TRA equivalent, emulating the US precedent. Ceteris paribus, such a law would appear to be the most relevant option in the sense that it would render regular military-to-military contacts between Tokyo and Taipei, and then a US military defense of Taiwan, more feasible through the support of the US–Japan alliance.

But, based on a comparative analysis of the US and Japanese cases, this chapter proposes that a Japanese TRA makes little politico-strategic sense, because the United States has legal benefit and protection regarding the TRA due to the potential client–agent relationship in military occupation of Taiwan after World War II. Conversely, Japan has no such legal benefit and protection, as it renounced all claims to Taiwan in the San Francisco Peace Treaty. It is perceived that a Japanese TRA would give Beijing a pretext for armed aggression against Taiwan, and further destabilize cross-strait relations.

Instead, this chapter urges the government in Tokyo to learn a lesson from the Kabul NEO in 2021, which ended in failure. The study has proposed amending Japan's Self-Defense Law in a way to enable military-to-military contacts with an unrecognized state, or the authorities thereof, for

---

reinforce the US–Japan alliance by providing rear-area support for US forces and exercising the right of limited collective self-defense with the United States.

As for operational electronic data, especially common operational pictures, Tokyo and Taipei can share important data via the United States, given that the United States operates the large ground-based early warning radar facility on the top of Mt. Leshan in Taiwan (Matsumura, 2017, pp. 21–22).

non-combatant evacuation of Japanese residents and travelers there. Such an amendment would be generally applicable to any NEO, including the case of a Taiwan crisis or war. Thus, without enacting a Japanese TRA, the Japanese government would be able to take advantage of an amended SDF Law to justify an extensive range and scope of semi-regular military-to-military contacts with the ROC authorities. It is high time that a Japanese TRA be dropped off completely from Taiwan policy agendas, both in Tokyo and Taipei, and be replaced by an amendment to the SDF Law.

Acknowledgments

This chapter is a result of the collaborative project "An Interdisciplinary Approach to Contemporary East Asia Studies" [21REN283] at St. Andrew's University Research Institute.

References

Bush, R. C. (2017). A one-China policy primer. Brookings Institution. *East Asia Policy Paper, 10*, 1–30. Retrieved August 5, 2023, from http://archive.today/GM4w4.

Davidson, P. S. (2021). Statement of Admiral Philip S. Davidson, US Navy Commander, US Indo-Pacific Command Before the Senate Armed Services Committee on US Indo-Pacific Command Posture. *US Senate.*

General Order No. 1 (1)a. (1945). Office of the Supreme Commander for the Allied Powers. Retrieved August 5, 2023, from http://archive.today/F4T3P.

Gordon, D. J. (1977). Use of force for the protection of nationals Abroad: The Entebbe incident. *Case Western Reserve Journal of International Law, 9*(1).

Hartzell, R. D. (2004, Fall). Understanding the San Francisco Peace Treaty's Disposition of Formosa and the Pescadores. *Harvard Asia Quarterly.* Retrieved August 5, 2023, from http://archive.today/WC0ri.

Jennings, R. Y. (1938, January). The Caroline and McLeod Cases. *American Journal of International Law, 32*(1) 82–99.

Jieitai Afugan-Haken no Shinsou: Nokosareta Genchi Kyoryokusha wa ima [The Depths of the Self-Defense Force Dispatch to Afghanistan: The Current State of Local Collaborators left in Afghanistan]. (2021, October 14). *NHK Closeup Gendai.* Retrieved August 5, 2023, from http://archive.today/csANF.

Kania, E. (2016, August 22). The PLA's Latest Strategic Thinking on the Three Warfares. *China Brief, 16*(13). Retrieved August 5, 2023, from http://archive.today/M4VIr.

Matsumura, M. (2023). *Nipponkokukenpo no Shotai to Kaiken: Jyoubun-, Bunr —
Kaishaku wo Koete* [The Essential Features of the Japanese Constitution
and its Amendment: Beyond Legal and Logical Interpretation]. *Momoyama-
Hougaku [St Andrew's Law Review] No. 38.* Retrieved August 5, 2023,
from http://archive.today/umqN2.

Matsumura, M. (2022a, September 9). Taiwan needs prudential realism. *Taipei
Times.* Retrieved August 5, 2023, from http://archive.today/DBT6E.

Matsumura, M. (2022b, March 21). Taiwan-Japan military ties possible. *Taipei
Times.* Retrieved August 5, 2023, from http://archive.today/mbnZd.

Matsumura, M. (2017). Exploring unofficial Japan-Taiwan security policy coor-
dination after the new guidelines for Japan-US defense cooperation. Osaka:
St. Andrew's University Research Institute, Monograph 31. Retrieved
August 5, 2023, from http://archive.today/uocg8.

Mayama, A. (2021). Zaigai-Jikokumin-Hogo no Kokusaihoujyou no Hyouka
[International legal Evaluation on the Protection of Overseas National] in
Yasuhiro Takeda, ed., Zaigai-Houjin no Hogo/Kyushutsu: Chosen-Hantou
to Taiwank-Kaikyo-Yuji heno Taiou [The Protection and Rescue of
Overseas Nationals: Coping with a Korean Peninsula and Taiwan
Contingency]. Tokyo: Toshindo, pp. 61–107.

Nakamura, S. (2022, February 18). Further Legal Changes Needed to Enable
Transport of Nonnationals: Ukraine's Lessons for a Taiwan Contingency.
International Information Network Analysis, Sasakawa Peace Foundation.
Retrieved August 5, 2023, from http://archive.today/RSFIU.

Rogoff, M. and Collins, Jr. (1990). The Caroline Incident and the Development
of International Law. *Brooklyn Journal of International Law, 16*(3).

Sekiguchi, T. (2021). *Chosen-Hanto oyobi Taiwan-Kaikyo-Yuuji niokeru Taihi-
Katsudou: Soute sareru Moderu-Ke-su no Kentou* [Rescue Operations in
Korea Peninsula and Taiwan Strait Contingencies: Examining expected
model cases]. Takeda, ed., *op. cit.*, pp. 253–288.

Siebens, J. and Lucas, R. (2022). Military Operations Other Than War in China's
Foreign Policy. *The Stimson Center.* Retrieved August 5, 2023, from http://
archive.today/Lo2gv.

*Taiwan ni Gen'eki Boueishou Shokuin haken he: Konka nimo Jyouchu Jyouhou-
Shushuu-Kyouka* [To strengthen information gathering, an MoD official
will be seconded to the *de facto* Embassy in Taipei as early as this summer].
(June 4, 2022). *Sankei Shimbun.* Retrieved August 5, 2023, from http://
archive.today/W0i7h.

Tanida, K. (2021, November 8). *Nihon no Afugan-Taihi-Sakusenn wo Kensho
suru* [Examining Japan's NRO from Afghan]. *Nippon.com.* Retrieved
August 5, 2023, from http://archive.today/iMrlS.

TAO and SCIO [The Taiwan Affairs Office of the State Council and The
State Council Information Office of the People's Republic of China].

(2022, August). The Taiwan Question and China's Reunification in the New Era. Retrieved August 5, 2023, from http://archive.today/0BZh6.

Tiezzi, S. (2022, October 18). Xi's Work Report to the 20th Party Congress: 5 Takeaways. *The Diplomat*. Retrieved August 5, 2023, from http://archive.today/KzHmo.

© 2025 World Scientific Publishing Company
https://doi.org/10.1142/9789811298301_0002

Chapter 2

Changes in Japan's Strategic Views on the Taiwan Emergency and Its Implications for Japan–Taiwan Relations

Sadamasa Oue

The recognition that "a Taiwan emergency is a Japanese emergency" has been widespread among the people of both Japan and Taiwan, thanks to the late former Prime Minister Shinzo Abe, who voiced this phrase in his virtual speech at the Institute for National Policy Research of Taiwan in December 2021 (Former Japan PM, 2021). However, with respect to what measures should be taken in a Taiwan contingency, the Japanese strategy is still unclear, not to mention national consensus. While concerns about China's rapid and opaque military buildup have long been pointed out by Japanese defense officials, it was Admiral Phil Davidson, then Commander of the US-Indo-Pacific Command, who galvanized the international security community, precipitating a sharp rise in concern about the Chinese Communist Party (CCP) and their objective to annex Taiwan. He testified in the Senate Armed Services Committee of the US Congress in March 2021 that "Taiwan is clearly one of their ambitions before that, and I think the threat is manifest during this decade, in fact in the next six years" (Shelbourne, 2021). As for US strategy toward China, the 2015 National Security Strategy (NSS) of the Obama administration stated that it "welcomes the rise of a stable, peaceful and prosperous China." In the 2018 NSS announced by the Trump administration, the statement changed to

"China and Russia are trying to erode the safety and prosperity of the United States by challenging the power, clout, and national interests of the United States." That is to say, it was only four years ago that the US completely abandoned its engagement policy on China and recognized it as a strategic competitor, or pacing threat. The Biden administration, while maintaining strategic ambiguity as a declared policy on Taiwan's defense, is stepping up its commitment to the defense of Taiwan, including military cooperation. However, looking at the response to the Russia-Ukraine war, it is impossible to predict whether the United States will intervene militarily in Taiwan despite the risk of a full-scale conflict that could escalate to a nuclear war with China. Japan is currently reviewing strategic documents such as the National Security Strategy, and it is no exaggeration to say that how China is recognized in the New Strategy, announced at the end of 2022, will characterize Japan's future security strategy, guiding how Japan and the Japan–US alliance deter and deal with a Taiwan contingency. Against these backdrops, this chapter outlines the basic stance of Japan, the United States, Taiwan, and China concerning "the Peace and Stability in the Taiwan Strait," and discusses Japan's shifting strategic views, including Japan's national interests that are at stake, and its possible strategies in the event of a Taiwan crisis. Next, the chapter will analyze factors that influence Japan's strategic approach, followed by the implications to the Japan–Taiwan relationship learned from the Taiwan Strait Crisis Policy simulation in which the author was engaged. Finally, some policy recommendations will be proposed.

2.1 Basic Stance on the Taiwan Issue of China, Taiwan, US, and Japan

There are three aspects of the Taiwan issue that the four countries must consider in order to orient their security policies: First, the fixation on domestic divisions caused by the Chinese Civil War, put on hold under the Cold War structure; second, the realization of the "One Country, Two Systems" model, made impossible by the democratization of Taiwan; and third, the militarization based on the lessons learned from the Third Taiwan Strait Crisis (1995–1996). Japan, the United States, and China have each adopted a strategic approach to the Taiwan issue based on their own assertions for these aspects in pursuit of their own national objectives.

The People's Republic of China (PRC) aims to finally put an end to the Chinese Civil War by achieving a national unification that will cement the legitimacy of CCP rule. Beijing has made every effort to build up a military posture that prevents, and if necessary, expels US intervention by force. Taiwan has become a full-fledged democracy after 38 years of martial law and the dictatorship of the Chinese Nationalist Party, or Kuomintang (KMT), and Taipei needs to protect this democracy and the Taiwan identity it has acquired through many civil movements. The United States continues to pursue a policy of strategic ambiguity to balance its commitment to the defense of Taiwan under the Taiwan Relations Act (TRA) while avoiding war with China. Japan's basic stance is to maintain economic relations with China and to maintain the *status quo* through the Japan–US Alliance. In short, while the three countries are firmly holding on to a strategy to maintain the *status quo*, China is pursuing efforts to change it, resulting in a confrontation in which it will be impossible to find a compromise between the two parties. China's President Xi Jinping has repeatedly stated that "the Taiwan issue is a pure internal affair of China, and we will not allow any interference from outside" and that "the split of 'Taiwan independence' is the biggest obstacle to the unification of the homeland, and is a serious danger to the restoration of Chinese ethnicity" (Sacks, 2021). He clearly stated that China would never abandon military means for the annexation of Taiwan. Accordingly, Japan, the United States, and Taiwan, who desire to maintain the *status quo*, need to collaborate to deter a PRC military invasion of Taiwan and, if deterrence fails, to defend Taiwan to bring back the *status quo ante* in the security order after any such military conflict.

2.2 Changes in Japan's Strategic Views on the Taiwan Contingency

2.2.1 *Review of the National Security Strategy*

The government of Japan is now reviewing the National Security Strategy, the National Defense Program Guidelines, and the Mid-Term Defense Program (three strategy documents) as promised by Prime Minister Fumio Kishida. Japan's first current national security strategy was formulated in 2013 under the second Abe government. Since then, Japan's security environment has drastically changed for the worse. The liberal international order suffered a major setback, and the world transformed into a competitive structure between the liberal democratic system and the authoritarian dictatorship system as symbolized by the US–China strategic confrontation. Russia's invasion of Ukraine, which broke out in February 2022, demonstrates that a large-scale military conflict between nations cannot be ruled out as a real threat. Japan is forced to deal with three fronts: China, which aims at annexation of Taiwan including Japan's Senkaku Islands with its enormous military power; North Korea, which is striving to strengthen its nuclear and missile capabilities; and Russia, which is engaged in a kinetic war with the threat of nuclear escalation. Conversely, the United States, Japan's only ally and security guarantor, is suffering a relative decline in its national power and domestic social divisions, thus revealing its intention to rely more on its allies including Japan to secure international order. Moreover, due to remarkable advances in information and communications technologies, the future "battle" will expand from traditional land, sea, and air space to new domains including space and cyberspace, as well as to cognitive areas. The coming war with China, if materialized, will become a comprehensive war that mobilizes not only military but also diplomatic, economic, intelligence, technology, and other means. Considering these factors, in order to ensure Japan's safety and prosperity, it is essential to fundamentally review existing security policies and establish a comprehensive strategy that unifies the efforts of the entire government, adapting to the emerging security paradigm. At the same time, Tokyo needs to dispatch strong messages to the international community that Japan will cooperate with an ally and like-minded countries to build a favorable security environment while upholding the values Japan believes in, such as the rule of law, basic freedoms, and human rights.

2.2.2 Changes in strategic views concerning the Taiwan Strait crisis

The new strategy is required to present how realistic prescriptions can be drawn against existing threats. In other words, this is the answer to the task of identifying the most serious threats to Japan's vital national interests, and formulating the optimal means and ways for securing national interests through deterrence and limiting their loss by effective responses if deterrence fails. The National Security Strategy of the United States, announced in October 2022, identifies China as "the only competitor with

Changes in Japan's Strategic Views on the Taiwan Emergency 23

both the intention to rewrite the international order and the more increasing capability to implement it," and articulates that the US will compete effectively with China "while blocking dangerous Russia" (Biden, 2022). Conversely, Japan's current strategy recognizes China as "a matter of concern for the international community, including Japan." It further states that from a broader perspective, Tokyo is building and strengthening a "mutually beneficial relationship based on common strategic interests," while with regard to China's attempts to change the *status quo* by force, "Japan will continue to respond calmly and firmly, demanding restraint from the Chinese side, without escalating the situation." As for relations across the Taiwan Strait, it remarks that "movements for stabilization and potential instability coexist" (Secretariat, 2013). However, this perception has dramatically changed due to the sharp increase in the number of Chinese vessels patrolling the waters around the Senkaku Islands and the intrusions into Japanese territorial waters since 2013, when the current strategy was formulated. Recent Defence White Papers of Japan have come to recognize China's attempts to change the *status quo* by force as a serious threat. In particular, President Xi Jinping, who insists that unification of Taiwan is essential for "the great rejuvenation of the Chinese ethnicity," refuses to renounce the use of force and frequently instructs the People's Liberation Army (PLA) to build the capacity to fight and win wars.[1] Admiral Davidson's (2020) comment that a Taiwan Strait crisis is likely to become manifest within six years created a serious sense of crisis within Japan. Abe warned that "a Taiwan emergency is a Japan emergency, and an emergency for the Japan–US alliance." Furthermore, President Xi Jinping, who had assumed the CCP Secretary position for an exceptional third term at the 20th Communist Party Congress and stacked the CCP Standing Committee with loyal subordinates, was more likely to use force due to overconfidence and miscalculation. Given that there are no viable candidates as his successor in the Supreme Leadership, the next decade of Xi's fourth term will overlap with the period covered by the new Japan NSS. In a military exercise conducted by the PLA after then US House Speaker Nancy Pelosi's visit to Taiwan, China established six exercise areas surrounding the main island of Taiwan, as if to rehearse a blockade of the island. In this "exercise," the PLA launched scores of ballistic

---

[1] For example, the most recent Defense of Japan 2022 allocates more pages to analyzing Chinese policy on Taiwan and the military balance in the strait (Japan Ministry of Defense, 2022, pp. 65–76).

missiles, five of which landed inside Japan's Exclusive Economic Zone, near Yonaguni Island. The military exercises also hinder vessels and aircraft navigating through the Taiwan Strait and the Bashi Channel, and the need to protect the citizens of the Sakishima Islands, including Yonaguni Island, has been raised. As such, serious discussions have been taking place among the Japanese public regarding specific responses to, and preparations for, the coming Taiwan Strait crisis.

2.2.3 *Japan's vital national interests in the Taiwan Strait crisis*

In the new strategy, the most important challenge is to formulate measures and methods to deter China's military invasion to annex Taiwan. This task should start to clarify Japan's vital national interests, which will likely be threatened in a Taiwan emergency. Although the sense of crisis that "a Taiwan emergency is a Japanese emergency" is shared by the majority of the Japanese, there is not necessarily a common understanding of why it is so. In order to promote cooperation with the United States and Taiwan, it is also necessary to understand the vital national interests of each other. The following are the vital national interests that Japan must protect in the event of a Taiwan crisis.

(1) **Defense and civil protection of the Senkaku Islands and the Southwest Islands:** As indicated in the military exercise in August, a PLA operation to unify Taiwan will be conducted over a wide area, including the Southwest Islands of Japan. The possibility of a simultaneous invasion of the Senkaku Islands, over which China claims territorial sovereignty, cannot be ruled out. Thus, the defense of the Senkaku Islands and the Southwest Islands, as well as ensuring safety of residents in the area, are of vital importance to Japan.

(2) **Maintenance of sea lanes indispensable for Japan's survival:** The Straits of Taiwan and Bashi are the main choking points of maritime traffic that carries energy, resources, food, products, etc. Maintaining free navigation in both straits is indispensable for the lives of Japanese citizens.

(3) **Ensuring the safety of Japanese nationals and companies in China and Taiwan:** There are some 130,000 Japanese companies and 0.8 million Japanese in China, while 25,000 Japanese nationals live in

Taiwan. Ensuring the safety of these Japanese companies and citizens must be given the highest priority.

(4) **Defending common values such as democracy, freedom, the rule of law, and human rights:** The Taiwan contingency is no longer a domestic issue for China, but a global race between an authoritarian dictatorship and a liberal democratic system over upholding their values. The imposition of authoritarian values on Taiwan by China's military power cannot be misinterpreted or misrepresented as two Chinese-speaking countries that share the same values.

(5) **Defending the geopolitical fortress located in the center of the first archipelago:** If the naval and air forces of the PLA advance into Taiwan, they will be able to freely deploy to the western Pacific, and the military balance in East Asia will shift overwhelmingly, conferring superiority to China. As US regional hegemony would be lost, the credibility of the Japan–US alliance could be seriously undermined. Japan might consider another option for its national security in lieu of the alliance with the US.

Considering the dire situation of the Russian–Ukrainian war, it is certain that once a military invasion is initiated, the above-mentioned vital national interests will be seriously damaged. In some cases, it cannot be denied that the war could expand to a total war between the United States and China, both of which wield nuclear weapons. Therefore, Japan needs to make deterrence of a Taiwan Strait crisis the first priority of its strategy toward China.

2.3 Japan's Strategic Approach to Taiwan Emergency

2.3.1 Challenges to deter the Taiwan Strait crisis

The West failed to deter Russia's invasion of Ukraine, but each country must learn from the lessons and use them to deter China's invasion of Taiwan. Conversely, China must have also learned from the huge suffering and difficulties that Russia is facing, recognized the enormous costs and risks of waging war, and convinced themselves of the need to prevent tangible and intangible military support to Taiwan as well as direct US military intervention. However, for President Xi Jinping, the unification of Taiwan is his personally declared commitment. Although the hurdle of the use of force has risen, it is unlikely to be abandoned. The annexation of Taiwan (the unification of the fatherland) is the last trump card to show the legitimacy of the CCP's one-party rule, which can never be abandoned, but could be a double-edged sword that, if it fails, risks leading to the collapse of the CCP itself. Consequently, the possibility of successful deterrence will increase by having Xi judge that the United States, Japan, and the international community must defend Taiwan by taking various measures to demonstrate their willingness and capacity, concluding that the possibility of a successful armed invasion is too low for Xi to afford the unacceptable risk of failure.

Conversely, it is also important that China should not be cornered into a situation that forces Beijing to use force, such as a declaration of independence by Taipei. The Republic of China (ROC) President Tsai Ing-wen, while resolutely refusing Xi's offer of a "One Country, Two Systems" solution, has refrained from making inadvertent statements that provoke China and has carefully pursued a policy of maintaining the current *status quo*. While Tsai will be handing over her government to her successor in the 2024 presidential election, Japan and the United States should clearly convey to the next president that they will support the same thoughtful attitude to maintain the *status quo*. At the same time, it is necessary to avoid a situation in which Taiwanese citizens perceive a Chinese military invasion as inevitable and are forced into a self-defeating declaration of independence. The realities of limited US and NATO support for Ukraine greatly reduced the trust that ROC citizens had in US military assistance in the event of a PLA attack. According to a public opinion poll conducted by the Taiwan Foundation for Democracy, the number of respondents who "trusted" such support declined from 65.0 percent in October last year to 34.5 percent in March this year, and the trust in Japan's support also fell from 58.0 percent to 43.1 percent (Ishida, 2022). While Taiwan itself needs to become more serious about national defense and strengthen its own military capabilities, it is equally important for Japan and the United States to convey practicable commitments to their involvement in the defense of Taiwan, providing reassurance to Taiwan's citizens in a timely and appropriate manner.

At the 20th Party Congress of the CCP, in which Xi Jinping began his third term in office, he stated that China would have to overcome "an unimaginably rough sea" in the future, and that the Taiwan issue was China's "historic challenge," promising that China would "not postpone it to the next generation" (Tian and Blanchard, 2022). It is not unlikely that Xi, who has solidified the center of leadership with his aides, will make a self-righteous and optimistic judgment of the situation, as is the case with Russian President Vladimir Putin. In order to transform Xi Jinping's optimism, in which unification can be achieved through the use of force if not peaceful means, into pessimism, in which a military invasion would directly lead to the collapse of the CCP's one-party system and his own ruin, cooperation among Japan, the United States, and Taiwan in practical ways, as well as strategic communication, is required.

2.3.2 *Credibility of US military intervention*

American President Joe Biden declared long before Russia's invasion that he would not dispatch US military forces to defend Ukraine, and in fact, he has been carefully avoiding a direct confrontation with Russia (Egan, 2021). As Ukraine is not an ally of the United States, nor is it a member of NATO, the US response against the Russian invasion cannot be condemned. It also makes sense from the perspective of avoiding escalation to a nuclear war. Taiwan has no alliance with any country, including the US, and the Taiwan Relations Act of the United States does not explicitly stipulate an obligation to defend Taiwan. Therefore, the situation in Taiwan is basically the same as that of Ukraine. For Xi, the credibility and mode of American military intervention are the most important determinants of his decision to undertake the use of force. For Japan, dealing with a Taiwan crisis alone would be almost impossible, and disadvantageous. Tokyo must adopt a joint approach based on the premise of the Japan–US alliance. Although the United States has not changed its policy of strategic ambiguity regarding its involvement in a Taiwan contingency, President Biden has stated four times that the US is "committed to defending Taiwan" (Johnson, 2022). It is reasonable to assume that the United States will intervene militarily for the following reasons. First of all, the United States recognizes China as a top-priority strategic competitor, and if Taiwan is annexed without any direct US military intervention against China's invasion, its power relationship with China will be so decisively disadvantaged that Washington would have to admit defeat in the strategic competition. In addition, in the event of a Taiwan emergency, Japan's vital national interests would be threatened, and in some cases, China may make preemptive attacks on the Japan Self-Defense Forces (SDF) and US bases in the Southwest Islands or the Senkaku Islands. In particular, an invasion of the latter would be an effective option for China, as this would force Japan and the United States to conduct two-pronged operations with the defense of Taiwan. In both cases, the situation would become more serious than an "important influence situation" for Japan, in which a joint response with US forces would be necessary. Finally, Taiwan, which has realized a mature democracy, is an important partner in the race against authoritarianism, and Taiwan's defense is likely to gain support from both the US public and Congress. As military intervention would be therefore justified, Biden would be forced to keep his word.

As noted above, the credibility of US military intervention can be highly appreciated, but the devil is in the details, particularly with regard to the timing and content of American military operations. It does not appear as though a Japan–US bilateral joint operational plan for a Taiwan emergency has yet been formulated, and a bilateral defense plan for the United States and Taiwan also remains to be developed. In September of last year, a delegation of retired Japan Air Self-Defense Force (JASDF) generals, including the author, visited the US Indo-Pacific Command to exchange ideas and get briefed on the US Pacific Air Force's operational concept of Agile Combat Employment (ACE). We understood that the ACE concept seriously considers the PLA's various missile threats in China's Anti-Access/Area Denial (A2/AD) posture and how American military planners are struggling to combine forces within the A2/AD threat zone (Stand-in Force) with forces outside it (Stand-out Force). Moreover, in order to prevent a direct engagement with China from escalating into a full-scale war, the main targets of air attack are vessels and ships proceeding through the Taiwan Strait, instead of military bases and facilities in China. While taking out air bases in China would be indispensable for establishing air superiority, it is estimated that only temporary air superiority can be obtained with the current force balance. Moreover, as attacking the mainland of China would increase the risk of nuclear escalation, the approval of the highest command authority would be required to conduct such an operation. The US Pacific Air Forces (PACAF) are currently preparing for the ACE operation, which requires bases for distributed deployment of air assets, logistical support functions, and pre-accumulation of military supplies and munitions. However, to secure access will depend on future negotiations with each country in the region, including Japan. The credibility of US military intervention can be further enhanced by promoting these preparations and demonstrating to China that these bilateral talks are progressing apace. Japan and the

United States need to begin by holding frank talks on the concept of responding to a Taiwan contingency.

2.3.3 *Window of opportunity for China's military invasion*

Some Chinese experts in the United States view China as a major power reaching its peak and the window of opportunity for China to annex Taiwan is narrowing (Brands and Beckley, 2022). Economic growth has substantially slowed down due to various factors including Beijing's Draconian COVID-19 lockdown policies, and the negative repercussions of "Wolf Warrior diplomacy," leading to China's being besieged by concerned nations. At the same time, the PLA military forces that have consistently been strengthened will maintain the momentum and be ready to be deployed in actual operations. In contrast, the US military buildup to cope with China has been slow despite a recent increase in the defense budget for the Pacific Deterrence Initiative. To make matters worse, the United States is consuming its stockpiles of military supplies and ammunition to support Ukraine. The military balance between the United States and China will become favorable to China in the short term, whereas China's superiority will be gradually lost in the long run. Therefore, it is highly likely that President Xi Jinping will make a big bet in the near future, according to the more pessimistic analyses. In contrast, optimists believe that Xi recognizes that he has obtained at least five more years in his third term in power — possibly ten, with a fourth term — which pushes back the deadline for him to act on his political (and personal) agenda of annexing Taiwan. According to game theory, the time to make a big decision is more likely during the latter half of a given period. Nevertheless, Japan and the United States must endeavor to grasp the signs of whether to make decisions and maintain efforts to make Xi Jinping incline toward a pessimistic strategic estimate at any time. It is of particular importance for Japan and the United States to promptly implement joint measures to close China's window of opportunity in the short term.

It is also important to share an understanding of whether the time that is elapsing will work in favor of Taiwan or China. Self-identification on the island is trending more toward "Taiwanese" rather than "Chinese" as the younger generation increases their participation in public discourse. If this trend continues, there will be increasingly less of the population willing to accept a "One Country, Two Systems" model for unification, not to mention a PLA military occupation. According to the latest Public Opinion Survey (February 24, 2020), the percentage of people who perceive themselves as Taiwanese has dramatically increased to 83.2 percent, whereas that of people who perceive themselves as Chinese has decreased to 5.3 percent (Everington, 2020). This is probably a reflection of the strong sense of crisis among the Taiwanese citizens who watched closely the situation in Hong Kong where the "One Country, Two Systems" concept was implemented but then was quickly abrogated by the CCP. Taiwanese citizens' awareness of national defense is also growing due to the devastation of the Ukraine War. According to a survey conducted in March last year, the number of respondents who answered yes to whether they would participate in Taiwan's defense against Chinese invasion doubled — to 70 percent — from the level it was prior to the Ukraine invasion (Inoue, 2022). The more belligerent Xi becomes, the more rebellious Taiwan's people tend to be. Attention should be paid to how Xi Jinping evaluates this dilemma and the possibility that Taiwan's unification by force will be initiated earlier rather than later. It is also important for Japan, the United States, and Taiwan to respect Taiwan's identity while not giving Xi Jinping a pretext for the use of force.

2.4 Suggestions for Japan–Taiwan Relations to Prepare for the Taiwan Crisis

2.4.1 *Overcoming the "One China" policy constraint*

Japan's sense of crisis regarding Taiwan has increased rapidly in the past few years. The first Policy Simulation of the Taiwan Strait Crisis, which the author organized and held in August 2021 with a number of retired generals and admirals of SDF, was featured by NHK, a Japanese public broadcaster, as a special program, drawing surprising attention from domestic as well as international audiences. The second simulation in August of last year, which happened to be held in parallel with the PLA exercise after Pelosi's visit, was reported on by scores of media outlets. The number of incumbent Diet members participating has increased from three in the first simulation to 10 in the second, including former Defense Minister Itsunori Onodera, who played the role of Prime Minister in the war game. As a result of these simulations, a number of policy issues that should be addressed by the Japanese government were identified, and one of the highest priorities that was highlighted to be overcome was the "One China" policy dilemma (Iwata *et al.*, 2022).

Tokyo has consistently maintained the position of the Japan–China Joint Statement of 1972, which states, "The Government of Japan recognizes the Government of the People's Republic of China as the sole legal Government of China. The Government of the People's Republic of China reiterates that Taiwan is an inalienable part of the territory of the People's Republic of China. The Government of Japan fully understands and respects this stand of the Government of the People's Republic of China, and it firmly maintains its stand under Article 8 of the Potsdam Proclamation" (Communique, 1972). Former Ambassador to the United States Takakazu Kuriyama (2007), who participated in the negotiations for the Statement as Chief of the Treaty Section, MOFA, at the time, explained this point as follows.

> Japan's hope is that the Taiwan issue will be settled peacefully through talks between the parties on both sides of the Taiwan Strait. If Taiwan is to be unified into the People's Republic of China as a result, Japan will naturally accept this (which is the meaning of the third paragraph of the Joint Statement). As long as the talks between the parties concerned are conducted, the Taiwan issue is perceived as China's domestic issue, which should not be intervened by a third party. Given this recognition, under the current situation where there is no possibility of armed conflict, there will be no operational problems with the Japan–US Security Treaty concerning Taiwan. However, if China were to attempt to unify Taiwan by force in the future, the situation would be fundamentally different, so Japan's response would have to be put on hold." (Kuriyama, 2007)

The government of Japan has also consistently proposed a peaceful settlement of the issue. As stated in the 1969 Sato-Nixon Joint Statement (November 21), "the Prime Minister stated that the maintenance of peace and security in the Taiwan region is also an extremely important factor for the security of Japan," and that it will "encourage the peaceful resolution of cross-strait issues" in the Taiwan Strait (Sato, 1969). The 2021 Suga-Biden Joint Statement (April 16) reconfirmed this policy. Against these backdrops, the 1996 Taiwan Strait Crisis reaffirmed that "the Situation in Areas Surrounding Japan" could include a Taiwan emergency, but preparing for a specific crisis was perceived as being against the promotion of a "peaceful resolution." Therefore, the situation became a dilemma in that measures could not be taken until the crisis occurred. As a result, the government of Japan has few channels, infrastructure, or track record for public dialogue with Taiwan. Hence, Japan's response in the event of an armed conflict has not yet been clarified.

The consistent promotion of a peaceful resolution by the Japanese government is a consideration to prevent the Taiwan issue from becoming a trilateral political problem among Japan, the United States, and China. The United States has its own "One China" policy in accordance with historical documents (Bush, 2017). However, Taiwan has never been ruled by the People's Republic of China, and the reality is that the large majority of Taiwanese people reject unification with the PRC, which has a radically different political and economic system. Even if Taiwan is prudent about independence and wants to maintain the *status quo*, China will not abandon the option to use force to annex Taiwan. Facing this reality, and following the American example, Japan must muster the wisdom and ingenuity to strengthen substantial communication with Taiwan while maintaining its conventional position.

2.4.2 *Importance of strategic communication with China and Taiwan*

The Taiwan issue is derived from the collision of three aspects, as stated at the beginning of this chapter, in which the countries concerned each interpret the historical background from their own standpoints. In this regard, acquiring the narrative advantage is crucial. For this reason, Japan needs to drastically strengthen its power of discourse and its strategic communications capacity. To avoid acting after the event, the government of Japan should take immediate actions including the establishment of specialized organizations for this purpose, the use of supercomputers to discriminate false information, the use of social-network influencers, and the enhancement of messaging capacity in Chinese and English. In addition, strategic communication will be the key to coping with cognitive warfare, on which the PLA puts a priority. It is necessary not only to enhance a systematic response by the government but also to enlighten the Japanese public about the need to raise their literacy in the cognitive domain (Iwata *et al.*, 2023).

While getting domestic preparedness ready, Japan must further strengthen its strategic communication with the PRC and Taiwan, in order to better deter a Taiwan Strait crisis. To Beijing, Tokyo should convey the following messages, while coordinating closely with the United States. First, the deterrence of a crisis is Japan's foremost purpose. Second, Japan may have to engage in the unfortunate event that such deterrence collapses. Finally, Japan will strengthen its defense posture in the Southwest Islands, which will also contribute to regional stability. In doing so, both Japan and China need to cooperate to establish a communication route that top leaders can trust so that messages can be accurately as well as securely exchanged with President Xi Jinping, enabling straightforward dialogue to prevent misunderstandings.

Japan should start with the opening of reliable communication channels with Taiwan. A trusted communication channel is required between the political leaders of Japan and Taiwan. Taking advantage of both countries being democracies, various channels can and should be established. Through top-level political dialogue as well as diverse bilateral communications, Japan needs to repeatedly convey the following messages. Again, first and foremost is that deterrence of the crisis is Japan's primary objective. Second, a unilateral declaration of independence would give China a pretext for an armed invasion, and therefore it would not be in the interests of Japan, the United States, or Taiwan itself. At the same time, Japan should clearly state that if deterrence fails, a Taiwan contingency would highly likely involve Japan so that Japan, together with the United States, will engage in support of Taiwan. Thus, Japan should start discussions on specific ways of coordination. If Japan is forced to choose whether to fight alongside the United States for the defense of Taiwan, especially against possible nuclear intimidation, the sorts of communications and decisions that will be made by top political leaders will be crucial not only for Japan's security but also for the Japan–US security alliance as well as for the regional security order. The government of Japan needs to acknowledge the status of Taiwan as an unrecognized state so that a broad and multilayered official working relationship can be developed during peacetime. At the same time, public understanding of why the defense of Taiwan is important for Japan should be disseminated and shared.

2.4.3 *Issues requiring coordination with Taiwan*

Japan needs to overcome the dilemma of maintaining the "One China" policy based on the Japan–China Joint Statement to proceed to coordination with Taiwan. Beijing will certainly protest if Tokyo discusses prevention and preparation of a Taiwan crisis with Taipei. However, Japan, in concert with the United States, should argue that China's bellicose moves have compelled Japan to consider the collapse of its premise for the "One China" policy and that Japan will stick to the joint statement unless China undertakes the use of force. Having this in mind, Japan should establish a framework for communication with Taiwan and plan various means of responding before the crisis arises, including a confidential communication system between Japan and Taiwan (signing a memorandum of understanding, if needed), alternative communication methods when Taiwan is isolated due to the disruption of submarine cables and satellite communication networks, and enhancing formality by dispatching defense officials and attachés (Taiwan ni Gen'eki, 2022).

In addition, discussions on the transportation of Japanese nationals and the response to displaced citizens must be held as soon as possible. In the absence of an embassy in Taiwan, the government of Japan needs to clarify the roles and responsibilities of the Taipei Office of the Japan–Taiwan Exchange Association, develop a practical plan and capacity for the evacuation of Japanese nationals in Taiwan, and formulate a basic policy for the acceptance of refugees from Taiwan. As noncombatant evacuation operations (NEO) in a Taiwan contingency would require bilateral and multilateral cooperation, Japan as a neighbor country should take the lead in establishing a coordination framework for NEO with Taiwan and other volunteer countries. In implementing NEO, understanding by local governments and residents is essential to accept displaced people. The government of Japan needs to provide practical requirements for transportation, accommodation, as well as health and welfare treatment based on realistic simulations. If necessary, it should take actions in advance concerning the use of private transportation, commercial accommodation, and specific public facilities.

Finally, Japan should prepare beyond a Taiwan crisis, taking into account the possibility of China collaborating with Russia and North Korea, as well as a complex contingency in anticipation of an invasion of the Senkaku Islands. Every response of the government of Japan will require the recognition of survival-threatening situations in accordance with security bills, which is very difficult for the United States and Taiwan to comprehend. It is important to gain the understanding of the ROC government, military, and other relevant institutions regarding the basic policy and the legal constraints on Japan's response from gray zone activity to armed attack, as well as the operational guidelines of the security organizations and the SDF.

2.5 Conclusion

Prime Minister Kishida expressed his concerns on May 6, 2022, in London where he met with his UK counterpart for coordinating sanctions against Russia and enhancing Japan's security ties with UK, saying "Ukraine Today may be East Asia Tomorrow" (*Kishida shushō*, 2022). The new NSS and related security documents which his cabinet and Kishida himself have committed to reflect his serious concerns in dire security situations, particularly a militarized China. Japan should not lose time to prepare itself for possible crisis. As things keep changing, the government of Japan should adapt its strategic approach to meet future security requirements, starting with the "One China" policy dilemma, while enhancing strategic communication with Taipei and Washington, as well as Beijing.

Acknowledgments

This chapter is a result of the collaborative project "An Interdisciplinary Approach to Contemporary East Asia Studies" [21REN283] at St. Andrew's University Research Institute.

References

Biden, J. (2022). National Security Strategy. The White House, 23.

Brands, H. and Beckley, M. (2022, August 16). *Danger Zone: The Coming Conflict with China*. New York, NY: W W Norton & Co Inc.

Bush, R. (2017). A One-China policy primer. Brookings Institutions. Retrieved from https://www.brookings.edu/wp-content/uploads/2017/03/one-china-policy-primer-web-final.pdf.

Communique, C. J. J. (1972, September 29). Joint communique of the government of Japan and the government of the People's Republic of China. Retrieved August 5, 2023, from http://archive.today/pZHRO.

Davidson, P. S. (2021, March 9). Statement before the Senate Committee on Armed Services). Retrieved from https://www.armed-services.senate.gov/imo/media/doc/Davidson_03-09-21.pdf.

Egan, L. (2021, December 9). Biden says U.S. will not unilaterally send troops to defend Ukraine. *NBCNews.com*. Retrieved August 5, 2023, from http://archive.today/7KR1b.

36 S. Oue

Everington, K. (2020, February 24). Record 83% of people in Taiwan identify as Taiwanese amid Wuhan virus outbreak. *Taiwan News*. Retrieved August 5, 2023, from http://archive.today/u6RFk.

Former Japan PM tells China, 'a Taiwan emergency is a Japanese emergency'. (2021, December 1). *CNN*. Retrieved August 5, 2023, from http://archive.today/mw4xk.

Government of Japan (2013, December 17). *National Security Strategy* (Provisional Translation). Cabinet Secretariat. Retrieved November 30, 2023, from https://www.cas.go.jp/jp/siryou/131217anzenhoshou/nss-e.pdf

Inoue, Y. (2022, April 24). *Ukuraina no teikō o mite chōhei-sei fukkatsu no shiji takamaru Taiwan* [Ukrainian resistance boosts support for Taiwan to restore conscription]. *Wedge Online*. Retrieved August 5, 2023, from http://archive.today/8StTj.

Ishida, K. (2022, March 22). *Taiwan de beigun no shinrai kyūraku yūji sansen meguru seronchōsa jieitai ni kitai 43-pāsento* [Confidence in U.S. forces plummets in Taiwan Opinion poll on emergency warfare: 43 percent expected for Self-Defense Forces]. *Asahi.com*. Retrieved August 5, 2023, from http://archive.today/bHglP.

Iwata, K., Takei, T., Oue, S., and Kanehara, N. (2022, May). *Jieitai Saikokanbu ga Kataru Taiwan Yuji* (SDF's top leaders talking on Taiwan Crisis). Shincho-sha.

Iwata, K., Takei, T., Oue, S., and Kanehara, N. (2023). *Kimitachi, Chugoku ni Katerunoka* [Can SDF win against China?]. Sankei Shinbun Shuppan.

Japan Ministry of Defense (2022). Defense of Japan 2022. Retrieved from https://www.mod.go.jp/en/publ/w_paper/index.html.

Johnson, J. (2022, September 19). Biden says U.S. would defend Taiwan in 'unprecedented attack'. *Japan Times*. Retrieved August 5, 2023, from http://archive.today/eAwKX.

Kishida shushō, 'Ukuraina wa ashita no Ajia' to kiki-kan tai Ro tsuika seisai [Prime Minister Kishida feels threatened that 'Ukraine will be the Asia of tomorrow,' additional sanctions against Russia] (2022, May 5). *Japan Reuters*. Retrieved August 5, 2023, from http://archive.today/d12tR.

Kuriyama, T. (2007, October 24). *Taiwan Mondai ni tsuite no Nihon no Tachiba — Nichu Kyoudou Seimei Dai Sankou no Imi* [Japan's Position on the Taiwan Issue-The Meaning of the Third Clause of Japan-China Joint Statement], *The Japan Institute of International Affairs*. Retrieved August 5, 2023, from http://archive.today/zvM4f.

Sacks, D. (2021, July 6). What Xi Jinping's major speech means for Taiwan. *Council on Foreign Relations*. Retrieved August 5, 2023, from http://archive.today/0JbTs.

Sato, E. (1969, November 21). Joint statement of Japanese Prime Minister Eisaku Sato and US President Richard Nixon. Washington, DC. Retrieved

August 5, 2023, from https://worldjpn.net/documents/texts/docs/19691121. D1E.html.

Shelbourne, M. (2021, March 9). Davidson: China could try to take control of Taiwan in 'Next Six Years'. *USNI News*. Retrieved August 5, 2023, from http://archive.today/6Fm90.

Taiwan ni Gen'eki Boueishou Shokuin haken he: Konka nimo Jyouchu Jyouhou-Shushuu-Kyouka [To strengthen information gathering, an MoD official will be seconded to the *de facto* Embassy in Taipei as early as this summer]. (June 4, 2022). Sankei Shimbun. Retrieved August 5, 2023, from http://archive.today/W0i7h.

Tian, Y. L. and Blanchard, B. (2022, October 16). China will never renounce right to use force over Taiwan, Xi says. Reuters. Retrieved August 5, 2023, from http://archive.today/4QjUm.

© 2025 World Scientific Publishing Company
https://doi.org/10.1142/9789811298301_0003

Chapter 3

Establishing Military Cooperation Between Taiwan and Japan: Policy Suggestions and Problems

Kuo Tzu-Yung

Officials in Japan have signaled growing concerns regarding potential tensions in the Taiwan Strait as China is pressuring Taiwan using military means, such as sending military aircraft into the air defense identification zone (ADIZ) of the Republic of China (ROC) and vessels into the waters surrounding the island. Therefore, for the first time, the Ministry of Defense of Japan explicitly framed stability in the Taiwan Strait as being important to Japan's own security in the Defense of Japan 2021 white paper, released in July 2021 (Onuorah, 2021).

In addition, in a December 1, 2021, forum organized by the Institute for National Policy Research, a Taiwanese think tank, former Japanese Prime Minister Shinzo Abe stated that "A Taiwan emergency is a Japanese emergency, and therefore an emergency for the Japan–US alliance. People in Beijing, President Xi Jinping in particular, should never have a misunderstanding in recognizing this." An armed invasion of Taiwan would be a grave danger to Japan, he explained (Former Japan PM, 2021).

Abe's rhetoric does reflect a sense of crisis in Japan. Furthermore, from August 4 to 7, 2022, the People's Republic of China (PRC) held its largest-ever military exercises around Taiwan, following then US House Speaker Nancy Pelosi's visit to the island democracy. During these exercises, five ballistic missiles fired by China landed in the waters of Japan's

Exclusive Economic Zone (EEZ) — the first time Chinese missiles have splashed down in what is unambiguously Japanese territory. Japan lodged a strong protest with China through diplomatic channels, calling the matter "a serious problem that affects our national security and the safety of our citizens" (Chinese missiles, 2022).

According to a *Taiwan News* report, the China Power Project, which is operated by the Center for Strategic and International Studies (CSIS), conducted a survey of 64 experts on China, Taiwan, and cross-strait relations from August 10 to September 8, 2022. These experts included former US government officials, policy and intelligence analysts, and experts from academia and think tanks. The survey found that 63 percent of respondents believe China will invade Taiwan within 10 years (Everington, 2022).

On October 16, 2022, at the 20th National Congress of the Chinese Communist Party (CCP), China's biggest political event, Chinese President Xi Jinping said that "We insist on striving for the prospect of peaceful reunification with the greatest sincerity and best efforts, but we will never promise to give up the use of force, and reserve the option to take all necessary measures" (Tian and Blanchard, 2022).

On October 17, 2022, US Secretary of State Antony Blinken warned that Beijing is pursuing its plans to annex Taiwan on a "much faster timeline" under Xi Jinping. Senior US and ROC military figures have said the Chinese People's Liberation Army (PLA) would have the capability within a few years, while analysts point to Xi's goal of national rejuvenation by 2049 as a potential deadline (Davidson, 2022).

Moreover, on November 14, 2022, Japanese Prime Minister Fumio Kishida told Asian leaders at the Association of Southeast Asian Nations (ASEAN) summit in Phnom Penh, Cambodia, that ensuring peace and stability in the Taiwan Strait was important for regional security, and that China is increasingly escalating tensions in the region. This was the first time the Prime Minister had ever discussed Taiwan-related issues at an ASEAN summit (Liu, 2022).

Against this backdrop, Japan does not have the luxury of eschewing military cooperation with Taiwan. Shinzo Abe transformed Japan's relationship with Taiwan to counter threats from China (Davidson, 2022; Sacks, 2022). However, compared with the dynamism of economic and unofficial interactions between the two countries in recent years, their military ties are lacking, and are believed to be the weakest link in this complex relationship.

This chapter provides some policy suggestions for areas of possible military cooperation between Taiwan and Japan in the near future, especially in terms of intelligence cooperation, mutual exchanges of military personnel, military technical cooperation, and even joint military exercises designed to deter a Chinese invasion of Taiwan. This chapter also highlights potential problems that could affect the prospects for military cooperation between Taiwan and Japan.

3.1 To Promote the Exchange of Military Intelligence

First, intelligence-sharing between the United States and Ukraine in the Russia–Ukraine War was robust. Intelligence always plays a crucial role in armed conflicts, and accurate intelligence is the key to success. Intelligence is an important weapon in the hands of policymakers and generals. Therefore, throughout The Art of War, the great military strategist of ancient China Sun Tzu emphasized the importance of intelligence (Utibe, 2017). Good intelligence can win battles and wars (Kahn, 2006), as the Russia–Ukraine War amply demonstrates. Joshua Rovner, an associate professor in the School of International Service at American University, said there are reasons to believe that intelligence played a critical role before and during Russia's invasion of Ukraine, and that it might prove vital to ending the war (Rovner, 2022).

Rovner added that the US intelligence community has unusually good access to Russian communications, and it seems likely that the intelligence provided more detailed and compelling insights about Russian plans. Some combination of human intelligence (HUMINT) and signals intelligence (SIGINT) sources may have provided insight into Putin's plans. This is why the US covert services were remarkably conspicuous before the war in Ukraine. So, American agencies can issue blunt assessments about Russian intentions and US policymakers used intelligence to rally support against Russian aggression (Rovner, 2022).

Besides, the exchange of intelligence cooperation and intelligence sharing are very important. The Biden administration has increasingly shared intelligence that has helped Ukrainian forces to target Russian forces (Rovner, 2022). During the war, Ukrainian fighters have mounted a fierce resistance, resisting Russian troops, targeting Russian convoys, and killing Russian commanders, largely thanks to real-time intelligence provided by the United States. According to the White House spokesperson, "We have consistently been sharing intelligence that includes

3.2 The Exchange of Military Intelligence Between Taiwan and Japan

The military threat that China poses to Taiwan grows increasingly with each passing year, and Japan is also threatened by an ascendant China (Ao, 2021). Recently, as the tensions between Taiwan and China intensified, conflicts between Japan and China have also increased. In the face of the imminent military threat from China, it is crucial that intelligence be exchanged in an effective manner between Taiwan and Japan.

The intelligence cooperation between the United States and Ukraine has provided a good example to the world. Thus, Taiwan and Japan should learn from this and strengthen cooperation on intelligence gathering and intelligence sharing. Fan Chen-kuo, deputy secretary-general of the Taiwan–Japan Relations Association, said that Taiwan and Japan should exchange security-related information in a systematic manner (Ihara, 2018).

Japan has robust intelligence, surveillance, and reconnaissance (ISR) capabilities that can provide Taiwan threat intelligence in the event of a potential conflict with China (Ao, 2021). It has been widely reported that Taiwan and Japan are believed to be sharing intelligence through back channels in the absence of formal diplomatic relations (Ihara, 2018).

Tokyo has sent a retired Japan Self-Defense Force (JSDF) officer to the office of the Japan–Taiwan Exchange Association — Japan's unofficial embassy in Taiwan, but the two sides still face obstacles in sharing intelligence and coordinating strategy in unforeseen circumstances (Shigeta, 2022). Yasuhiro Matsuda, a professor of International Politics in the Institute for Advanced Studies on Asia at the University of Tokyo, said there is no real-time information-sharing mechanism between Taiwan and Japan, such as the General Security of Military Information Agreement between Japan and South Korea, because Japan has no official relationship with Taiwan (Onuorah, 2021).

In order to resolve the problem and check China's hostility, Taiwan and Japan need an intelligence-sharing alliance, and can decide to make a secret agreement to promote more real-time defense intelligence cooperation. Through such a secret agreement between Taiwan and Japan,

Japanese and Republic of China (ROC) defense officers can share more real-time intelligence about China's military capabilities and behaviors, especially the intelligence of missile threats.

Eric Chan, a fellow at the Global Taiwan Institute, and Wallace "Chip" Gregson, a former US officer and marine, said that both Taiwan and Japan face similar constant, aggressive Chinese Air Force (PLAAF) incursions into their respective air defense identification zones (ADIZ), yet there is no coordination between Taiwanese and Japanese responses. Against surges of PLA activity, more robust coordination would be required. This would mean liaison officers embedded in respective air operation centers for real-time intelligence sharing and analysis would allow for crisis management between operational headquarters. This would form the basis for a coherent information network, vastly increasing each partner's situational awareness and combat capability (Chan and Gregson, 2022).

On June 4, 2022, the *Sankei Shimbun* reported that the significant increase in China's military exercises and incursions around Taiwan over the past few years has prompted calls for Japan to appoint an active-duty defense attaché to Taipei so as to enhance intelligence capabilities and facilitate communications with Taiwan. However, due to concerns that sending an active-duty defense attaché to Taipei might draw anger from China, the candidate would be a civil servant with the Ministry of Defense rather than a military officer (Yang *et al.*, 2022).

This is a significant step for the exchange of military intelligence between Taiwan and Japan. Kuo Yu-jen, executive director of the Institute for National Policy Research, said if the reported move goes ahead, it would represent a step forward in strengthening military relations between Taiwan and Japan (Yu and Lin, 2022a). We hope that the government of Japan would also allow Taiwan to send an active-duty defense attaché to Japan to facilitate intelligence cooperation with each other in the near future.

3.3 To Develop Exchanges of Military Personnel

According to Masahiro Matsumura, a professor of international politics at St. Andrew's University in Osaka, apart from promoting the exchange of military intelligence, Taiwan and Japan should develop bilateral exchanges of military personnel, particularly among high- and mid-level commanders. However, since Japan ceased recognition of the ROC in 1972, Tokyo has strictly avoided direct official-to-official interaction with Taipei, adhering instead to a non-governmental framework (Matsumura, 2022a).

Therefore, Japanese officials are banned from meeting publicly with their Taiwanese counterparts, let alone engaging in exchanges of military personnel from both countries. Professor Matsumura added this means that Japan's defense policymakers and military leaders must not have official policy talks and exchanges with Taiwan's counterparts, but only informal Japan–Taiwan defense interaction through low-profile, non-governmental, unofficial, and informal contacts and channels (Matsumura, 2022a).

For example, former Japanese Defense Minister Shigeru Ishiba, who led a parliamentary delegation to Taiwan on July 27, 2022, said the trip was aimed at fostering exchanges on Japan–Taiwan security, and that the delegation held talks with ROC officials on regional security issues. Kuo Yu-jen said that this was the highest-level delegation from Japan to visit Taiwan since the severing of diplomatic relations (Yu and Yeh, 2022).

Apart from the visits of former Japanese military officers to Taiwan, we hope that incumbent military officers, particularly the high- and mid-level commanders, could be allowed to visit Taiwan. We also encourage the Japanese military to invite their Taiwanese counterparts to visit Japan. Exchanges of military personnel can bolster the exchange of strategic information and thinking between military officers of Taiwan and Japan, which could help both cope with a military crisis across the Taiwan Strait.

Besides, various units of Taiwan's armed forces have begun reviewing and analyzing the tactics employed by the PLA in its drills held around Taiwan, and the information gathered from this analysis will serve as a useful reference for the military in the future (Yu and Lin, 2022b). Japan's military can send high- and mid-level commanders to Taiwan to study the PLA's tactics with Taiwan military officers.

Hence, Taiwan and Japan should create a bilateral officer exchange program to build a strong military relationship. Building bilateral ties between Taiwanese and Japanese militaries to share standards, processes, and procedures would constitute the bedrock relationship they will need to fight together during a crisis. Frequent exchanges would begin to build bridges between early and mid-career professionals. This officer exchange program could grow into an official training process (Noon and Ross, 2022).

3.4 To Build Military-Technical Cooperation

Paul Leaf, a former editor of the *Stanford Law Review* and an attorney at an international law firm, said Taiwan is focusing on building asymmetric combat capabilities to deter China's potential invasion. Submarines are valuable to Taiwan because they can offer an asymmetric response to target Chinese warships. For instance, submarines could contest a Chinese maritime blockade and attack Beijing's amphibious vessels if China tries to invade the island by sea (Leaf, 2014). However, Taiwan's small fleet of conventional submarines is insufficient on its own to deter a Chinese invasion. Therefore, Taiwan wants to build submarines.

On November 24, 2020, Taiwan officially began work on its first domestically produced submarine in an effort to beef up its coastal defenses against any invasion from China. Under the program, Taiwan will build eight new diesel-powered attack submarines, which will substantially rejuvenate its fleet of two World War II-era vessels and two Dutch-made submarines built in the 1980s. The first submarine is expected to be completed by 2024 (Hale, 2020).

Foreign submarine companies, with the approval of their governments, are aiding in the secretive program to build submarines in Taiwan. Taipei has stealthily sourced technology, components, and talent from at least seven nations, including America, Britain, Australia, South Korea, India, Spain, and Canada, to help Taiwan build an underwater fleet (Saito *et al.*, 2021).

Japan has the most advanced submarines in the world. It also has capabilities and sophisticated technology to build advanced conventional submarines. For example, on March 9, 2022, Japan commissioned the first of a new class of diesel-electric submarines *Taigei* (meaning "Great Whale") built by Mitsubishi Heavy Industries, Ltd., a leading Japanese submarine manufacturer, bringing the planned expansion of its submarine fleet to 22 boats when it enters service (Yeo, 2022).

Moreover, in a television interview with the *Australian Broadcasting Corporation* ahead of the eighth Australia–Japan 2+2 Foreign and Defense Ministers' meeting held on October 10, 2018 in Sydney, then-Japanese Foreign Minister Taro Kono said that Japan was prepared to sell its submarines to Australia should protracted negotiations between state-owned French shipbuilder Naval Group and the Australian government for the construction of 12 French-designed diesel-electric boats collapse (Gady, 2018). Hence, Japan has the capacity to help Taiwan build new submarines.

Japan, however, is hesitant to do this because of fear of Chinese pressure. According to two senior defense ministry sources in Tokyo, the idea of helping Taiwan was informally discussed in Japan but was dropped out of concern over how Beijing might react. Retired Vice Admiral Yoji Koda, a former fleet commander of the Japanese Maritime Force, said that one reason for Japan's hesitancy is fear of the economic consequences of offending Beijing (Saito *et al.*, 2021). Paul Leaf said if Japan refuses to strengthen Taiwan's defensive capabilities, China will infer that its willingness to take Taiwan outweighs other nations' readiness to stop it. Therefore, Japan should help Taiwan acquire modern submarines (Leaf, 2014).

Aside from submarines, according to several documents obtained by Janes, the global open-source intelligence company, from the Ministry of Defense (MoD) in Tokyo, Japan is developing two advanced standoff hypersonic warheads that will be fitted onto two hypersonic weapons, namely, the Hyper Velocity Gliding Projectile (HVGP) and the Hypersonic Cruise Missile (HCM), with the "Sea Buster," which is being specifically developed to target enemy surface vessels, most likely larger warships (Takahashi, 2020).

In order to deter attacks by aircraft carriers of the PLA Navy, Taiwan is developing its own missiles, particularly the Hsiung Feng III medium-range supersonic missiles that can attack Chinese aircraft carriers. In this regard, Japan could help Taiwan develop advanced anti-ship missiles for use against attacking Chinese warships. Taiwan and Japan could reach an agreement whereby Taiwan would dispatch technicians to Japan for short-term research and study, and Taipei could invite Japanese experts to Taiwan to conduct field instruction so as to strengthen military technical cooperation.

According to media reports in November 2022, Japan has begun to consider relaxing export conditions on used Self-Defense hardware to include tanks and missiles, which are now prohibited from being supplied to foreign countries. It will also look into offering Asian countries such equipment free of charge to enhance defense cooperation as China expands its military power (Miki, 2022).

3.5 To Conduct Joint Military Exercises

Japan conducts military exercises with several other nations, including the United States, South Korea, India, and the Philippines, among others. For example, the naval forces of Japan, the United States, and South Korea conducted joint military drills in September 2022. Japan and the United States conducted a joint military drill involving the US aircraft carrier *Ronald Reagan* in areas around Japan in light of North Korea's continued missile launches in October 2022. Besides, Japanese defense forces also participated for the first time in Indonesia's military exercises in August 2022.

Moreover, the air forces of Japan and the Philippines held their first-ever joint exercises in July 2021. According to Sebastian Strangio (2021), Southeast Asia editor at *The Diplomat*, "the exercises are also a clear indication of the increasing level of security cooperation between Manila and Tokyo in the face of China's expansive claims and the build-up of its naval and maritime capabilities."

On June 24, 2021, Japan's then-deputy defense minister warned of a growing threat posed by Chinese and Russian collaboration, warning that his country would have to "wake up" to the realities of Chinese coercion and help to protect Taiwan "as a democratic country." He pointed out that Japan and Taiwan were geographically close, and an attack on Taiwan would impact Okinawa, which is home to thousands of US military personnel, as well as their families (Brunnstrom, 2021).

On August 3, 2022, Japanese Cabinet Affairs Minister Hirokazu Matsuno said that Japan was concerned about China's military activities near the island of Taiwan because the relevant area overlaps with Japan's EEZ (Japan Conveys Concern, 2022). In face of China's challenges, Japan should work with Taiwan to deter a Chinese attack on Taiwan and prepare a joint military response. However, Taiwan and Japan don't have formal diplomatic ties, so conducting joint military exercises between the two militaries is not feasible under China's protest.

In order to overcome this dilemma, the United States could invite Taiwan to participate in international military exercises. For example, the US House of Representatives on July 14, 2022, passed an annual defense policy bill with provisions to reinforce the partnership between Washington and Taipei, including requiring the US President to invite Taiwan to join US-led military exercises in the region (Chiang and Huang, 2022). The ROC military could take this opportunity to conduct joint military exercises with the Japanese military.

3.6 To Enable Direct Talks Between the Militaries of Taiwan and Japan

Because there are no diplomatic relations between Taiwan and Japan and the Japan government's self-imposed restriction, there is no way for Japan to conduct direct and meaningful policy coordination with Taiwan, not to mention working together militarily to deter or repel an invasion by China. Yoichi Kato, a visiting research fellow at the Institute for National Defense and Security Research, observed that official communication channels between Taipei and Tokyo are close to nonexistent (Kato, 2021). For this reason, Taiwan and Japan conduct diplomatic affairs through civilian channels, and the two countries can currently only discuss these and other security-related issues through unofficial channels.

On August 27, 2021, Taiwan and Japan's ruling parties held a virtual meeting, discussing possible military exchanges and how to handle the rising challenge they both face from their neighbor China. The talks were attended by two senior lawmakers, one from Taiwan's Democratic Progressive Party (DPP) and one from Japan's Liberal Democratic Party (LDP). The DPP's Lo Chih-Cheng and Tsai Shih-Ying said that the talks focused on areas including semiconductors, China's nearby military activities, and possible cooperation among Taiwan, Japan, and the United States. Possible cooperation between the Coast Guards of the two sides was also discussed. Masahisa Sato, a lawmaker who runs the LDP's foreign affairs team, said the dialogue would help inform the Japanese ruling party's policymaking (Blanchard *et al.*, 2021).

Russell Hsiao, executive director of the Global Taiwan Institute in Washington, DC, emphasized that the time is now for direct high-level security talks between Taiwan and Japan, and there must be direct high-level security dialogues between Taipei and Tokyo. In 2019, President Tsai Ing-wen stated that "Taiwan and Japan are confronted with the same threats in the East Asian region" and "it is vital that talks be raised to the level of security cooperation" (Hsiao, 2022). We hope direct talks between the militaries of Taiwan and Japan can be carried out as soon as possible.

3.7 The Problems of Military Cooperation Between Taiwan and Japan

3.7.1 *No diplomatic relations*

It is necessary and urgent to establish military cooperation between Taiwan and Japan in the face of the imminent threat posed by China. Yet, according to professor Matsumura, given that there is no diplomatic recognition between Taiwan and Japan, there is also no formal mechanism for such communication and coordination between Taipei and Tokyo (Matsumura, 2022b).

In order to overcome this diplomatic dilemma for military cooperation between Taiwan and Japan, Taipei and lots of pro-Taiwan Japanese politicians are calling on the government of Japan to emulate America's Taiwan Relations Act (TRA) and enact a Japanese version of the TRA to improve bilateral cooperation on security and render a Japan military defense of Taiwan more feasible.

On December 25, 2021, at the inauguration ceremony of the Japan–Taiwan Co-Prosperity Chiefs Alliance, which comprises 127 city and village mayors in Tokyo, Kaga Mayor Riku Miyamoto, the chairman of the alliance, called on Tokyo to draw up a Japanese version of TRA to improve bilateral cooperation on security. He said that a Japanese version of the TRA would create a bilateral channel for security and political dialogues that both countries need (Lin and Chin, 2021).

3.7.2 *China's pressure*

The government of Japan is very concerned about China's attitude when dealing with Taiwan. Tetsuo Kotani, a professor of global studies at Meikai University and a senior fellow at the Japan Institute of International Affairs, said that whether Tokyo will seek more official relations with Taipei largely depends on Beijing's behavior (Kotani, 2022).

Professor Kotani added that in order to enhance intelligence exchanges with Taiwan, Tokyo dispatched a retired (i.e., not on active-duty) SDF officer in 2003 to be stationed at the Japan–Taiwan Exchange Association due to concerns about a backlash from Beijing. As tensions across the Taiwan Strait have grown in recent years, there have been calls in Tokyo for dispatching active-duty SDF officers to Taipei instead of retired officers. The government of Japan, however, dispatched a civilian official for fear of provoking China (Kotani, 2022).

3.8 China's Huge Market

According to Niklas Swanström (2022), a fellow at the Foreign Policy Institute of the Johns Hopkins University School of Advanced International Studies (SAIS), Japan is instinctively positive toward Taiwan and its democratic development; however, at the same time, it is also concerned about the economic impact of potential Chinese reactions in light of Japan's growing relations with Taiwan. Beijing's boycott of South Korea when Seoul placed a Terminal High Altitude Area Defense (THAAD) system on its soil is fresh enough in Japanese memory.

Swanström added that Japan's weakness and strength is its economy, and Beijing is more than aware that economic pressure on Tokyo is a robust tool. Japan depends on China both for trade and supply chains, with 21.6 percent of its exports and 23.3 percent of its imports going to and coming from China, respectively. This makes Japanese trade and economic growth especially vulnerable to Chinese pressure. There is no doubt that Beijing will weaponize this to leverage Tokyo into submission (Swanström, 2022).

3.9 Conclusion

According to Sabrina Shaffer, an intern at the Foreign Policy Research Institute, although Japan has committed itself to promoting a "free and open Indo-Pacific," it has not clarified whether it would provide aid to Taiwan in the event of a Chinese invasion. As a close neighbor of Taiwan, Japan is vulnerable to any such Chinese attacks. Moreover, Japan's close military ties with the United States will likely embroil Tokyo in any conflict with Beijing. Hence, it is becoming increasingly clear that "Taiwan's problem is also Japan's problem" (Shaffer, 2022).

After Pelosi visited Taiwan in August 2022, China flexed its military muscles around the nation in the hopes of deterring Taiwan from independence (Sang, 2022). If China's military measures are left unchecked, it would spiral up its pressure over Taiwan, leading to a big threat to neighboring countries, particularly Japan (Sang, 2022). Therefore, it is time for Japan to take concrete actions — not merely provide lip service — and to join the United States in defending Taiwan from Chinese expansionism.

According to Ben Noon, the CEO of Talon Cyber Security, and Joseph Ross, a research assistant at the Center for Strategic and Budgetary Assessments, if a war broke out tomorrow between Taiwan and China, the militaries of Taiwan and Japan would have almost no ability to coordinate their actions. Only disaster awaits on the current trajectory (Noon and Ross, 2022). Therefore, Taiwan and Japan should conduct military cooperation, to exchange military intelligence, military personnel, and military technical cooperation, and for joint military exercises, as soon as possible.

Ben Noon and Joseph Ross added that coordinated efforts between Taiwan and Japan could be the most effective strategic deterrence against Beijing's reckless activities. Bilateral military cooperation alone will not be a silver bullet to deter Chinese aggression over Taiwan, but it is a necessary first step for them to effectively coordinate during a crisis (Noon and Ross, 2022). Hence, the two nations should make joint efforts to build a sound, stable, and mature military relationship.

However, there are no official diplomatic ties between Taiwan and Japan, so any cooperation to solidify bilateral military relations must be handled with caution. According to Thomas Wilkins, a senior fellow at the Australian Strategic Policy and International Relations at the University of Sydney, instead of direct military cooperation, Taiwan and Japan might profitably explore collaboration on nontraditional security issues such as climate change, pandemics, and transnational crime. In particular, both countries' recent national defense white papers place emphasis on Humanitarian Assistance and Disaster Relief (HADR) operations. Joint cooperation in this sphere would strengthen bilateral relations and lay the foundation for a deeper and expanded partnership (Wilkins, 2012).

What is more, according to Shaffer, the Global Cooperation and Training Framework (GCTF) — which consists of four core members: the United States, Taiwan, Japan, and Australia — provides another potential avenue for ROC–Japanese military coordination. GCTF is a platform that encourages information sharing and interstate collaboration on humanitarian issues such as HADR, women's rights, public health, media literacy, and clean energy. By collaborating on HADR efforts, Japan and Taiwan can more closely align their militaries and practice joint exercises without major policy changes that could alarm Beijing (Shaffer, 2022).

Finally, the United States cannot be ignored for military cooperation between Taiwan and Japan, as Washington always plays a vital role in facilitating bilateral relations between Taipei and Tokyo. In the absence of a TRA in Japan, observers argue that the role of the US–Japan security alliance must serve as the foundation for enhancing Taiwan–Japan security cooperation (Hsiao, 2022).

According to Hal Brands (2022), a professor at Johns Hopkins University's School of Advanced International Studies, military cooperation between Japan and the United States is deepening, with American and Japanese forces stepping up and training together — including large-scale exercises off several southern islands — and preparing joint-operational plans in case war breaks out over Taiwan.

Yoichi Kato mentioned that the need for this trilateral framework stems from Japan's limits to having only "working relations on a non-governmental basis" with Taiwan. He added that the only way to overcome this systemic challenge and to coordinate effectively with Taiwan is to go through the United States, which has a deeper, wide-ranging relationship with Taipei based on the TRA. The law stipulates that it is the policy of the United States to assist Taiwan to defend itself (Kato, 2021).

In just over a year, US President Joe Biden has publicly stated four times that US forces would defend Taiwan if it is attacked by China, the clearest response to the issue of whether the United States will come to the aid of Taiwan (Cooper, 2022). In April 2021, when Japan's former Prime Minister Yoshihide Suga visited the United States, Joe Biden urged Japan to back Taiwan (Sevastopulo and Harding, 2021). The joint leaders' statement included the first reference to Taiwan since 1969 (Brunnstrom *et al.*, 2021). The January 2022 US–Japan alliance's Security Consultative Committee's (SCC) statement again explicitly underscored the importance of peace and stability in the Taiwan Strait (Hughes, 2022).

According to Chris Hughes, a professor of International Politics and Japanese Studies at the University of Warwick in the UK, Japan's preparedness to openly identify the importance of Taiwan's security has been a relatively new departure, given that the last US–Japan discussion of the issue at summit level was the 1969 joint communiqué between President Richard Nixon and Prime Minister Satō Eisaku that noted Taiwan was "the most important factor for Japan's security" (Hughes, 2022).

China will be more emboldened in its regional and global ambitions if Taiwan falls by force (Chong and Keat, 2022). In July 2021, then-Deputy Prime Minister Taro Aso said that "if a major problem occurred in Taiwan, it would not be going too far to say that it could be an existential threat for Japan." He added that "in such a case, Japan and the United States will have to work together to defend Taiwan" and "we need to consider seriously that the southern islands of Okinawa could be next (Parry and Tang, 2021)."

However, Adam Liff, an associate professor of East Asian International Relations at Indiana University's Hamilton Lugar School of Global and International Studies, explained that though Japanese leaders in 2021 made high-profile statements concerning Taiwan, recent developments do not indicate a major change in Japan's official posture (Liff, 2021). According to a report in *The Diplomat*, preparedness of Japan for a cross-strait emergency has been far behind what is necessary (Takahashi, 2022).

The government of Japan must recognize that Taiwan and Japan are in the same boat. What is more, according to Akihisa Nagashima, a member of the House of Representatives of Japan and a visiting professor at Chuo University's Graduate School of Public Studies, Japan and Taiwan share the same fate. There is a Chinese idiom saying that "if the lips are gone, the teeth will be cold." Taiwan can prove an invaluable partner given its experience fighting against the CCP.

Therefore, the government of Japan should not hesitate and must take the decisive step to establish military cooperation with Taiwan so as to protect regional democracy, peace, stability, and freedom. To paraphrase John Weston (2022), a former Canadian member of parliament, "Japan's policy on Taiwan is out of date, failing to recognize Japan's need to respond to Beijing's threats." Taiwan needs the help of Japan and vice versa. Taiwan is ready, willing, and able to support such an effort. What is Japan waiting for?

References

Ali, I. and Stewart, P. (2022, March 4). U.S. providing intelligence to Ukraine, officials say. *Reuters*. Retrieved August 5, 2023, from http://archive.today/MX3jZ.

Ao, J. (2021). Japan as the sixth eye: Benefits and challenges from the perspective of a Taiwan Conflict Scenario. *Air University Advanced Research Group*. Retrieved August 5, 2023, from https://www.airuniversity.af.edu/Portals/10/ISR/student-papers/AY21-22/Japan_as_the_Sixth_Eye_Ao.pdf.

Blanchard, B., Lee, Y., and Saito, M. (2021, August 27). Taiwan, Japan ruling parties discuss China, military cooperation. *Reuters*. Retrieved August 5, 2023, from http://archive.today/LVcW3.

Brands, H. (2022, November 7). Why Japan is gearing up for possible war with China. *Bloomberg*. Retrieved August 5, 2023, from http://archive.today/zjRs8.

Brunnstrom, D., Hunnicutt, T., Nomiyama, C., and Spetalnick, M. (2021, April 16). Biden and Japan's Suga project unity against China's assertiveness. *Reuters*. Retrieved August 5, 2023, from http://archive.today/zHejH.

Brunnstrom, D. (2021, July 2). Japan minister says necessary to 'wake up' to protect Taiwan. *Reuters*. Retrieved August 5, 2023, from http://archive.today/U7pz2.

Chan, E. and Gregson, W. (2022, August 10). The future of Taiwan-Japan Defense Cooperation. *Global Taiwan Brief*, Vol. 7, Iss. 16. Retrieved August 5, 2023, from http://archive.today/GNnE7.

Chiang, C.-Y. and Huang, F. (2022, July 15). U.S. House passes defense bill with Taiwan provisions. *Focus Taiwan.*

Chinese missiles suspected of landing in Japan's economic zone (2022, August 4). *Al Jazeera.* Retrieved August 5, 2023, from http://archive.today/Zxwov.

Chong, C. and Keat, Y. (2022, October 20). Taipei must stay wise facing China. *Taipei Times.* Retrieved August 5, 2023, from http://archive.today/gAmz9.

Cooper, Z. (2022, September 19). The Fourth Taiwan strait slip-up. *American Enterprise Institute.* Retrieved August 5, 2023, from http://archive.today/wow1h.

Davidson, H. (2022, October 19). PRC has faster timeline on Taiwan: US. *Taipei Times.* Retrieved August 5, 2023, from http://archive.today/Qnlvb.

Everington, K. (2022, September 20). 63% of experts think Chinese invasion of Taiwan possible in 10 years: ChinaPower. *Taiwan News.* Retrieved August 5, 2023, from http://archive.today/TmQJD.

Former Japan PM tells China, "a Taiwan emergency is a Japanese emergency" (2021, December 1). *CNN.* Retrieved August 5, 2023, from http://archive.today/mw4xk.

Gady, F.-S. (2018, October 11). Japan offers to build Australia's $50 billion submarine fleet if French deal falls through. *The Diplomat.* Retrieved August 5, 2023, from http://archive.today/EbTUj.

Hale, E. (2020, November 24). Taiwan begins building first domestically produced submarines. *Al Jazeera.* Retrieved August 5, 2023, from http://archive.today/VfQuh.

Hsiao, R. (2022, January 6). The urgency of direct Japan-Taiwan security talks. *Japan Forward.* Retrieved August 5, 2023, from http://archive.today/ep5Hk.

Hughes, C. (2022, September 27). Japan's integration into US-Japan alliance strategy *vis-à-vis* Taiwan. *Italian Institute for International Political Studies.* Retrieved August 5, 2023, from http://archive.today/WymHU.

Ihara, K. (2018, January 26). Taiwan wants intelligence-sharing arrangement with Japan. *Nikkei.* Retrieved August 5, 2023, from http://archive.today/tOOJz.

Japan Conveys Concern to China over Planned Military Exercises near Taiwan (2022, August 3). *QNA.* Retrieved August 5, 2023, from http://archive.today/WZd12.

Kahn, D. (2006, September–October). The rise of intelligence. *Foreign Affairs.* 85(5), pp. 125–134.

Kato, Y. (2021, October 27). How should Taiwan, Japan, and the United States cooperate better on defense of Taiwan? *Brookings.* Retrieved August 5, 2023, from http://archive.today/oaiN7.

Kotani, T. (2022, August 4). Japan to upgrade defense ties with Taipei by dispatching a MOD official. *The Prospect Foundation.* Retrieved August 5, 2023, from http://archive.today/9JhU8.

Leaf, P. J. (2014, December 19). The US and Japan should help Taiwan acquire modern submarines. *The Diplomat*. Retrieved August 5, 2023, from http://archive.today/Grxf8.

Liff, A. P. (2021, August 23). Has Japan's policy toward the Taiwan strait changed? *Brookings*. Retrieved August 5, 2023, from http://archive.today/qSQrj.

Lin, T.-Y. and Chin, J. (2021, December 25). Japanese "Taiwan Relations Act" urged. *Taipei Times*. Retrieved August 5, 2023, from http://archive.today/cB4O3.

Liu, T.-H. (2022, November 14). Peace in Taiwan strait key: Kishida. *Taipei Times*. Retrieved August 5, 2023, from http://archive.today/zS7BL.

Matsumura, M. (2022a, May 21). Taiwan-Japan military ties possible. *Taipei Times*. Retrieved August 5, 2023, from http://archive.today/mbnZd.

Matsumura, M. (2022b, November 18). Establishing Japan-Taiwan military ties: A legal breakthrough. *The Third Annual Workshop between St. Andrew's University in Osaka and IIR Taiwan Center for Security Studies*.

Miki, R. (2022, November 6). Japan weighs allowing secondhand tank and missile export. *Nikkei Asia*. Retrieved August 5, 2023, from http://archive.today/XV598.

Noon, B. and Ross, J. (2022, May 12). The U.S. and Japan need training with Taiwan to deter China. *Real Clear Defense*. Retrieved August 5, 2023, from http://archive.today/mNuNP.

Onuorah, D. (2021, December 23). The 2021 Defense White Paper and Japan's Taiwan Policy: Interview with Yasuhiro Matsuda. *The National Bureau of Asian Research*. Retrieved August 5, 2023, from http://archive.today/4kjFH.

Parry, R. L. and Tang, D. (2021, July 7). Japan pledges to defend Taiwan if China attacks, says deputy prime minister Taro Aso. *The Times*. Retrieved August 5, 2023, from http://archive.today/oTq91.

Rovner, J. (2022, May 23). Intelligence and War: Does secrecy still matter? *Texas National Security Review*. Retrieved August 5, 2023, from http://archive.today/V9gQS.

Sacks, D. (2022, July 13). Shinzo Abe transformed Japan's relationship with Taiwan to counter threats from China. *Council on Foreign Affairs*. Retrieved August 5, 2023, from http://archive.today/Pr5UJ.

Saito, M., Lee, Y., Park, J.-M., Kelly, T., Macaskill, A., Wu, S., and Lague, D. (2021, November 29). T-DAY: The battle for Taiwan. *Reuters*. Retrieved August 5, 2023, from http://archive.today/xxFGa.

Sang, H. T. (2022, October 14). Constraining China's "new normal." *Taipei Times*. Retrieved August 5, 2023, from http://archive.today/bOXun.

Sevastopulo, D. and Harding, R. (2021, April 14). US pushes Japan to back Taiwan at Biden-Suga summit. *Financial Times*. Retrieved August 5, 2023, from http://archive.today/QHYan.

Shaffer, S. (2022, October 14). Why Japan needs to talk to Taiwan. *The Foreign Policy Research Institute*. Retrieved August 5, 2023, from http://archive.today/JGfV1.

Shigeta, S. (2022, October 1). Japan risks security lapses in Taiwan crisis, lacking formal ties. *Nikkei*. Retrieved August 5, 2023, from http://archive.today/dk4tS.

Strangio, S. (2021, July 2). Japan, Philippines to hold first ever joint air exercises. *The Diplomat*. Retrieved August 5, 2023, from http://archive.today/bRIBT.

Swanström, N. (2022, September 27). China: Can it control Japan's Taiwan policy? *Italian Institute for International Political Studies*. Retrieved August 5, 2023, from http://archive.today/MxS5z.

Takahashi, K. (2020, March 12). Japan developing new anti-surface warheads for future hypersonic weapons. *Janes*. Retrieved August 5, 2023, from http://archive.today/MiGXp.

Takahashi, K. (2022, August 20). How would Japan respond to a Taiwan contingency? *The Diplomat*. Retrieved August 5, 2023, from http://archive.today/59knQ.

Tian, Y.-L. and Blanchard, B. (2022, October 16). China will never renounce right to use force over Taiwan, Xi says. Reuters. Retrieved August 5, 2023, from http://archive.today/4QjUm.

Utibe, T. M. (2017). Sun Tzu's strategic thought and counterinsurgency in Nigeria: Issue and theoretical explanations. *Research on Humanities and Social Sciences*, 7(7), pp. 27–30.

Weston, J. (2022, November 7). Canada could learn from Taiwan. *Taipei Times*. Retrieved August 5, 2023, from http://archive.today/5gt16.

Wilkins, T. S. (2012, January 31). Taiwan–Japan Relations in an Era of Uncertainty. *Asia Policy*, 13, pp. 113–132.

Yang, M.-C., Yu, M., and Shih, H.-C. (2022, June 4). Japan to send active-duty defense attaché to Taipei: Report. *CNA*.

Yeo, M. (2022, March 11). Japan commissioned first of new submarine class. *Defense News*. Retrieved August 5, 2023, from http://archive.today/2J40l.

Yu, M. and Lin, K. (2022a, June 4). Stationing of Japanese defense attaché would boost exchanges: Analysts. *CNA*.

Yu, M. and Lin, K. (2022b, August 15). Taiwan military reviewing PLA tactics applied in recent drills. *CNA*.

Yu, M. and Yeh, J. (2022, July 27). Japan delegation eyes security exchanges with Taiwan visit. *CNA*.

© 2025 World Scientific Publishing Company
https://doi.org/10.1142/9789811298301_0004

Chapter 4

Russia–China Entente and the Challenge to East Asian Security

Michał Lubina

The current Russia–China relationship can be described as a contemporary equivalent of a political entente (Lukin, 2021) that is based on three interdependent pillars: "strategic rears," global revisionism, and economic cooperation. The first, "back-to-back" (*bei kao bei*, per Yu, 2021) relations means that Moscow and Beijing can concentrate their efforts elsewhere, on more important priorities (the Asia-Pacific for China; the "near abroad" for Russia), and challenge the current international values-based order. Until 2022, both Moscow and Beijing were "soft revisionists" (Ferguson, 2012), but this changed in the case of the Russian Federation on February 24, 2022, when Russia launched its full-scale invasion of Ukraine. Since then, Russia has turned from a soft revisionist to a hard revisionist. Finally, intensive economic cooperation (previously mostly in trade in military technologies, currently in raw materials: oil, gas, coal, wood, etc.) although asymmetric in nature, is acceptable for both sides. In terms of East Asian security, both Russia and China would love to change the current architecture, yet they are still too weak to do so. That is why they test the waters: to check how far they can go in undermining the current international order.

4.1 The Literature

The literature on Russia–China relations is burgeoning. This was not so a mere decade ago. Of course, the Sino-Soviet split has been covered extensively in global academia, but contemporary relations between these two powers have not been a hot topic. Since 2008, this gradually started to change. The economic crisis hit the West that year without undermining China, and not breaking Sino-Russian ties, spurring interest in Moscow–Beijing ties. Interest intensified after the 2014 annexation of Crimea and the real start of Russia's war on Ukraine (then widely referred to as a "crisis" or "hybrid conflict"). By the mid-2010s, studying Sino-Russian ties had become trendy, and this accelerated after Russia's full-scale invasion of Ukraine in 2022. Nowadays, one can read almost anything on Russia–China relations, from profound research to pure fantasy. The most important publications are presented here.

It is fair to start from the official and semiofficial perspective on Russia–China from these two countries, even if this will be *pro forma* only as these two authoritarian states do not present a good habitus for independent scholarship. The official line of both Russia and China can be summarized as "official optimism:" relations are excellent and have never been better. It is a "new model of major power relations" (Ministry of Foreign Affairs of the People's Republic of China, 2023b), "no limits relations" (Kremlin, 2022), that "reached unprecedented level" (Kremlin, 2019) of "all-weather friends" (Office of the Commissioner of the Ministry of Foreign Affairs of the People's Republic of China, 2021), and so on. While appreciating the bureaucratic poetry emanating from these statements — "the democratization of international relations," for example (e.g., Kremlin, 2002; more about it: Lubina, 2017) — much of it can be written off as propaganda, pure and simple. Yet, as with all propaganda, it is not totally groundless: Good propaganda should be based on at least a modicum of truth. And so it is in this case. Indeed, Russia–China relations are the best they have been in history, though a cynic would add that they were rarely good in the past. But this is precisely the point. The goal of such joint statements is to show the current state of Russia–China relations as better than they are in reality. If they are good, and indeed they are, then they are shown as excellent.

This official narrative is supplemented by semiofficial discourse in both countries, controlled more or less tightly by the political authorities. The supervision is not always 100 percent strict: In the last two decades, from time to time, one could have found a critical voice here or there, both in Russia (e.g., Trenin, 2000; Gabuev, 2015) and in China (e.g., Fu Ying, 2016). Nevertheless, these rare examples were never totally independent and one could only wonder about their hidden agendas. Control became much tighter in China after Xi Jinping, so unsurprisingly little was published that does not toe the line (for an exception, see Hu, 2022). In Russia, censorship after the full-scale invasion of Ukraine became much tighter and even previously critical authors started following the Kremlin line (e.g., Trenin, 2023) or went abroad. A distinct genre is the work of Russian researchers in English; usually they present a softened version of the "official optimism" line (e.g., Lukin, 2018).

Naturally, a much greater degree of pluralism appears in global (read: English-language) academia and in various think tanks and other analytical centers. Here, 2008 once again marks the turning point, as this was the year when the seminal book *The Axis of Convenience* (Lo, 2008) was published. Although the major theses of this book — such as the notion that the Sino-Russian relationship is little more than an anti-Western relationship of convenience — the book was so elegantly and conveniently written that it influenced many, if not the majority, of researchers and analytics (in some cases bordering on partial copy-pasting, e.g., Petersen and Barysch, 2011). One could even argue that this approach had been the dominant one for almost two decades in the West. Even now, there are books following this same line of reasoning (e.g., Berzina-Cerenkova, 2022), which only proves that in the analytical world the ability to write convincingly and in good English is at least as important — if not more so — as the correctness of the observations and forecasts.

The other major narrative involves the Sino-Russian alliance (e.g., Blank, 2020; Bogusz *et al.*, 2021). According to authors writing from this point of view, although Russia and China are not treaty allies, they are political, and therefore *de facto*, allies, as they are both revanchist states struggling to undermine the rules-based (read: American) international global order. This anti-hegemonism (read: anti-Americanism) is believed to be overshadowing everything else in this relationship, including problems, anxieties, and contradictions. As long as there is a common foe, Sino-Russian relations will remain strong. To paraphrase Mao Zedong, contradictions between the People's Republic of China (PRC) and Russia are non-antagonistic whereas contradictions between China and the United States as well as between Russia and the United States are antagonistic. The informal division of labor between China and Russia means that both Moscow and Beijing undermine the rules-based international order from both sides of Eurasia (Bogusz *et al.*, 2021). The peak of this narrative came during the Beijing Winter Olympics when Moscow and Beijing signed yet another bombastic joint statement, proclaiming their "no limits friendship" (Kremlin, 2022). Aside from these two major narratives, there are also others that try to move beyond these two, using such buzzwords as "fellow travelers" (Kaczmarski, 2018), "entente" (Lukin, 2021), or "asymmetric win–win" (Lubina, 2017), nevertheless, these are less influential than the two major narratives mentioned previously.

4.2 The Burden

Sino-Russian relations have a history going back 400 years. Yet the past is not a good heritage. For much of that time it had been a burden for both Moscow and Beijing (Lo, 2008) despite all the proclamations to the contrary. During most of this time, both Russia and China were indifferent to one another, and at times hostile. Now the past is usually overlooked. When Dmitri Medvedev, then the President of Russia, visited Beijing September 26–28, 2010, Chinese state TV showed a chronology of events in recent history: PRC–USSR "friendship" of the 1940s and 1950s, followed immediately by the resumption of cooperation in the 1980s. The 1960s and 1970s were simply erased, as if nothing happened, split or no split.

There was much in the prehistory of Sino-Russian relations. Roughly speaking, at the beginning, in the 17th and 18th centuries, China was stronger, which is not well remembered in Russia or in the West (but quite well in the PRC). This was confirmed by the Nerchinsk (1689) and Kyakhta (1727) treaties, which were essentially compromises on Chinese terms. Moscow pulled back from Priamure (near the Amur region) and in return was granted trade concessions, which they managed quite well (Mancall, 1972; Lukin, 2013; Voskresenskiy, 2004; Afinogenov, 2020).

It worked until the mid-19th century when China became seriously weakened by Western colonialism. Russia used this opportunity to turn the tables. Since then, Russia became stronger and China, weaker. Using the turmoil caused by the Taiping rebellion and by the second opium war, Tsarist Russia not only got the upper hand in the old dispute over the Amur region, seizing it and legalizing the seizure via the Aigun (1858) and Peking (1860) treaties, but also conquering the strip of Pacific coast now known as the Primorsky Krai, an example of imperialism pure and simple, as these lands had never been historically Russian or Slavonic in any regard. Throughout the second part of the 19th century, Russia continued its economic and political expansions into Manchuria until it was stopped by Japan during the 1904–1905 Russo–Japanese War (Fairbank and Goldman, 2006).

The dynamics of a strong Russia and a weak China continued during the Soviet period. The USSR supported, if not created, the communist movement in China by founding and financing the Chinese Communist Party (CCP) and by forging the First United Front: a Kuomintang (KMT)–CCP alliance in 1921. Their influence was halted by Chiang Kai-shek in the mid-1920s during his anti-communist purges (Mirovitskaya, 2000). However, Chiang had won only the first half of his struggle with the communists. After 1945, he lost the second half, in the resumption of the Chinese Civil War against the Chinese communists, who were backed by the USSR and forced the KMT to flee to Taiwan. The USSR, however, was not entirely happy. Apparently, Stalin would have preferred a divided China along the lines of Vietnam, Germany, and (later) Korea, with the communists controlling the north and the KMT, the south (Polit, 2004). Yet, the CCP won anyway, and the Kremlin accepted it as a *fait accompli*. As long as Stalin was alive, Mao Zedong and the rest of the PRC leadership had to keep their heads low, and accept the hierarchy in the socialist bloc with the USSR at the top (Dziak and Bayer, 2007). Once Stalin was dead and gone, however, and Khrushchev, assessed as being incompetent and weak by Zhongnanhai, came to power, Mao felt that his time had arrived. He challenged the USSR's leadership in the bloc by the late 1950s and the early 1960s, when a full-blown Sino-Soviet split revealed itself (Lüthi, 2008).

Ultimately, the PRC lost this struggle, as most of the communist and socialist parties in the world backed Moscow, but for the Kremlin, it was a Pyrrhic victory, as the struggle against both the West and China overstretched the Soviets. Sino-Soviet relations hit rock bottom in 1969 when PRC forces seized the empty Zhenbao/Damanskiy Island on the Ussuri River (Dziak and Rowinski, 2017). The military clash that followed was won by the Soviets, and PRC leadership panicked, to the point of considering a Soviet invasion of China a possibility. Although it never came, this threat influenced Mao Zedong's willingness to mend fences with the United States, a vital event for the PRC, and for the ultimate defeat of the Soviet Union. Moscow did not manage to confront its two rivals at once, and by the mid-1980s, tried to appease both the West and China. Although this strategy worked, with Mikhail Gorbachev, the last President of the Soviet Union, charming the Western public and restoring relations with China under Deng Xiaoping in 1989 (at the cost of concessions), this proved to be of little value, since the USSR itself dissolved in 1991 (Dmochowski, 2008). This was bad news for China, which had hoped for preservation of the first communist state. Beijing was particularly anxious about Boris Yeltsin, a person accused of splitting the USSR and being too pro-Western (Dmochowski, 2008). Yet, it was Yeltsin himself who came to power in the Russian Federation, the successor of the USSR, in 1991.

As seen from this short summary, the past is a burden for Russia–China relations, as both sides have long looked at one another with suspicion and anxiety.

4.3 From Turned Backs to Back-to-Back

In December 1991 and the first half of 1992, the PRC and the Russian Federation clearly had reservations about one another. Russia oriented itself to the West and hoped for Western help with market reforms; it also dreamed that by doing so Moscow would keep its great power status. The CCP had just perpetrated the Tiananmen Massacre, and was busy trying to break out of a Western-imposed isolation by reaching out to Asia-Pacific partners. These dynamics kept bilateral relations low and cool (Wilson, 2004; Tsyganov, 1999). This changed in December 1992 when Boris Yeltsin visited Beijing. Disappointed with the results of Russia's turn to the West, Yeltsin wanted to improve Russia's position by upgrading its relations with China (Wilson, 2004). This motive would come to be a leitmotif of Russia's foreign policy from then on. China, conversely, was happy to mend fences with Russia and to realize that "Yeltsin's anti-communism is not anti-Chinese" (Li, 2000). Besides these strategic considerations, there was one more thing, and an essential one, that glued Russia–China relations: the booming arms trade. China needed to buy arms, preferably cheap arms, but was embargoed by the West after Tiananmen; Russia, with their military-technical industry, was almost bankrupt, so they needed exports to survive. They found themselves perfect partners, a match made in heaven (or rather in hell). The arms trade became the glue of their relations throughout the 1990s and 2000s (Yuan, 2010; Garnett, 2000; Wilson, 2004; Tsyganov, 1999).

Since then, Russia–China relations intensified quickly. In 1994 they engaged in a "constructive partnership" (Karasin, 2007, pp. 271–273), which quickly evolved into a "strategic partnership" in 1996 (Karasin, 2007, pp. 333–337). It was already then, in the 1990s, when Russian and Chinese elites realized that their countries were first and foremost "strategic rears" for each other (Lo, 2008). Thanks to normalized relations with China, Russia can keep its eastern flank covered, while the same is true for China of its northern flank. With their strategic rears covered, both sides could (and did) focus on more important foreign policy dimensions. In particular, these included the West, especially Western Europe, and particularly Germany for Russia; the Asia-Pacific, and the continuous opening to the world, in the case of the PRC (Lo, 2008). This is how the first pillar of Russia–China relations, the strategic rears, or what the Chinese analysts call "back-to-back" (Yu, 2021) relations was born.

The decade of the 1990s was uneven, however. Successes were mixed with problems. The former included demilitarization of the border and almost full demarcation; non-interference in each other's domestic affairs; institutionalization of relations; and above all, the arms trade (Garnett, 2000). This was the essence of the Moscow–Beijing bilateral relations during that period. The problems included Sinophobia in East Siberia and in the Russian Far East, with fears about the "Chinese demographic threat," which made these regions anti-Chinese and thus complicated people-to-people relations for two decades (Larin, 2009; Lukin, 2007; Rozman, 2000; Vitkovskaya *et al.*, 2000). Outside of the trade in weapons, the two sides had only low levels of economic cooperation, making the economy the weakest link in their relations in the 1990s (Wilson, 2004).

The early 2000s saw a repetition of the scheme from the early 1990s. After 9/11, Russia strongly supported the United States, making another pivot to the West, after the early 1990s, and pushing relations with the PRC to the background. Yet, the "second political honeymoon" between Washington and Moscow would prove to be as short-lived as the first one, and ended in the same, bitter disappointment (Kaczmarski, 2006). By 2003, Russia, strengthened by petrodollars, believed it could balance US dominance, and this assumption made the PRC attractive again to the Kremlin. Beijing was more than happy, as it considered President Vladimir Putin's earlier pro-US turn a potentially dangerous move with negative consequences for the security of China's western (Central Asia) and northern borders. Now, when the Kremlin had sobered up in the eyes of Zhongnanhai, the CCP leadership really welcomed Russia's new approach (Wilson, 2004). Soon there was a breakthrough in the most toxic issue in the bilateral relations, the border demarcation (Iwashita, 2006). In October 2004, Putin met in Beijing with then PRC President Hu Jintao and reached a compromise about the three outstanding islands, dividing two in half (Bolshoi Ussuriskiy/Heixiazi and Abaigatu) and returning Yinlong (Tarabarov) to the PRC (Lu, 2018; Iwashita, 2006). This was indeed a compromise, as international law would have given all three islands to China, as they lie closer to the Chinese banks of their respective rivers, the Amur (Heilongjiang) and Aigun.

In the mid-2000s (roughly between 2004 and 2008), Russia–China relations remained good but limited (Lo, 2008). Both sides shared the same strategic goals of limiting US unilateralism as well as tactical cooperation in Central Asia; both used their bilateral relations to strengthen their own position vis-à-vis Washington. At the same time these relations were limited by a lack of full trust, by Russia's "energy geopolitics," and by China's disinterest in closer economic cooperation with Russia beyond the spheres of resources and arms (Yu, 2006). Moscow dreamed of playing the PRC, Japan, and South Korea off against each other by manipulating the Eastern Siberia–Pacific Ocean (ESPO) oil pipeline, which frustrated an oil-hungry China. Beijing, conversely, was not eager to invest too heavily in Russia; it just wanted Russian resources and weapons. This led to bilateral disappointment, skillfully concealed by political propaganda proclaiming very good ties (Lubina, 2017). Already before 2008 the PRC had become richer and globally more influential than Russia, and the latter hoped this would only be a temporary situation.

The 2008 crisis affected both Russia and the West, yet the PRC managed to survive the crisis — it even strengthened Beijing's position. It also strengthened the growing sense of Sinocentrism among the Chinese. After three decades of successful reforms, and after the showcase of the 2008 Beijing Olympics, the CCP ceased to "keep a low profile." Already then, during the late period of Hu Jintao, Zhongnanhai's assertiveness started emerging (tentatively at first, unlike during the Xi Jinping era, after 2012). As far as Russia was concerned, it tried to reset its relations with the United States, but after an initial improvement of relations in 2009 and 2010, they proved to be a failure by around 2012. In the meantime Moscow has quietly accepted the Chinese terms of cooperation, in oil (ESPO credits, 2008), arms sales, and a Russian Far East development program (Kaczmarski, 2015). The latter proved to be a psychological breakthrough (though not material, as the program failed to make a difference) as for the first time, Russia considered the PRC as a power that can help to develop the region instead of considering it a potentially hostile force only waiting to reconquer these lands in the future (Kaczmarski, 2015).

In 2012, Xi Jinping came to power and Vladimir Putin returned to the Russian presidency. Simultaneously, Russia and China were losing hopes for a structural deal with the West. On the Russian side, the pivotal role in this process was played by the Bolotnaya Square protests in Moscow; these more than anything else made the Putin regime realize the strength of the democratic threats emanating from the West. Then came the annexation of Crimea, the first invasion (a hybrid one) of Ukraine, and Western sanctions on Russia in 2014. Between 2014 and 2022, the Kremlin was disillusioned about the prospects of mending fences with the United States but hoped for continuous cooperation with Western Europe, to distance it from the United States (Bogusz *et al.*, 2021). These hopes were dashed by the second, full-scale invasion of Ukraine in 2022. This unified the West and made Russia a pariah state in the eyes of the Western public and politicians. As for the PRC, the decisive year was 2018. Until then, Beijing had hoped to win over then US President Donald Trump in order to keep the Sino-American relations as they were (which were beneficial for China), but by 2018 it proved impossible. The Trump administration moved assertively on the PRC; trade and propaganda conflicts soon started. Since then, despite the occasional improvement, Sino-American relations have been clearly on a "strategic competition" basis (Heath, 2021).

All these factors drew Moscow and Beijing closer to one another. This was demonstrated by the ostentatious political friendship between Putin and Xi (Bērziņa-Čerenkova, 2022). The success of this rapprochement was based on Russia's quiet consent to becoming the junior partner in this relationship (Bogusz *et al.*, 2021). Moscow burned previous anxieties and decided that China was more of an opportunity than a threat, as it offers a chance for a more just (from Moscow's perspective) international order. It was in the 2012–2022 period that the three pillars of the Russia–China relations were formed. First, back-to-back relations. Second, revisionism, or anti-Americanism, meaning an attempt to limit US domination, and to end Pax Americana and replace it with a more just world order. Although both Russia and China lack a clear vision of the future, in Russia's case it is something of a contemporary equivalent of the 19th century concert of powers; in the PRC's case, a new version of the *Tianxia* world order

(Nathan and Zhang, 2022). This lack of an alternative is not (yet) a problem as they focus on the present; on limiting the United States and undermining the current rules-based international order. Finally, the third pillar is economic cooperation. Initially, it was arms sales, yet the importance of this sphere has diminished since the mid-2010s. Since 2008, resources replaced arms as the major item in Russia–China trade; mostly oil, followed by gas and coal. This is beneficial for both sides, even if more so for the PRC, as Russia developed an alternative; an insurance card in case of a deterioration in relations with the West (which indeed happened after 2022).

To conclude, on the eve of Russia's full-scale invasion, Russia–China relations were strong despite being asymmetric. Neither the Trump presidency, COVID-19, nor Russia's invasion of Ukraine undermined them. The latter, however, proved to be the biggest test for these relations since 9/11.

4.4 The Art of Ambivalent Support

Just weeks prior to Russia's full-scale invasion of Ukraine, Vladimir Putin went to Beijing for the opening ceremony of the Winter Olympics. He was given a red carpet welcome, met with Xi (which was shown on the first page of *Renmin Ribao*), and signed yet another joint statement, this time about "no limits" to Russia–China relations (Kremlin, 2022). This was not a new phrase; it was coined for the first time a year prior by Wang Yi (Yu, 2021), yet the world took note of it only in 2022. It strengthened speculation about China's role in Russia's war against Ukraine.

It is unknown what Putin said or did not say to Xi about his planned invasion. Or rather, how much information he shared. Since then, there have been many leaks presenting contradictory pictures, from Putin withholding his plans to fully briefing Xi. Maybe one day it will be known, yet for now analysts and commentators can only speculate. At least in public, the Chinese were surprised by the scale of invasion (Sun, 2022). But it does not mean they were against it. On the contrary: They shared Russia's reading of the origins of the conflict, with victim (Ukraine) blaming and accusing the West of instigating the root cause of the war (see e.g., PRC's 2023 "peace plan;" a statement containing neither peace nor a plan, FMPRC, 2023a). The US factor was decisive here (Repnikova and Zhou, 2022). For the PRC, the Ukraine is far away, in Russia's sphere of influence, whereas the United States is nearby and tries to contain the "great rejuvenation of the Chinese nation," so, to simplify, what is good for the United States is bad for China. A potential Russian victory would have further undermined the rules-based international order, weakened the global leadership of the United States, and strengthened revisionists' powers. Such a scenario offered a chance to fulfill the dream of a multipolar world order.

That is why the PRC hoped for a swift Russian victory. It also bet on Moscow's win. Although Chinese communiqués were ostensibly neutral (abstaining from votes at UN General Assembly and Security Council), in both official and semiofficial texts (Yu, 2022), this neutrality was biased in favor of Russia. This could be seen in not naming the war a "war" (but a "conflict," or a "crisis"), in confusing the realities and repeating Russia's "blame NATO" narrative. Since Russia's invasion of Ukraine was a clear-cut example of aggression and a violation of the UN Charter and the Five Principles of Peaceful Coexistence, the PRC stance was clearly one-sided.

To PRC's surprise, just like to Russia's surprise, the "special operation" did not go as planned. Instead of Kyiv falling in a couple of days, if not weeks, the war has lasted until the time of writing, and Russia is not winning it. Beijing was surprised by the weak performance of the Russian armed forces and by Ukrainians' staunch defense, but most importantly by the West's united stance against Russian aggression, including military support for Ukraine. The renewed transatlantic unity coupled with the strengthened US global leadership role became the two single most negative aspects of the war for the PRC. Despite that, and despite some gestures interpreted as distancing China from Russia, the PRC has not thrown Putin under the bus. Beijing did not criticize Moscow, and did not condemn the Russian atrocities in Bucha, Irpin, and elsewhere. Instead, Xi Jinping called Putin, met with him in Samarkand, and visited Moscow in March 2023. His men, like Li Zhanshu (Top Chinese legislator, 2022) and Wang Yi supported Russia in late 2022 (FMPRC, 2022). This is because Russia is considered by Zhongnanhai as "half of the sky" in terms of PRC security (Geddes, 2023).

Yet, at the same time as the PRC supports Russia politically, diplomatically, ideologically, and morally, Beijing is much more restrained in offering any economic help. Yes, it bought volumes of discounted Russian oil (as did India), as well as liquefied natural gas and coal (Murtaugh and Chakraborty, 2022; Chorzempa, 2022). However, private companies as well as major state banks remain wary of jumping into bed with Russia.

Fearing secondary sanctions, Beijing has not given Moscow new loans or new foreign direct investment. Since 2022, the PRC's alleged military aid became an issue, with reports claiming Beijing is covertly supporting the Russian army. Even if true, the scale is not decisive and it is all done covertly (through third countries and private companies), not openly because it follows the main line of Zhongnanhai: the PRC may wish Russia to win, but does not want to pay for Russian mistakes.

4.5 The Sino-Russian Challenge to East Asian Security

Seen from an East Asian perspective, the Russo-Ukraine war may seem a distant matter. Ukraine is far, poor, and strategically unimportant. Some East Asians may even share a sense of Schadenfreude, as for the last century it was Europe that conquered them, lectured them, and patronized them; pointing fingers at them as inhabitants of a conflict-prone region of the world. And now it is Europe where the bloody war is taking place, whereas East Asia, despite all the tensions over territorial claims, prospers as a peaceful place. Such an attitude would be understandable from a human perspective, yet Ukraine is not a faraway matter as the consequences of this war are global. This is a case study in how the Russia–China entente works in practice. One of the reasons (although not the major one) why Russia invaded Ukraine was because it felt secure in its east. Moscow knows well that good relations with China ensure it can fully concentrate on its western front, and dispatch human and capital resources from the Asian part of the country. To put it bluntly, if Sino-Russian relations were as tense as they used to be in the 1980s and early 1990s (not to mention the 1960s and 1970s), the Far Eastern divisions of the Russian Army, instead of slaughtering civilians in Bucha, would remain posted in the Khabarovsk Krai watching over the Amur River border. Thanks to the "back-to-back" logic, Moscow was free to use its Asian units in Ukraine, with well-known consequences. And now imagine the reverse scenario: Should the PRC decide to seize disputed islands in the East China Sea or the South China Sea, or should Xi dare to invade Taiwan, it would make a lot of sense for the People's Liberation Army (PLA) to know that it can dispatch almost all its resources without having to keep a watchful eye on its northern border. This "back-to-back" logic works as both a strategic and a psychological reassurance.

This is hardly the only example. When we look at Sino-Russian military cooperation, we can see a clear trend since the 2010s. Previously, joint military drills served as a means for political signaling and had little military value *per se* (Yuan, 2010). This was the case with the Peace Mission in 2005 and subsequent, regular Sino-Russian drills. During these drills, Moscow and Beijing wanted to convey a message to the world (read: to the United States): the PLA could learn a thing or two from more experienced Russian troops, and Chinese generals had a chance to see new equipment in action, ready for sale (Yu, 2005). All these aspects are still in place, even if their importance has diminished with time. However, since 2012, all this was complemented by Sea Cooperation, a maritime military drill, which outpaced the Peace Mission as the most important Sino-Russian exercise (Kaczmarski, 2015). This clearly serves Beijing's interests, as the PRC's only conceivable future conflicts are maritime ones; particularly over Taiwan. It makes a lot of sense for China to prepare for this, to train with (*de facto*) Russian political allies, and to exert pressure on regional rivals and foes. It makes much less sense for Russia to alienate non-PRC partners in the region, yet that is the consequence of the "PRC first" policy of Russia in the Asia-Pacific (Lo, 2015), as well as the asymmetric relationship with the PRC (Lubina, 2017). This is what happens when the PRC sets the agenda.

There is a similar story with Russo-Chinese joint patrols approaching — and in some cases, violating — Japanese and South Korean Air Defense Identification Zones. This happened to South Korea in November 2022 and in June 2023, and to Japan in May 2022 (S Korea, Japan scramble jets, 2023). These ongoing incidents show one thing: Beijing is testing reactions, following the Russian playbook in Europe, where Russian air forces from time to time would test NATO forces at their Eastern flank. Politically, it also serves PRC goals more than Russia's, as such actions alienate Russia from other East Asian partners and diminish Moscow's strategic space in the region. This is precisely in the PRC's interests, as Beijing wants to show that it has Russia on its side while diminishing Russia's political and strategic options in the region. Again, this is how the logic of Sino-Russian entente works to the advantage of the major revisionist power in the region, China. This automatically undermines the current security environment in East Asia.

The crucial point, then, is Taiwan. It is an obvious platitude to describe Taiwan's strategic, economic, and ideological importance to the rules-based international order and what may happen if the PRC decides to irrevocably alter the island's *status quo*. Much less known is Russia's important yet secondary role in the Taiwan Strait. Currently, Russia clearly sticks to its "One China" policy and fully supports Beijing. But this was not always the case. In the early 1990s, Russia was more ambivalent (Rigger, 2015; Tubilewicz, 2002; Lukin, 2007), and it could have pursued a less Sinocentric Taiwan policy, along the lines of certain Western countries that "acknowledge" or "respect" China's view that both sides of the strait belong to one China, while at the same time undermining it by developing political (e.g., parliamentary) ties with Taipei. Moreover, not so long ago, Moscow was in fact happy about Taiwan being independent as this guaranteed the security of the Russian Far East (Lo, 2008). Yet, this is all history now. By the 2000s, Russia chose to be just an appendix to the PRC, at least on the Taiwan issue, staunchly toeing the CCP line (Rigger, 2015). One can find parts about Taiwan in every joint statement and it is always following Beijing's script. This marks another consequence of Sino-Russian asymmetry. And this is again bad news for the security of the region, as the backing of Russia empowers Beijing to be even more assertive, as it knows it has a UN Security Council member behind it.

It is the same story with the disputes in the East China Sea and the South China Sea. Before the mid-2010s, Russia distanced itself from this topic and did not want to back Beijing. This changed around the year 2016, and since then the Kremlin has become a supporter of the Beijing line, conducting joint military drills with the PLA near disputed waters (Yu, 2016). This is clearly to the advantage of Zhongnanhai and to the detriment of the stability of the current security architecture in the region.

All these examples illustrate one thing: The PRC, regardless of Russia, would have behaved similarly in these matters, playing the role of a revisionist, and steadily undermining the rules-based international order in general and East Asian security in particular. Yet, having Russia as its junior partner — as its accomplice in this undertaking — strengthens and empowers Beijing even more. At minimum, the PRC has its back covered in the north and the west, and has diplomatic backing from a permanent member of the Security Council. Moreover, it can learn military skills from a more experienced army (and navy) and use the Russians for political signaling. At maximum, it can use the politically vassalized Russia to test the waters against Japan, South Korea, Taiwan, and most importantly, though indirectly, against the United States. These are the consequences of the Sino-Russian entente for East Asian Security.

4.6 Conclusion

The PRC and Russia do not want to spark a global war (although the latter clearly enjoys threatening the world with nuclear Armageddon). Zhongnanhai is more subtle. Their strategic calculus is to undermine the rules-based international order indirectly by making US partners and allies hesitate. Beijing and Moscow want to create serious doubts in certain capitals about Washington's ability and willingness to come with a helping hand in time of crisis. Should important partners distance themselves from the United States and decide that it does not pay to irritate Beijing, the PRC would find it much easier to pursue its goals and increase its power in East Asia and beyond. In other words, Beijing prefers to bully smaller powers without having to resort to the use of force. This is the difference between the PRC and Russia, for now at least, as the Kremlin has decided that any means, including a full-scale invasion, is acceptable. The PRC has not moved that far yet. Beijing desperately wants to seize Taiwan, and to control all the disputed islands in the East and South China seas, yet for now, the United States is still too strong and too committed to defending the *status quo*. This forces the PRC to work hard on undermining the rules-based international order indirectly, to plant the seeds of doubt in the hearts and minds of East Asian capitals, and to try to influence other actors by non-military means. Simultaneously, the PLA is undergoing an impressive military modernization, and the PRC has the political backing of Moscow — still a militarily powerful country, and one with the largest number of nuclear weapons in the world. Russia in this regard serves as the PRC's political bullterrier: Zhongnanhai does not have to use it, only signaling that it is willing to do so if push comes to shove. Therefore, the very fact that Russia is strategically aligned with the PRC, that it politically backs Beijing's stance on maritime disputes and on Taiwan, that it conducts joint aircraft patrols that approach or violate other countries' Air Defence Identification Zones, and accepts joint military drills with the PLA near disputed waters, all this strengthens Zhongnanhai and undermines the current security environment in East Asia.

That is why the Russian–Ukraine war is so politically crucial (albeit geographically distant) to East Asian security. A Russian win would seriously undermine the current rules-based international order. This would empower Beijing to be even more assertive in the region. Conversely, a Russian defeat in Ukraine would weaken the PRC's major accomplice and indirectly hurt Zhongnanhai as well. This will not change the general revisionist line of Xi Jinping, but Russia's failure would complicate matters for Beijing. So, even from the geographically distant perspective of East Asia, helping Ukraine in order to weaken Russia (and indirectly the PRC) is a game worth playing.

References

Afinogenov, G. (2020). *Spies and Scholars. Chinese Secrets and Imperial Russia's Quest for World Power*. Cambridge MA: Harvard University Press.

Bērziņa-Čerenkova, U. A. (2022). *Perfect Imbalance. Russia and China*. Singapore: WSPC, pp. 5–30.

Blank, S. (2020). The Un-Holy Russo-Chinese alliance. *Defense & Security Analysis, 36*(3), 249–274.

Bogusz, M., Jakóbowski, J., and Rodkiewicz, W. (2021). The Beijing-Moscow axis: The foundations of an asymmetric alliance. *OSW Report*. Retrieved August 5, 2023, from http://archive.today/A09bn.

Chorzempa, M. (June 27, 2022). Export controls against Russia are working — With the help of China. *Peterson Institute for International Economics (PIIE)*. Retrieved August 5, 2023, from http://archive.today/v0zHg.

Dmochowski, T. (2008). *Chińsko-radzieckie stosunki polityczne po śmierci Mao Zedonga [Sino-Soviet Political Relations after Mao Zedong's Death]*. Gdańsk: Wydawnictwo Uniwersytetu Gdańskiego.

Dziak Waldemar, J. and Bayer, J. (2007). *Mao. Zwycięstwa, nadzieje, klęski [Mao. Victories, hopes, failures]*. Warszawa: Trio.

Dziak, W. J. and Rowiński, J. (2017). *Chińsko-sowiecki spór graniczny. Wybór dokumentów [Sino-Soviet Border Dispute. A Collection of Documents]*. Warszawa: INP PAN.

Fairbank, J. K. and Goldman, M. (2006). *China: A New History*. Cambridge MA: Harvard University Press.

Ferguson, C. (2012). The strategic use of soft balancing: The normative dimensions of the Chinese-Russian 'strategic partnership'. *Journal of Strategic Studies, 35*(2), 197–222.

Gabuev, A. (April 30, 2015). Kitaytsy ponimayut, chto Rossiya yegradiruyet iz-za korruptsii i neeffektivnogo upravleniya [*The Chinese Understand that Russia is Degrading due to Corruption and Ineffective Administration*]. Retrieved August 5, 2023, from http://archive.today/VO4iH.

Garnett, S. (2000). Introduction. In: S Garnett (ed.), *Rapprochement or Rivalry? Russia — China Relations in a Changing Asia* (pp. 7–15). Washington DC: Carnegie.

Geddes, T. D. G. (2023). China-Russia relations since Ukraine: What Chinese scholars are saying. *Sinification.com*. Retrieved August 5, 2023, from http://archive.today/FP5dl.

Heath, T. R. (2021). U.S. strategic competition with China: A RAND research primer. Retrieved August 5, 2023, from http://archive.today/TB61q.

Hu, W. (2022). É wū zhànzhēng de kěnéng jiéguǒ yú zhōngguó de juézé [*The Possible Result of Russia-Ukraine War and China's Choice*]. Retrieved August 5, 2023, from http://archive.today/WVpHC.

Iwashita, A. (2006). *4000 kilometrov problem. Rossiysko-kitayskaya granitsa* [*4000 Kilometers of Problems. The Russian-Chinese Border*]. Moscow: ACT.

Kaczmarski, M. (2006). *Rosja na rozdrożu. Polityka zagraniczna Władimira Putina* [*Russia at the Crossroads. The Foreign Policy of Vladimir Putin*]. Warszawa: Sprawy Polityczne, pp. 43–57.

Kaczmarski, M. (2015). *Russia-China Relations in the Post-Crisis International Order* (pp. 24–100). London, New York: Routledge.

Kaczmarski, M. (2018). The Sino-Russian relationship: Fellow travellers in the West-dominated World. *The China Quarterly, 236*, 1197–1205.

Karasin, G. B. (ed.). (2007). *Sbornik rossiysko-kitayskikh dogovorov 1949–1999* [*The Collection of Russian-Chinese Treaties 1949–1999*]. Moscow: Terra-Sport.

Kremlin (2002). Sovmestnaya deklaratsiya Rossiyskoy Federatsii i Kitayskoy Narodnoy Respubliki [*Joint Declaration of the Russian Federation and the People's Republic of China*]. Retrieved August 5, 2023, from http://archive.today/XbiVu.

Kremlin (2019). Vecher, posvyashchonnyy 70-letiyu ustanovleniya diplomaticheskikh otnosheniy mezhdu Rossiyey i Kitayem [*Gala Marking the 70th Anniversary of Diplomatic Relations Between Russia and China*]. Retrieved August 5, 2023, from http://archive.today/727Up.

Kremlin (2022). Sovmestnoye zayavleniye Rossiyskoy Federatsii i Kitayskoy Narodnoy Respubliki o mezhdunarodnykh otnosheniyakh, vstupayushchikh v novuyu epokhu, i global'nom ustoychivom razvitii [*Joint Statement of the Russian Federation and the People's Republic of China on International Relations Entering a New Era and on Global Sustainable Development*]. Retrieved August 5, 2023, from http://archive.today/xr7OT.

Larin, A. (2009). *Kitayskiye migranty v Rossii. Istoriya i sovremennost'* [*Chinese Migrants in Russia. History and Contemporary*]. Moscow: Vostochnaya Kniga Publishing.

Li, J. (2000). From good neighbors to strategic partners. In: S Garnett (ed.), *Rapprochement or Rivalry? Russia — China Relations in a Changing Asia* (p. 71). Washington DC: Carnegie.

Lo, B. (2008). *Axis of Convenience. Moscow, Beijing and the New Geopolitics.* London: Chatham House.

Lo, B. (2015). *Russia and the New World Disorder.* London: Chatham House.

Lu, X. (2018). Sovetsko-kitayskiye pogranichnyye peregovory (1964–2004) [*Soviet-Chinese Border Talks 1964–2004*]. *Vestnik Yuzhno-Ural'skogo gosudarstvennogo universiteta* [*Bulletin of the South Ural State University*], *18*(3), 33–39.

Lubina, M. (2017). Russia and China. A political marriage of convenience: Successful and stable. *Oplanden-Berlin-Toronto: Budrich*, 114–137.

Lukin, A. (2018). *China and Russia: The New Rapprochement.* Cambridge: Polity Press.

Lukin, A. (2021). The Russia–China entente and its future. *International Politics, 58*, 363–380.

Lukin, A. B. (2007). *Medved' nablyudayet za drakonom. Obraz Kitaya v Rossii v XVII-XXI vekakh* [*The Bear Watches over Dragon. The Image of China in Russia in 17–21st Centuries*]. Moscow: East-West Publishers.

Lukin, A. B. (2013). *Rossiya i Kitay: chetyre veka vzaimodeystviya. Istoriya, sovremennoye sostoyaniye i perspektivy razvitiya rossiysko-kitayskikh otnosheniy* [*Russia and China: 400 Years of Interaction. History, Current Situation and Perspectives of Development of Russia-China Relations*]. Moscow: Izdatelstvo VES MIR (IVM).

Lüthi, L. (2008). *The Sino-Soviet Split: Cold War in the Communist World.* Princeton: Princeton University Press.

Mancall, M. (1972). *Russia and China. Their Diplomatic Relations to 1728.* Cambridge MA: Harvard University Press, pp. 51–150.

Ministry of Foreign Affairs of the People's Republic of China (FMPRC). (2022, October 27). Wang Yi Speaks with Russian Foreign Minister Sergey Lavrov on the Phone. Retrieved August 5, 2023, from http://archive.today/JwkZN.

Ministry of Foreign Affairs of the People's Republic of China (FMPRC) (2023a). China's Position on the political settlement of the Ukraine crisis. Retrieved August 5, 2023, from: http://archive.today/nr02A.

Ministry of Foreign Affairs of the People's Republic of China (FMPRC) (2023b). Forging ahead to open a new chapter of China-Russia friendship, cooperation and common development. Retrieved August 5, 2023, from http://archive.today/z25ug.

Mirovitskaya, R. A. (2000). *Kitayskaya gosudarstvennost' i sovetskaya politika v Kitaye 1941–1945* [*The Chinese Statehood and Soviet Policy in China, 1941–1945*]. Moscow: Pamyatniki istoricheskoy mysli.

Murtaugh, D. and Chakraborty, D. (2022, July 6). China and India funnel $24 billion to Putin in energy spree. *Bloomberg*. Retrieved August 5, 2023, from http://archive.today/8FxMg.

Nathan, A. J. and Zhang, B. (2022). "A shared future for mankind": Rhetoric and reality in Chinese Foreign policy under Xi Jinping. *Journal of Contemporary China, 31*(133), 57–71.

Office of the Commissioner of the Ministry of Foreign Affairs of the People's Republic of China (OCMFA) (2021, June 15). Foreign Ministry Spokesperson Zhao Lijian's regular press conference. Retrieved August 5, 2023, from http://archive.today/m5AV6.

Petersen, A. and Barysch K. (2011). Russia, China and the geopolitics of energy in Central Asia. *Centre for European Reform Report*. Retrieved August 5, 2023, from http://archive.today/ogJKq.

Polit, J. (2004). *Chiny* (China). Warszawa: Trio.

Repnikova, M. and Zhou, W. (2022). What China's social media is saying about Ukraine. *The Atlantic*. Retrieved August 5, 2023, from http://archive.today/NzzCk.

Rigger, S. (2015). The Taiwan issue and the Sino-Russian partnership. In: J. Bellacqua (ed.), *The Future of ChinaRussia Relations*. Kentucky: Kentucky University Press, 314–315.

Rozman, G. (2000). Turning fortress into free trade zone. In: S. Garnett (ed.). *Rapprochement or Rivalry? Russia — China Relations in a Changing Asia* (pp. 151–162). Washington DC: Carnegie.

S Korea, Japan scramble jets due to China-Russia joint air patrol (2023, June 7). *Aljazeera.net*. Retrieved November 7, 2023, from: http://archive.today/36Xag.

Sun, Y. (2022). Ukraine: Did China have a clue. *The Stimson Center*. Retrieved August 5, 2023, from: http://archive.today/Dw26I.

Top Chinese legislator pays official goodwill visit to Russia (2022, September 10). Xinhua. Retrieved August 5, 2023, from: http://archive.today/ovVSA.

Trenin, D. (2000). The China factor: Challenge and chance for Russia. In: S. Garnett (ed.), *Rapprochement or Rivalry? Russia — China Relations in a Changing Asia* (p. 41). Washington DC: Carnegie.

Trenin, D. (2023). Two worlds of Russia's Foreign policy. *Center for International Relations and Sustainable Development*. Retrieved August 5, 2023, from: http://archive.today/JP8rx.

Tsyganov, Y. V. (1999). Russia and China: What is in the pipeline? In: G. Chufrin (ed.), *Russia and Asia: The Emerging Security Agenda* (pp. 302–310). New York: Oxford University Press.

Tubilewicz, C. (2002). The little Dragon and the Bear: Russian-Taiwanese relations in the post-cold war period. *Russian Review, 61*(4), 282.

Vitkovskaya, G., Zayonchkovskaya, Z., and Newland, K. (2000). Chinese migration into Russia. In: S. Garnett (ed.), *Rapprochement or Rivalry? Russia — China Relations in a Changing Asia*. Washington DC: Carnegie, p. 347.

Voskresenskiy, A. (2004). *Kitay i Rossiya v Yevrazii. Istoricheskaya dinamika politicheskikh vzaimovliyanii* [China and Russia in Eurasia: The Historic Dynamics of Political Dual Influence]. Moscow: Muravey.

Wilson, J. L. (2004). *Strategic Partners. Russian-Chinese Relations in the Post-Soviet Era.* London: Routledge, pp. 112–145.

Ying, F. (2016). How China sees Russia: Beijing and Moscow are close, but not allies. *Foreign Affairs*, 95, 96.

Yu, B. (2005). The new world order according to Moscow and Beijing. *Comparative Connections, 7*(3). Retrieved August 5, 2023, from http://archive.today/J652N.

Yu, B. (2006). China's year of Russia and the gathering nuclear storm. *Comparative Connections, 8*(1). Retrieved August 5, 2023, from http://archive.today/tPXgA.

Yu, B. (2016). Politics of reluctant allies. *Comparative Connections, 18*(2), 129–144. Retrieved August 5, 2023, from http://archive.today/sC2Za.

Yu, B. (2021). Empire strikes back at Moscow and Beijing. *Comparative Connections, 23*(1), 139–150. Retrieved August 5, 2023, from http://archive.today/OX85I.

Yu, B. (2022). China-Russia relations: Ukraine Conflict Déjà Vu and China's principled neutrality. *Comparative Connections, 24*(1), 147–156. Retrieved August 5, 2023, from http://archive.today/ryCvn.

Yuan, Y. D. (2010). Sino-Russian defense ties. In: J. Bellacqua (ed.), *The Future of ChinaRussia Relations* (pp. 203–221). Kentucky: Kentucky University Press.

© 2025 World Scientific Publishing Company
https://doi.org/10.1142/9789811298301_0005

Chapter 5

An Evolving Approach Toward Japan–Taiwan Security and Defense Coordination

Hon-Min Yau

The world is getting more concerned about China's military expansion in East Asia. Since 2016, the People's Liberation Army (PLA) has rapidly shifted from being assertive to being more reckless in East Asia, and it has increased the intensity of its provocative behavior around the Taiwan Strait with military exercises of a larger scale and frequent aggressive air and naval activities. Traditionally, both Taiwan (Republic of China, ROC) and China (People's Republic of China, PRC) have restrained their military aircraft from the commonly accepted "median line" of the Taiwan Strait, which is an implicit boundary line that was in place during the Cold War to reduce the possibility of unwanted armed incidents and military escalation in the region. However, on June 15, 2021, it was recorded that a historically high number of military aircraft were dispatched by the PLA in a single air combat mission package, with 28 airplanes entering the adjacent airspace zone around Taiwan (Chan and Lindberg, 2021, p. 9). On October 4, 2021, in a single day, there were 52 aircraft in total intruding into the east side of the median line (Chung, 2021). After the then US House Speaker Nancy Pelosi's visit to Taiwan in August 2022 (US House Speaker, 2022), not only did China conduct multiple military drills in the adjacent area of Taiwan (Chin, 2022), but PLA air and naval platforms also attempted to enter Taiwan's territorial waters. China has completely

77

disregarded any concerns about military escalation, and by late 2022, a sudden increase in the number of Unmanned Aerial Vehicle reconnaissance activities over Taiwan's remote islands became another Chinese Communist Party (CCP) strategy to create a new normal (Ang and Suorsa, 2022). Furthermore, in April 2023, in protesting ROC President Tsai Ing-wen's meeting with the then newly elected US House speaker, Kevin McCarthy, the PLA conducted further so-called "encircling Taiwan" military drills and dispatched its aircraft carrier *Shandong* to the east of Taiwan (Shepherd and Chiang, 2023). It was noted on April 10, 2023, that a record-breaking number of 91 PLA aircraft intruded into the adjacent airspace of Taiwan (Yu and Lo, 2023).

The danger of these provocative and reckless actions by the PLA cannot be understated. In comparison, in the 1991 Gulf War, the first airstrike attack package in US Operation Desert Storm included a modest number of 25 aircraft that successfully paralyzed the command-and-control system of the Iraqi forces (US Air Combat Command, 2016). In addition, a modern PLA air brigade typically has 24 aircraft (Trevethan, 2018). When security analysts interpret China's air intrusions with these factual data and empirical developments, China's assertive behavior in this region is less likely to be considered simple accidents and more probably the result of meticulous political and military calculation. The conventional wisdom in the region often suggests that the international community should refrain from engaging with Taiwan in order not to "provoke" China. However, such a past belief ignores the fact that, under Xi Jinping's third term as the CCP General Secretary, China's irresponsible behavior is more the result of its endogenous motivation based on a power-seeking logic and less an exogenous response to developments in the international sphere. As the CCP already demonstrates strong expansionist intentions, the concern is no longer whether regional security actors are provoking China, but instead, whether the lack of collaboration in the region will in fact deliver a false signal and fuel Chinese miscalculation.

In response to such rapid dynamics and dangerous escalation in the region, both US President Joe Biden and Prime Minister Suga Yoshihide of Japan emphasized the need for peace and stability across the Taiwan Strait at their first summit in April 2022 (The White House, 2021). In September 2021, Japan's former Minister of Defense, Kishi Nobuo, highlighted the importance of the Taiwan Strait to his country in an exclusive interview with *CNN* (Chin, 2021). In December 2021, the late Prime Minister Shinzo Abe even remarked that "any emergency over Taiwan would mean an emergency for Tokyo as well" (China summons Japan envoy, 2021). Even in the subsequent video conference in January and the QUAD meeting in May 2022, both President Biden and Japanese Prime Minister Fumio Kishida reiterated the importance of "peace and stability across the Taiwan Strait" (The White House, 2022c, 2022d). In May 2023, G7 leaders met in Japan and released a joint communiqué reaffirming the importance of peace and stability across the Taiwan Strait (Yu and Chen, 2023). These political leaders have gradually come to understand that an accommodative approach may please China, but it affords no guarantee of regional security.

To maintain regional stability in the Taiwan Strait, some immediate efforts to change Xi's security perceptions of the region are required. Indeed, Taiwan needs to convince its public that the ROC military can do its job adequately through continuous self-enhancement and defense investments so that the Taiwanese society will be encouraged and mobilized in preparing for any Taiwan contingency. Likewise, supportive words from the international community also need to be matched by their own actions; otherwise, such efforts at stabilizing regional security will be destined to fail (Liu *et al.*, 2021). It is clear that to maintain regional prosperity, solid strategic partnerships and collective collaborations need to be demonstrated between Taiwan and security stakeholders in the region, in particular, Japan, in the hope of shifting China's perception of the region.

5.1 The Challenges and Opportunities of Taiwan–Japan Cooperation

Traditionally, both political and technical difficulties have hindered the prospects of any form of cooperation. From the political perspective, in consideration of China's reaction, the government of Japan has strictly adhered to its policy of having no official contact with Taiwan since its establishment of diplomatic relations with China in 1972 (Yamaguchi, 2021). From a technical perspective, not only has the territorial dispute in the East China Sea obstructed discussions of cooperation with Taiwan, but the strong pacifist tradition in Japan's post-war policy circles has traditionally increased the uncertainty regarding its active contribution to regional stability. In fact, Article 9 of the Japanese Constitution fundamentally renounces Japan's right to use force abroad (The House of Representatives, 1946). Since the 2015 revision of the Legislation for

Peace and Security (Soble, 2015), it is still very challenging for the Japanese Self-Defense Force (SDF) to use its military assets overseas, even if it could have a slight chance of receiving proper parliamentary approval from the Japanese Diet.

Nevertheless, amid China's intensifying military activities in East Asia, both aspects need creative conceptualization and reorientation. First, in terms of the aspect of political recognition, diplomatic relations and security partners do not need to go hand in hand. Just as China maintains diplomatic relations with many countries but is not a security partner with many of them at the same time, other regional actors could be Taiwan's security partners even without diplomatic recognition. That is to say, international relations in the 21st century are activities involving multilayered relations. The fact is that, even though China does not recognize Taiwan's political existence internationally, it still acknowledges Taiwan's global existence in the economic domain under the World Trade Organization (WTO) framework. Therefore, the bottom line is that cooperation is possible as long as it is a sovereign decision that is taken by Japan collectively.

Second, in terms of the technical aspect, the Japan–Taiwan Fishery agreement (signed in 2013 and revised in 2018) is actually a successful case of cooperation before any official diplomatic relation (DeAeth, 2018). In the context of the reality of there being no official recognition and without touching upon the issue of Taiwan's *status quo*, the two sides could still have a coordination committee, including specialists from the two governments, which could meet annually to discuss immediate maritime issues including maritime pollution, and illegal, unreported, and unregulated (IUU) fishing. In addition, Joe Biden's Indo-Pacific Strategy, released on February 11, 2022, explicitly highlighted the need to maintain peace and stability across the Taiwan Strait by strengthening relations with regional partners (The White House, 2022a). His administration has repeatedly expressed support for Taiwan without subscribing his country to any kind of timeless assumptions (Mendis & Yau, 2022). The National Security Strategy released in October 2022 further stated the need for America's "Indo-Pacific allies to be engaged cooperatively … on shaping the order to which we all aspire …" (The White House, 2022b, p. 17). The political reality is that, due to the lack of a supreme authority in the volatile international environment, the legitimacy of each country's external behavior is better judged by whether they are sensible in light of the changing dynamics of security realities, and correspondingly, they should not be self-constrained by their past policy positions. In December 2022, the Japanese government modified its three most important security documents, including the National Security Strategy, National Defense Strategy, and Defense Buildup Program, and identified China as Japan's "greatest strategic challenge" (Prime Minister's Office, 2022, p. 9). As we are seeing a gradual reorientation of Japanese government policy, the future delivery of such a new posture should be about how to overcome both resources challenges and political hurdles (Liff & Hornung, 2022). The issue now is not about whether Japan should passively continue a self-imposed policy of "working relations on a non-governmental basis" with Taiwan (Ministry of Foreign Affairs of Japan, 2021), but it is more about how Japan can be better prepared to actively readjust itself to the new security context in the Indo-Pacific region.

In retrospect, prior to the outbreak of the Russo-Ukraine War, the United States was the only country that repeatedly warned Ukraine of an incoming attack from the Russian military (Dettmer, 2022). But Ukraine was still strategically surprised, without having mobilized its reservists in a timely manner, which could be due to an intelligence failure. Hence, a good decision comes from good intelligence and cooperation in Human Intelligence (HUMINT), Imagery Intelligence (IMINT), Signals Intelligence (SIGINT), etc., which will be beneficial in helping regional security and deterring a potential miscalculation by China's leadership. For Taiwan and Japan to practically contribute to the region's security without breaking with Japan's pacifist tradition under its current legal constraints, creative collaborations are still required, and intelligence sharing would seem to be the first feasible road map for facilitating future cooperation.

5.2 Intelligence Sharing: A First Step to Improving Understanding

From the perspective of civilian engagement, academic exchanges between research institutes and conference events, with the aim of proposing policy recommendations, are among the broader forms of intelligence exchange. Workshops held to explore the field for bilateral cooperation and to shape the understanding between Taiwan and Japan are also value-added activities. It would also be constructive to conduct war-gaming exercises to deliberate upon the potential contingency scenarios over the

Taiwan Strait and to investigate possible responses to these situations. Visiting scholars, policymakers, officials, and even students posted at educational and research institutes on the other side are also another vital component of minimizing knowledge gaps and refining a future course of action.

If both parties want to engage with the security challenges and make bilateral cooperation workable and effective, some form of quasi-official or official engagement eventually needs to happen, in particular in the domain of high politics, defense, and security. In fact, before the modification of Article 9 of the Constitution, Japan could make a sovereign decision to expand its intelligence exchange with Taiwan without any involvement or use of its military overseas. However, past experience has shown that it is very often the government departments on the Japanese side who are self-constrained by the issue of the lack of formal diplomatic relations between the two sides (Shigeta, 2022). What the Japanese government may want to do more is, like the US, to remove the barriers to formal dialogue via the creation of domestic legislative tools to encourage cooperation and communication between Taiwan and Japan (Lin and Hetherington, 2022). For example, the US's Taiwan Relations Act (TRA) and the following bills, such as the Taiwan Travel Act, Asia Reassurance Initiative Act, Taiwan Allies International Protection and Enhancement Initiative Act, and Taiwan Assurance Act, have created multiple frameworks for bilateral dialogue. These US domestic tools could facilitate broader exchanges with Taiwan in multiple domains. Hence, in the context of intelligence cooperation, the obstacle for Japan to deepen its working relations with Taiwan is not whether Article 9 of the Constitution could be modified, but rather it is about coming to a Japanese decision regarding whether cooperation with Taiwan is more important than trying to accommodate China. In fact, there seems to be growing Japanese dissatisfaction with the current security realities, and Japanese policymakers are starting to exercise strategic autonomy; it was reported in June 2022 that the Japanese Ministry of Defense was having discussions regarding establishing military attachés in Taipei (Japan to send, 2022). In March 2023, the Japanese government first approved a new reciprocal access agreement with Australia and the United Kingdom (Miki, 2023), and it later conducted evacuation drills in Okinawa to practice its emergency protocols in response to a potential conflict in the region (Yang, 2022). The government of Japan has started to recognize the practical need to reorient its security posture. If this trajectory can be continued, some potential evolving works of exchange with Taiwan from non-political to highly political domains should be possible. If these initiatives are started properly, they might gradually spill over to create future solid realizations.

(1) **Economic intelligence:** Economically, Taiwan is a recognized member of the WTO and is known for being an innovative economic entity. Hence, this is an area that both sides could develop without suffering from China's political disruption. While China has been moving closer to Iran and Russia in the form of a "Cold War-style alliance" amid the Sino-US competition since 2016 (Li, 2022), the United States is also shifting its economic policy from a comparative advantage to a "complimentary [advantage] approach" (Office of the US Trade Representative, 2022). Nevertheless, Taiwan has a solid traditional manufacturing capability and information and communications technology (ICT) industry, not to mention its unique position in the semiconductor industry. Hence, establishing collaborations between Japan and Taiwan in the future in the direction of technology and the development of standards, and continuing to deepen their already interdependent manufacturing ecosystem would be extremely important in the foreseeable volatile economic environment.

(2) **Intelligence cooperation in global health:** As testified by the experience of fighting against COVID-19, in the 21st century, diseases have become a significant threat to global security. Unfortunately, China still prioritizes its own political interests without acknowledging the potential risk to global security and the actual needs of the Taiwanese people, and Taiwan is still excluded from the World Health Organization (WHO) and World Health Assembly (WHA). Given that Taiwan and Japan are geographically close, culturally appreciated, and economically intermingled, a future outbreak of an infectious disease could quickly traverse from one country to the other. Not only should Taiwan and Japan continue to deepen their existing exchanges based on the COVID-19 experience, but the challenge to global health and the risk to Japanese well-being also provide sound legitimacy for such a plan. Hence, both sides should not only develop a platform to share disease intelligence but also support and create a biotechnology industry ecosystem with talent from both countries.

(3) **Military industry exchange:** Another lesson learned from the Russo-Ukraine conflict is that Ukraine could adopt a strategy of trading

space with time due to its position as the second-largest country in Europe. In addition, it has land borders with many NATO states, such as Poland and Slovakia, with direct connections of highways and railways. Ukraine continues to receive military supplies during wartime, but Taiwan, as a relatively small island, is obstructed by its surrounding ocean regarding its material supply during wartime. Furthermore, Taiwan imported most of its natural gas from the Middle East, but the PLA's A2/AD capabilities and the huge size of its air force and navy are expected to work on blockading the island. This makes Taiwan's defense not only about capabilities but also about capacities. Given that it is unlikely that Taiwan could receive wartime supplies like Ukraine during the Russo-Ukraine war starting in 2022, Taiwan is hedging toward a more resilient and controllable defense strategy, which relies on indigenized defense production. Compared to Taiwan, Japan has a more comprehensive experience in designing and integrating self-defense weapons for land, air, and sea. Japan has built its own submarines, ships, anti-submarine warfare capabilities, and aircraft. Conversely, Taiwan has the National Chung-Shan Institute of Science and Technology (NCSIST) and Aerospace Industrial Development Cooperation (AIDC), which are continuously investing in missiles and indigenous defense aircraft together with other suppliers in aeronautics and shipbuilding. Hence, Taiwan established the Taiwan National Defense Industry Development Association (TW-DIDA) in 2017 to promote its domestic defense industry. It is very likely that there are broader fields of technology in which Japan and Taiwan could conduct exchanges within the guidelines of Japan's 2014 "The Three Principles on Transfer of Defense Equipment and Technology," as long as these transfers and cooperation are defensive in nature (Ministry of Defense of Japan, 2014). Given that Taiwan is a reliable partner with a track record of strong manufacturing capabilities, this is certainly a direction that both Taiwan and Japan could work on together toward better deterring the CCP and Xi Jinping's ambitions.

(4) **Cybersecurity intelligence:** One of the unique characteristics of cyberattacks is that they are often a transnational activity, respecting no borders. In fact, cyberattacks are similar to ballistic missile attacks. Without good intelligence, it is very challenging for defenders to know where a ballistic missile is coming from and going to, and what kind of payload it carries. Likewise, a cyberattack can be quick and

stealthy, and these attacks often give defenders very little time to react. Hence, the defense against these time-sensitive threats requires collaborative intelligence and well-coordinated international response by surveillance sensors along their attack trajectories. In the Asia-Pacific region, the Asia Pacific Computer Emergency Response Team (APCERT) was initiated by the Japanese Computer Emergency Response Team/Coordination Center (JPCERT/CC) in 2002 to encourage international cooperation and support, and there are about 28 organizations from 20 areas on a regional level that are collaborating today. As state-sponsored cyberattacks often come with implications of economic and political signaling, Taiwan and Japan should continue to deepen and broaden these existing "technical only" structures of cyber cooperation to evolve toward a possible "cyber regime complex" (Nye Jr, 2017), which could work to secure cyberspace through multiple collaborations among governments, the private sector, the technical community, and non-governmental organizations in the region.

(5) **The intelligence of maritime security and humanitarian assistance:** Given that both Taiwan and Japan are maritime countries, in the hope of improving the livelihoods of the general public, an immediate step would undoubtedly be establishing better intelligence sharing to facilitate better Humanitarian Assistance and Disaster Relief (HADR) capabilities. Simple naval drills would be ideal, like a "passing exercise" (PASSEX), in which both sides practice how to communicate with each other in order to build interoperability. In addition, in 2014, the United States and Japan established a form of maritime domain awareness (MDA) collaboration in order to improve maritime intelligence over the East China Sea (The White House, 2014), and this may be another direction that both Taiwan and Japan could develop. By increasing the visibility of maritime activities in the region, both sides could reduce miscommunication and improve their response times to any emergency.

(6) **Intelligence/Surveillance/Reconnaissance (ISR) collaboration:** During the fourth Taiwan Strait Crisis after the Pelosi visit, it was reported that there was a discrepancy in terms of the quantity of the PLA's ballistic missiles that landed in the waters east of Taiwan and in the Japanese Exclusive Economic Zone (EEZ). Taiwan reported that 11 ballistic missiles were launched during the PLA military drills (Ministry of National Defense of the Republic of China, 2022), but

Japan only reported nine missiles (Dooley, 2022). This discrepancy indicates that the lack of ISR sharing could equally harm both sides' battlefield visibility and deny the possibility of coordinated actions. Another lesson from the Russo-Ukraine War was that the weaker party could not continue its war effort without enough time-sensitive data. Hence, it is NATO that has constantly dispatched surveillance aircraft, such as Airborne Warning and Control Systems (AWACS), to provide real-time feeding to improve the transparency of the battlefield for the Ukraine military (Common, 2022). In addition, the Starlink satellite internet constellation operated by the US aerospace company SpaceX offers communication with hospitals and regional governments, and has been an essential part of Ukraine's resilient community, contributing to the sustainability of the Ukrainian resistance during wartime (Roulette, 2023). As such, given that China is always looking for a quick and decisive campaign, it is naturally expected that China's use of force upon Taiwan would certainly be an invasion involving military assets from PLA's multiple military theatres, attacking from the Bohai Sea, Yellow Sea, East China Sea, and South China Sea. In order to identify military threats at the earliest stage, it is crucial for both Taiwan and Japan to share and protect information and intelligence while developing and maintaining common situational awareness. Both governments could invest resources to institutionalize not only the system collaboration but also for organizations to align with the new security challenges in the region. Their intelligence agencies could establish a dialogue to share HUMINT, IMINT, SIGINT, Electronic Intelligence (ELINT), Satellite Intelligence (SATINT), etc., and even include time-sensitive surveillance information from the military organizations in overlapping jurisdictions and other specific areas of interest. Nevertheless, there is no General Security of Military Information Agreement (GSOMIA) between Taiwan and Japan. In addition, this would elevate bilateral cooperation, similar to the joint ISR mechanism specified within the US–Japan Defense Cooperation (Ministry of Defense of Japan, 2015). Regardless of the above concerns, internationally, such cooperation could still be done as a Japanese sovereign decision overriding potential political protests from China. Domestically, Japan still needs to develop innovative tools to ease domestic legal concerns. If this is a long-term vision of intelligence cooperation, Japan may need to domestically develop creative legal tools, like the US's Taiwan

Relations Act (TRA) initiated by Congress, in order to deepen bilateral ISR collaboration. In addition, given that the United States has formal or quasi-formal cooperation with both countries, any kind of intelligence-sharing framework would have a better chance of success if it could be blessed by the security guarantor in the region.

5.3 Chartering Toward Defense Cooperation: A Needed but Challenging Step to Increase Interoperability

If the above intelligence exchanges could be realized, it would signify the beginning of the social agency of the Japanese government and the reorientation of its strategic autonomy toward prioritizing Japan's security needs over China's interests. Considering that Japanese air and sea ports are geographically located in critical locations in any future Taiwan Strait conflict, and the US has a huge number of military bases in Japan, the above frameworks could slowly be elevated to further defense cooperation and eventually improve the interoperability of these two militaries. However, given that defense cooperation during peacetime will be a sensitive issue in Japanese society due to the traumatic memory of WWII, such a proposal would still require a certain legal relief from its current domestic constraints. Before the realization of the modification of Article 9 of the Japanese Constitution, one possible leeway might be to claim a form of cooperation between Taiwan and Japan for the purpose of the evacuation of Japanese nationals abroad according to Article 84-4 of the Japan SDF Law. Nevertheless, from Taiwan's domestic perspective, the revelation of such cooperation could likely do more harm than good. In fact, such cooperation could be misinterpreted by Taiwanese society as the Japanese government being more concerned about evacuating its own people than helping Taiwan, and it could also be used as political propaganda by China to divide and conquer the hearts and minds of people in Taiwan. Eventually, to deepen its defense cooperation with Taiwan, Japan needs to enact a challenging relaxation of its constitutional constraints in order to allow for a certain level of international military cooperation.

Once the constraints from Japan itself can be released, the other concern would be Taiwan's ambiguous international status (Crawford, 2006, p. 219). Given that Japan has no diplomatic relations with Taiwan, the only option is to use domestic legal tools to compensate for the lack of official ties, as mentioned earlier. In fact, scholars argue that the United States was able to use the TRA to regulate its relations with Taiwan due to the US's "residual legal power" over this legally undecided territory (Matsumura, 2022). In addition, China repeatedly criticizes the United States for using domestic law to allow official contact with Taiwan and for unilaterally "violating the international law and basic norm in international relations" (Ministry of Foreign Affairs, 2022). Superficially, these viewpoints present an international obstruction to any possibility of cooperation between Taiwan and Japan. Nevertheless, the above arguments ignore the fact that it is also a recognized norm that many countries, such as the United States, see international laws as not necessarily superior to domestic laws (Paulsen, 2008, p. 1770). In reality, the TRA is a domestic law approved by the US Congress that supersedes the three Communiqués established by the US executive branch (DeLisle, 2019, p. 36). Furthermore, there are critical scholars who argue that Taiwan's existence already manifests the international practice of self-governance based on the principles of democratic values, and the constant existence of Taiwan on the global stage is already a political and social reality that the international community cannot ignore (Chen, 2016). While the debate continues and an international consensus on Taiwan's status has yet to emerge, it is up to Japan to decide which viewpoint it wants to side more closely with. Just like the Japanese government's participation in the Global Cooperation and Training Framework (GCTF) since 2019 (Shattuck, 2022), an initiation created by Taiwan and the United States to host workshops on public health, law enforcement cooperation, cybersecurity, humanitarian assistance, etc., the big question is whether Japan's foreign policy would rather remain reactive to the regional dynamics or choose to actively shape the Indo-Pacific environment.

5.4 Reducing China's Ability to Exploit the Security Context Over the Taiwan Strait

Any cooperation between Japan and Taiwan would demonstrate the regional actors' intentions to maintain peace and prosperity over the Taiwan Strait, but it would also carry the risk of providing China with a pretext to protest strongly. However, if both Taiwan and Japan feel a sense of urgency in terms of Xi's growing ambition in the following years of his regime, it will also be a necessary evil to take such risks.

While China has constantly escalated the Taiwan Strait tensions by sending 1,727 PLA sorties over the region in 2022 (China's warplane incursions, 2023), China's foreign minister Wang Yi diplomatically called for the international community to "give peace a chance" without providing military weapons to the Russo-Ukraine War (Ng, 2023). Hence, CCP's propaganda apparatus is certainly going to name any form of international exchange with Taiwan as challenging Beijing's so-called "One China" principle and disrupting regional stability, but we should not forget that it is China that is using military means to reshape the strategic environment in the Taiwan Strait without reaffirming the rules-based international order. In addition, Taiwan's ambiguous international status is probably the biggest vulnerability, and one that has been constantly exploited by China to disrupt the region's stability. From the incursions into Taiwan's airspace to China's economic coercion of Lithuania in protesting the development of its relationship with Taiwan (Reynolds & Goodman, 2022), not only will China miss any good opportunity to turn constructive initiatives aimed at enhancing peace and prosperity by regional actors into a weapon for destructive propaganda, but it is also very likely that any future form of deeper cooperation would be labeled by China as "Cold War mentality" or "foreign interference" to rally its domestic audience around the flag and to divide and conquer the already contested society in Taiwan (Xi, 2022). Hence, some kind of mitigation strategy needs to be employed.

At the beginning of the Russo-Ukraine War in 2022, Japan joined the international effort and imposed harsh sanctions on Russia. According to the then Japanese Defense Minister Nobuo Kishi, "If the international community somehow allows or condones Russia's aggression against Ukraine, it might send a wrong message that such actions can be tolerated in other parts of the world" (Hudson, 2022). Likewise, both Japan and the US should make their strategic communication toward China clear, that its aggressive behavior in the region will only force them to deliver more policy initiatives of defense collaboration with Taiwan. In addition, there is no regional security governance mechanism in East Asia, and China constantly criticizes the US's hub-and-spokes approach as a so-called Cold War alliance, but not a partnership. Hence, being multilateral or regional is always better than being bilateral in order to deny China's manipulative campaign and improve the credibility of the exchange. China would frame any bilateral cooperation as an act of geopolitical calculation, but a multilateral format can be perceived more as a collective concern among the international community. Therefore, multilateral dialogue is always better than trilateral or bilateral cooperation.

5.5 Conclusion: From Risk Management to Conflict Management

Both Japan and Taiwan are robust liberal democracies, and true liberals know that "the only certainty in this life is change, but ... the change can be directed toward a constructivist end."[1] During the 1950s and 1960s, there was a history of Japanese military advisors, using the code name "white group," sharing their military knowledge with Taiwan to help defend against the aggression of the CCP (Cheung, 2018). Indeed, the Japanese government could play a more proactive role instead of continuing to respond passively to regional developments, and with creative thinking and innovative planning, a new cooperation framework can be renewed and developed by both sides in order to reorient the CCP's perception.

To conclude, as we march through the third term of Xi Jinping's leadership, China is increasing its military presence in the region, either as the result of Xi's personal ambitions in the short term, or contextual developments in the long run. As the Taiwan Strait is a vital transportation and trade route linking the prosperous countries of East Asia, this development is continuing to cause regional security and stability to deteriorate. Although Taiwan is committed to defending itself, this goal is still very challenging to achieve by its efforts alone. Proper support and cooperation from the international community is an essential factor in maintaining regional peace. A country's security policy needs to be revised regularly to reflect the dynamics of regional development. It may be time for these regional security actors to reassess their strategic posture toward the region in order not to fuel China's misguided ambitions.

References

Ang, A. U.-J. and Suorsa, O. P. (2022, September 27). The 'new normal' in PLA incursions into Taiwan's ADIZ. *The Diplomat*. Retrieved August 5, 2023, from https://archive.vn/9LXpq.

---

[1] From Henry A. Wallace.

Chan, C. and Lindberg, K. S. (2021, June 15). China sends 28 planes near Taiwan in year's largest exercise. *Bloomberg News*. Retrieved August 5, 2023, from http://archive.today/szF42.

Chen, L.-C. (2016). *The US-Taiwan-China Relationship in International Law and Policy*. Oxford, UK: Oxford University Press.

Cheung, H. (2018, October 28). Taiwan in time: Military advice from the former enemy. *Taipei Times*. Retrieved August 5, 2023, from https://archive.vn/jGBSX.

Chin, J. (2021, September 17). Japan to defend against Chinese aggression: Minister. *Taipei Times*. Retrieved August 5, 2023, from https://archive.vn/teOfV.

Chin, J. (2022, August 5). PLA starts live-fire drills near Taiwan. *Taipei Times*. Retrieved August 5, 2023, from https://archive.vn/ww2yJ.

China summons Japan envoy over former PM Abe's comments on Taiwan (2021, December 2). *Reuters*. Retrieved August 5, 2023, from http://archive.today/nZTYN.

China's warplane incursions into Taiwan air defence zone doubled in 2022. (2023, January 2). *The Guardian*. Retrieved August 5, 2023, from http://archive.today/9hGro.

Chung, L. (2021, October 4). Beijing sends record 52 fighter jets to test Taiwan, raising fear of mishaps. *South China Morning Post*. Retrieved August 5, 2023, from http://archive.today/isQ4R.

Common, D. (2022, October 22). Flying just outside Ukraine, NATO's sentinel planes warn of Russia's battlefield moves. *CBC News*. Retrieved August 5, 2023, from https://archive.vn/FY6HE.

Crawford, J. (2006). *The Creation of States in International Law*. Oxford, UK: Oxford University Press.

DeAeth, D. (2018, March 20). Taiwan-Japan revise bilateral fishery agreement around Diaoyu Islands. *Taiwan News*. Retrieved August 5, 2023, from http://archive.today/AqI0f.

DeLisle, J. (2019). The Taiwan relations Act at 40. *Asia Policy, 14*(4), 35–42.

Dettmer, J. (2022, February 23). Zelenskyy under pressure to mobilize Ukrainians, start serious defense planning. *VOA*. Retrieved August 5, 2023, from http://archive.today/8SjQe.

Dooley, B. (2022, August 4). With 5 Missiles, China sends stark signal to Japan and U.S. on Taiwan. *The New York Times*. Retrieved August 5, 2023, from http://archive.today/hbGT6.

Hudson, J. (2022, May 6). Confronting Russia will deter China, says Japanese defense minister. *The Washington Post*. Retrieved August 5, 2023, from http://archive.today/xRGSX.

Japan to send active-duty defense attaché to Taipei: Report (2022, July 4). *Focus Taiwan News*.

Li, C. (2022). Biden's China strategy: Coalition-driven competition or Cold War-style confrontation? *Brookings*. Retrieved August 5, 2023, from US: http://archive.today/hV7WS.

Liff, A. P. and Hornung, J. W. (2022). Japan's new security policies: A long road to full implementation. *Brookings*. Retrieved August 5, 2023, from US: http://archive.today/4e20e.

Lin, T.-Y. and Hetherington, W. (2022, October 17). Japanese officials oppose '*status quo*' shift. *Taipei Times*. Retrieved August 5, 2023, from http://archive.today/XxR35.

Liu, F.-K. L., Karalekas, D., and Matsumura, M. (2021). *Security Turbulence in Asia: Shaping New Strategy in Japan and Taiwan*. Taipei, Taiwan: Taiwan Center for Security Studies.

Matsumura, M. (2022, May 21). Taiwan-Japan military ties possible. *Taipei Times*. Retrieved August 5, 2023, from http://archive.today/mbnZd.

Mendis, P. and Yau, H.-M. (2022). Can America prevent a Chinese invasion of Taiwan? *The National Interest*. Retrieved August 5, 2023, from http://archive.today/3X5oY.

Miki, R. (2023, March 1). Japan defense pacts with U.K. and Australia move closer to approval. *Nikkei Asia*. Retrieved August 5, 2023, from http://archive.today/BiGe3.

Ministry of Defense of Japan (2014). The three principles on transfer of defense equipment and technology. Retrieved August 5, 2023, from https://www.mofa.go.jp/fp/nsp/page1we_000083.html.

Ministry of Defense of Japan (2015). The guidelines for Japan-U.S. Defense Cooperation. Retrieved August 5, 2023, from https://www.mod.go.jp/en/j-us-alliance/guidelines/index.html.

Ministry of Foreign Affairs (2022). Foreign Ministry Spokesperson Hua Chunying's Regular Press Conference on August 3, 2022. Retrieved August 5, 2023, from http://archive.today/Q0WoF.

Ministry of Foreign Affairs of Japan (2021, January 14). Taiwan (Basic Data). Retrieved August 5, 2023, from http://archive.today/WRs3W.

Ng, T. (2023, March 21). Ukraine: China says its refusal to condemn Russia gives peace a chance. *South China Morning Post*. Retrieved August 5, 2023, from http://archive.today/RjXS8.

Nye Jr, J. S. (2017). Deterrence and dissuasion in cyberspace. *International Security*, *41*(3), 44–71.

Office of the U.S. Trade Representative (2022). *Remarks by Ambassador Katherine Tai at the Roosevelt Institute's Progressive Industrial Policy Conference*. Washington, DC, USA: Office of the U.S. Trade Representative.

Paulsen, M. S. (2008). The constitutional power to interpret international law. *Yale LJ*, *118*, 1762.

Prime Minister's Office (2022). *National Security Strategy of Japan.* Tokyo, Japan: Prime Minister's Office.

Reynolds, M. and Goodman, M. P. (2022, May 6). China's Economic Coercion: Lessons from Lithuania. *Center for Strategic and International Studies.* Retrieved August 5, 2023, from http://archive.today/Rb7b5.

Roulette, J. (2023, February 9). SpaceX curbed Ukraine's use of Starlink internet for drones-company president. *Reuters.com.* Retrieved August 5, 2023, from http://archive.today/HGGMd.

Shattuck, T. (2022, March 28). Expanding the scope of the GCTF. *Taipei Times.* Retrieved August 5, 2023, from http://archive.today/FutSH.

Shepherd, C. and Chiang, V. (2023, April 8). Chinese military starts drills encircling Taiwan after Tsai's U.S. visit. *The Washington Post.* Retrieved August 5, 2023, from http://archive.today/RYBwT.

Shigeta, S. (2022, October 1). Japan risks security lapses in Taiwan crisis, lacking formal ties. *Nikkei Asia.* Retrieved August 5, 2023, from http://archive.today/dk4tS.

Soble, J. (2015, September 18). Japan's Parliament Approves Overseas Combat role for military. *The New York Times.* Retrieved August 5, 2023, from http://archive.today/yWPLo.

Taiwan defence ministry: China launched 11 ballistic missiles into waters near Taiwan (2022, August 4). *Reuters.* Retrieved August 5, 2023, from http://archive.today/90CN4.

The House of Representative (1946, November 3). The constitution of Japan. Retrieved August 5, 2023, from http://archive.today/tXgXM.

The White House (2014, April 25). U.S.-Japan joint statement: The United States and Japan: Shaping the future of the Asia-Pacific and beyond. Retrieved August 5, 2023, from http://archive.today/r7Ttv.

The White House (2021, April 16). U.S.-Japan Joint Leaders' Statement: "U.S. — JAPAN GLOBAL PARTNERSHIP FOR A NEW ERA." Retrieved August 5, 2023, from http://archive.today/BusAF.

The White House (2022a, February 11). FACT SHEET: Indo-Pacific Strategy of the United States. Retrieved August 5, 2023, from http://archive.today/ecVbb.

The White House (2022b, October). *National Security Strategy.* Washington DC, USA: The White House.

The White House (2022c, January 21). Readout of President Biden's Meeting with Prime Minister Kishida of Japan. Retrieved August 5, 2023, from http://archive.today/PrgRF.

The White House (2022d, May 23). Remarks by President Biden and Prime Minister Kishida Fumio of Japan in Joint Press Conference. Retrieved August 5, 2023, from http://archive.today/ptFvp.

Trevethan, L. S. (2018). 'Brigadization' of the PLA air force. China Aerospace Studies Institute. Retrieved August 5, 2023, from https://apps.dtic.mil/sti/pdfs/AD1082606.pdf.

US Air Combat Command (2016, February 11). DESERT STORM: The strike Eagle's opening act. Retrieved August 5, 2023, from http://archive.today/Wm4NC.

US House Speaker Pelosi arrives in Taiwan (2022, August 2). *Reuters*. Retrieved August 5, 2023, from http://archive.today/NmNDa.

Xi, J. (2022, October 16). Hold High the Great Banner of Socialism with Chinese Characteristics and Strive in Unity to Build a Modern Socialist Country in All Respects. Retrieved August 5, 2023, from http://archive.today/S4gZv.

Yamaguchi, M. (2021). Japan says ties with Taiwan are only unofficial. Retrieved August 5, 2023, from http://archive.today/dGSAw.

Yang, W. (2022, March 28). Japan holds evacuation drills amid Taiwan invasion fear. *Deutsche Welle*. Retrieved August 5, 2023, from http://archive.today/GhfFw.

Yu, M. and Lo, J. (2023, April 10). Record-breaking 91 Chinese planes detected around Taiwan in 12 hours. *Focus Taiwan News*. Retrieved August 5, 2023, from http://archive.today/tM40i.

Yu, M. and Chen, C. (2023, May 20). Taiwan thanks G7 for stressing importance of cross-strait peace. *Focus Taiwan News*. Retrieved August 5, 2023, from http://archive.today/3z3Vk.

© 2025 World Scientific Publishing Company
https://doi.org/10.1142/9789811298301_0006

Chapter 6

Is a Taiwan Crisis Also a Japan Crisis? Japan's Complicated Security Laws

Takeuchi Toshitaka

The world is no longer a tranquil place, to say the least. A war has been raging in Ukraine since February 2022 due to the Russian invasion of that country. There are also heightened tensions in the Taiwan Strait. On the one hand, the People's Republic of China (PRC) claims Taiwan (the Republic of China, or ROC) as its own, dubbing it a "renegade province" that must be united with the mainland by force, if necessary. On the other hand, Taiwan wants to maintain the *status quo* of *de facto* independence. The tensions in East Asia increased after Nancy Pelosi, Speaker Emerita of the US House of Representatives, visited Taiwan and met ROC President Tsai Ing-wen in August 2022. China's reaction was furious, launching missiles around Taiwan, five of which landed in Japan's exclusive economic zone (EEZ). This intentional landing must be read as a warning to Japan, suggesting that the PRC leadership believes that Japan would very likely get involved in some way in a Taiwan contingency. This showed that there was a good chance that Japan would become entangled, if not directly attacked. This chapter examines how Japan might deal with a Taiwan contingency, if it is indeed possible. It discusses Japan's legally possible actions in the case of a Taiwan contingency and also explains the complicated nature of Japan's security legislation that might hinder its actions even if there existed the political will to do so.

Section 6.1 discusses the Pelosi visit and its aftermath. Then, in Section 6.2, we look at public opinion in Taiwan, Japan, and the United States, citing opinion polls and pronouncements by prominent politicians. In Section 6.3, the Taiwan Relations Act (TRA) and the Japan–US Security Treaty are explained in the context of Taiwan. In Section 6.4, Japan's constitutional restrictions and the new 2015 national security laws are explained in detail because they are complicated and determine what Japan can legally do in a Taiwan crisis. In Section 6.5, the proceedings of a tabletop exercise (TTX) on a Taiwan crisis conducted in Japan are explained to see how these legal complications would affect on-the-ground decision-making. Finally, we finish with some concluding remarks.

6.1 The Pelosi Visit and Its Aftermath

6.1.1 *The Pelosi visit and China's missile launch*

House Speaker Nancy Pelosi, the second in line to succeed to the US presidency, visited Taiwan and met with Tsai Ing-wen in August 2022 to show her strong support, and that of the US Congress, for Taiwan. This was a controversial visit because China would surely regard it as far too provocative, especially as Xi Jinping was concurrently seeking an unprecedented third term in a few months. He must have been very sensitive about his image as a strong and effective world leader. He might have viewed it as an affront and felt that he had lost face.

China's reaction was indeed furious, conducting the so-called exercises in six areas around Taiwan, the purpose of which is said to demonstrate how China can isolate and attack Taiwan. Significantly, it launched eleven (according to Taiwan and China, but nine according to Japan) missiles into the waters surrounding Taiwan, five of which fell within Japan's EEZ southwest of Hateruma Island near Taiwan. This was the first time in history that China fired missiles into Japan's EEZ. It should also be noted that half of the missiles that were launched landed in Japan's EEZ. This must be read as a stern warning to Japan not to interfere in what Beijing considers an internal matter. One might suspect that the whole thing was intended more as a warning to Japan, rather than Taiwan.

The crux of the matter for Japan is that the act was intentional and reportedly decided upon by PRC President Xi Jinping himself. When he was provided with the option of whether or not to launch missiles directly into Japan's EEZ, he chose to do so in a provocative decision (Nakazawa, 2022). The AP confirmed that this was intentional as well, reporting that "China conducts 'precision missile strikes' in Taiwan Strait" and "the People's Liberation Army announced that 'all missiles hit the target accurately,' suggesting that China may have intentionally targeted Japanese waters." Also, it reported that "China's official Xinhua News Agency reported the exercises were joint operations focused on 'blockade, sea target assault, strikes on ground targets, and airspace control'" (Lai and Wu, 2022).

6.1.2 Japan's concerns and reactions

Japan, of course, strongly protested this provocation. China merely responded that it did not recognize the EEZ and accused Japan of heightening unnecessary tensions. The *Global Times* said it all: It argued that China has the right to conduct military exercises in what Japan claims to be its EEZ because "there is no delimitation between the relevant waters surrounding China and Japan, so there is no such thing as a so-called Japanese exclusive economic zone." Furthermore, it warned Japan that it is easier to strike Japan than the United States, and Japan should be aware that "anyone who wants to meddle in China's domestic affairs will inevitably have to pay the price" (Japan's 'sense of insecurity,' 2022). If what China did in Japan's EEZ is acceptable, it should be acceptable for other countries to launch missiles into areas that China claims to be its EEZ in the South China Sea because many countries (including Japan) do not recognize many of the PRC's claims over the vast expanse of the South China Sea. One wonders how China would react to such an eventuality. Not only is what China did a dangerous act of provocation, but the fact that Xi Jinping himself decided to commit the act is chilling.

The *Global Times* is a nationalistic newspaper and ostensibly does not represent the Chinese government as such. However, it is said that its views tend to reflect those of the Chinese government. No matter how China rationalizes it, the fact remains that China knows what Japan claims and intentionally landed missiles in this EEZ. China must have expected Japan's strong reactions but still took action. This means that it prefers to warn Tokyo that it is determined to strike Japan militarily if Japan comes to the aid of Taiwan. Another point that one can glean from this is that the

Chinese government believes that Japan is very likely to involve itself in a Taiwan contingency. This suggests that China would probably make aggressive first moves against Japan itself, including striking the bases and facilities of Japan's Self-Defense Forces (SDF), as well as those of the US forces stationed in Japan, even should Japan hesitate to get involved. China must take the possible reactions of Japan and the United States into account when contemplating offensive scenarios. This makes their calculations more complicated, with increased uncertainty, which should hopefully force China to take a more cautious approach.

Compared to the 1995–1996 Third Taiwan Strait Crisis, Japan's reaction was much stronger this time. The intentional landing of missiles in Japan's EEZ must have had a big impact. For example, Prime Minister Kishida Fumio called it "a serious issue that affects our national security and the safety of our citizens" (Gu and Hwang, 2022). Further, then Foreign Minister Hayashi Yoshimasa stated, on the occasion of the ASEAN Regional Forum (ARF) Ministerial Meeting in August 2022, that China's missile launches near Japan were a "grave incident concerning the security of Japan and safety of its people" (Sasaki, 2022).

The Pelosi visit, along with a second high-level visit by Tsai with Kevin McCarthy, then the speaker of the House, in April 2023 — this one taking place in the United States — clearly showed the unwavering bipartisan support of the US House for Taiwan. However, critics of the meeting called it too provocative, giving China a chance to change the *status quo*. This is true because China has established a "new normal" in which the People's Liberation Army (PLA) operates much closer to Taiwan than it ever has before, and more regularly. For example, China nowadays routinely ignores the median line, which the two sides had heretofore tacitly recognized in the Taiwan Strait, and sends incursions into Taiwan's Air Defense Identification Zone (ADIZ) on a daily basis. The visit has been called symbolic grandstanding and a kind of gesture that could "threaten the delicate *status quo* that has enabled Taiwan to maintain its *de facto* sovereignty and protect its way of life" (Hsieh and Hsu, 2023).

6.2 Opinions in Taiwan, Japan, and the US

6.2.1 *Taiwan*

What do people in Taiwan think about unification and independence? In a public opinion survey by the Election Study Center of National

Chengchi University, the vast majority of respondents support the *status quo*, at more than 90 percent — whatever the *status quo* actually represents. It is almost equally divided among those who say, "decide the status later," "maintain it indefinitely," and "more inclined toward independence." A tiny minority of about 6 percent is inclined toward unification. It seems, though, that those who are more inclined toward independence increased significantly between 2018 and 2020, and have remained flat since then. Those who support unification as soon as possible remain at around 1 percent, whereas those who support independence as soon as possible are at around 5 percent. It is not clear, however, among those who support unification, whether sooner or later, under what kind of conditions they envision unification: Is it under the PRC or the ROC, or may they be possibly hoping for an amicable unification, which seems practically impossible at present? No matter how small it may be, one cannot rule out the theoretical possibility that there are some who may want unification under the PRC. It is usually assumed that the PRC will conduct a disinformation campaign first to break the will of the people of Taiwan. Then, the PRC can achieve unification without resorting to kinetic means — the preferred outcome for China. However, this may be based on a nativistic feeling, as the quote in the following paragraph shows.

Another crucial indicator is how respondents identify themselves, either as Taiwanese or Chinese. According to polling conducted by the same center cited above, those who identify as Taiwanese come in at around 60 percent or more, those who identify as both Chinese and Taiwanese are at around 30 percent, and those who identify as Chinese reach only 2–3 percent: a tiny minority. The reason that some people identify themselves as exclusively Chinese and support unification with the PRC may be coming from a very simple, nativistic feeling, as the following quote attests: "He supports unification with China simply because it is the land of his ancestors. People with the same heritage, and culture should, he believes, be one nation." "He would still fight if war broke out, although for his home, family and village" (Lung, 2023). This may especially be the case for some ROC citizens who escaped from China when it was taken over by the Chinese Communist Party (CCP) in 1949.

As cited in the *Taipei Times*, according to an Election Studies Center survey conducted in March 2019, it is clear that people in Taiwan reject the "one country, two systems" formula that the PRC hopes will entice the people of Taiwan to accept unification. The result was that 79 percent rejected the formula, with only 10.4 percent accepting it. A majority,

87.7 percent, said that Taiwan's future and cross-strait relations should be decided by Taiwan's 23 million people ("One country, two systems," 2019). The survey was conducted around the time when the democracy movement in Hong Kong was underway, being televised widely in Taiwan and around the world. The protest movement was brutally suppressed by the Chinese state, which was legalized through the implementation of China's national security law passed in June 2020. The events in Hong Kong proved that the "one country, two systems" formula was nothing more than a facade designed to lure Taiwan to China. The PRC broke its promise with the United Kingdom to apply the "one country, two systems" model for half a century after the reversion in 1997. This must have hardened the attitude of the people in Taiwan.

6.2.2 *Japan*

What about Japan? Here, we discuss what the Japanese public and prominent Japanese politicians are thinking about the Taiwan issue. At a summit meeting in April 2021, then-Prime Minister Suga Yoshihide and US President Joe Biden stated that they "underscore the importance of ensuring peace and stability in the Taiwan Strait" and "urge for a peaceful solution to the cross-strait issue" (House, 2021). This was the very first reference to the Taiwan Strait in any US–Japan summit statement since 1969. However, on his return to Japan, Suga said in the Diet that it "does not presuppose military involvement at all," keeping in line with the official position (Ryall, 2021). Then Defense Minister Kishi Nobuo was more direct in saying that "the peace and stability of Taiwan are directly connected to Japan" in June of the same year (Reynolds and Nobuhiro, 2021). Suga's successor, Kishida Fumio, at a summit meeting with Biden in May ·2022, also confirmed what Japan and the United States had agreed upon the previous year. Kishida stated in a press conference after the summit, "We stressed the importance of ensuring peace and stability in the Taiwan Strait, which is an essential element for the peace and prosperity of the international community." Biden agreed, saying, "We support the One China policy," but added, "That does not mean that China has the ability […] the jurisdiction to go in to use force to take over Taiwan. So, we stand firmly with Japan and with other nations not to let that happen" (Kishida, Biden reaffirm, 2022). This makes two Japanese prime ministers in a row to explicitly express Japan's concerns about the Taiwan Strait issue.

Deputy Prime Minister Aso Taro said, without mincing words, that an attack on Taiwan would be a "Survival-Threatening Situation" for Japan, which makes the use of force possible (Johnson, 2021). This is tantamount to pledging that Japan will help defend Taiwan if China attacks. This requires prior Diet approval, except in some extremely urgent cases, however. Ex-Prime Minister Abe Shinzo said in December 2021 that "[a] Taiwan contingency is a contingency for Japan. In other words, it is also a contingency for the Japan-US alliance. People in Beijing, particularly President Xi Jinping, should not misjudge that" (Taiwan contingency, 2021). So, Japan's prominent politicians, especially those in the ruling Liberal Democratic Party (LDP), are inclined to support Taiwan, notwithstanding the constitutional and legal difficulties that Japan faces in doing so.

What about the Japanese public? In a public opinion poll which asked about a potential Taiwan crisis, 81 percent replied that they feared that Japan would become entangled, and 14 percent said they did not. They were just asked whether or not Japan would be entangled, not what they thought Japan should do in a Taiwan contingency (Taiwan yūji, Nihon hakyū, 2022). Still, this means that the vast majority of the Japanese surveyed think that Japan would have to react in some way, most likely through the mobilization of the SDF. It may be for Japan's defense only, but the term "entangled" might connote US forces in Japan. When asked directly what Japan should do to prepare for a Taiwan contingency, 40 percent said that Japan should enhance its capabilities to deal with it, including amending existing laws. Nearly half said that we should prepare for it, which implies enhancing capabilities, but within the confines of the current laws. Therefore, almost all Japanese support enhancing its capabilities, which in essence means SDF capabilities.

In Okinawa prefecture, the most likely place to be affected, they were asked the following question: In the event that China and the United States are involved in an armed conflict over Taiwan, what is the possibility that Okinawa will be entangled? 44 percent answered that they feared it a great deal, and 41 percent said they were somewhat afraid. So, 85 percent are afraid that Okinawa will become entangled. This is similar to the poll cited above. On the question on the importance of the US bases in Okinawa for Japan's national security, 20 percent said "plenty," and 49 percent replied "to some extent." So, even in Okinawa, nearly 70 percent regard the US forces positively. This is somewhat surprising because Okinawa is where the anti-base sentiment is most prevalent (Isoda, 2022).

In sum, the polls tell us that the vast majority of Japanese people believe that Japan would very likely become entangled in a Taiwan Strait conflict, and Japan should enhance its capabilities in preparation for this. This is in line with what prominent politicians, such as those cited above, are saying. Then, one can conclude that Japan as a whole is aware that it must do something to defend itself. In the worst-case scenario, Japan itself would be attacked, and US forces in Japan would be dispatched from their bases in Japan. In that case, Japan would be inclined and most likely do something to help Taiwan defend itself.

What about the expectations that people in Taiwan have about Japan's involvement? The *Asahi Shimbun* cited a survey that the Taiwan Foundation for Democracy conducted in November 2021. According to the survey, 58 percent believed that Japan would dispatch the SDF to help defend Taiwan, whereas 35.2 percent said that Japan would not. On the other hand, in the case of the United States, 65.0 percent replied that the US forces would intervene, and 28.5 percent said they would not (Ishida, 2021). Thus, it is safe to say that the large majority of people in Taiwan expect that both Japan and the United States would intervene militarily in some form. Japan, in its 2021 White Paper on National Defense, mentioned "the vital importance of a stable security scenario across the Taiwan Strait," which seems to suggest that it would be forthcoming to do something for Taiwan and support the United States in such a defensive action.

6.2.3 *The United States*

What about general opinion in the United States? The United States is the linchpin in any Taiwan Strait crisis, as a matter of course. Let us see first what public opinion is like. An August 2021 survey report titled "For First Time, Half of Americans Favor Defending Taiwan if China Invades" was released by the Chicago Council on Global Affairs. Its key findings are as follows:

- The majority favors US recognition of Taiwan as an independent country (69 percent).
- A slimmer majority (53 percent) supports the United States' signing a formal alliance with Taiwan, and a plurality (46 percent) favors explicitly committing to defend Taiwan if China invades.
- Just over half of Americans (52 percent) favor sending US troops to defend Taiwan if China were to invade the island.

- Americans are divided over whether the United States should (50 percent) or should not (47 percent) sell arms and military equipment to Taiwan (Smeltz and Kafura, 2021).

It should be noted, first of all, that over a two-thirds majority supports outright independence for Taiwan, which is a definite *casus belli* for war according to the PRC. Also, about one-half of Americans support sending the US military if China invades Taiwan. Then, it is not much of a surprise that one-half support signing a formal alliance with Taiwan. All these findings seem to show that the majority supports a policy of strategic clarity, not ambiguity. On the other hand, it is somewhat surprising that only one-half is willing to sell arms and military equipment, which is what the TRA authorizes and what the United States has been doing for decades. It seems logical to say that if one favors Taiwan's outright independence, one should definitely support arms exports as a means of defense. Given this somewhat perplexing, if not contradictory, finding, one might wonder that many respondents do not necessarily have detailed knowledge about the intricacies of the situation in the Taiwan Strait. One thing is clear, however: It is highly likely that the majority of the American public is going to support Taiwan if and when a Taiwan contingency occurs.

Another survey report by the same Chicago council in August 2022 had the following key findings:

- Three-quarters of Americans (76 percent) think it is likely that China will see Russia's invasion of Ukraine as a precedent, encouraging it to invade Taiwan.
- In the event of a Chinese invasion of the island, the majority would support imposing diplomatic and economic sanctions (76 percent), sending additional arms and military supplies to the ROC government (65 percent), and using the US Navy to prevent Beijing from imposing a blockade against Taiwan (62 percent).
- Four in 10 would support sending US troops to Taiwan to help the ROC government defend the country against China (40 percent) (Smeltz and Kafura, 2022).

It says that 62 percent support sending in the US Navy to prevent a potential Chinese blockade. This is a significant finding in that China is expected to initiate a disinformation war and then an economic blockade. After all, Taiwan is economically dependent on China and is not prepared to withstand an economic blockade. One retired high-ranking defense official is quoted as saying that "China could simply blockade Taiwan, which has only about an eight-day supply of natural gas; sever undersea telecommunication cables; or strangle us economically by cutting off trade." After all, "around 40 percent of Taiwan's exports go to China or Hong Kong" (Lung, 2023). It is noteworthy that 40 percent support sending US troops to Taiwan to help.

What about the US government? It has maintained a cross-strait policy marked by strategic ambiguity since 1979. The US Congress also enacted the TRA that year, which will be examined in more detail in the following section. The point of the TRA is that these pledges or commitments are political in nature. Therefore, what the US presidents (the executive branch) and Congress will do, or think, is crucial. The current Biden administration has been following the traditional Taiwan support policy. For example, "Asked if the United States would be willing to get involved militarily to defend Taiwan," Biden said "Yes," and "That's a commitment we made," although he added, "We agree with the 'One China' policy. We signed on to it and all the attendant agreements made from there" (Johnson, 2022). Biden has repeatedly said "yes" to similar questions. It cannot be said to be a gaffe of some sort because he replied "yes" continuously and consistently. The US Congress, no matter which party is in control, is strongly in favor, as the Pelosi visit and McCarty meeting show. Moreover, in 2022, Congress passed the Taiwan Enhanced Resilience Act, which enables the use of Foreign Military Financing (FMF) assistance for US arms sales to Taiwan. This helps Taiwan buy more US arms.

6.3 The Taiwan Relations Act and Japan–US Security Treaty

6.3.1 *The Taiwan Relations Act*

Let us briefly discuss the TRA. It states the following:

> Section 2.2.d: To consider any effort to determine the future of Taiwan by other than peaceful means, including by boycotts or embargoes, a threat to the peace and security of the Western Pacific area and of grave concern to the United States.

Section 2.2.f: It is the policy of the United States [...] to maintain the capacity of the United States to resist any resort to force or other forms of coercion that would jeopardize the security, or the social or economic system, of the people on Taiwan.

Section 3.3: The President is directed to inform the Congress promptly of any threat to the security or the social or economic system of the people on Taiwan and any danger to the interests of the United States arising therefrom.

The act merely mentions "the social or economic system of the people of Taiwan," a phrase that makes broad interpretations possible. In other words, possible applications can be very broad and are subject to political considerations in practice. The United States is neither obliged nor committed to come to defend Taiwan. It is merely suggested or implied. This ambiguity is the point on which proponents of strategic clarity disagree, if not outright object to it. They argue that making it clear will increase America's deterrence power by making China more conscious and cautious. This logic is straightforward and understandable. However, it does not necessarily enhance the credibility of US involvement, if not the other way around. As explained above, the PRC leadership already assumes that the United States would intervene in a cross-strait conflict. An unconditional US defense commitment would, however, likely undercut the essential component of assurance in deterrence and might also upset the *status quo* by increasing the likelihood of conflict. For example, it might embolden the proponents of *de jure* independence in Taiwan, which is a *casus belli* for the PRC.

6.3.2 *Japan–US Security Treaty*

What is often overlooked is the relevance of the Japan–US Security Treaty. Preventing and coping with a military crisis across the Taiwan Strait has been one of the *raisons d'être* of the treaty. It says that US military bases in Japan are for "the maintenance of international peace and security in the Far East." It states as follows:

Art. IV: The Parties will consult together from time to time regarding the implementation of this Treaty, and, at the request of either Party, whenever the security of Japan or international peace and security in the Far East is threatened.

Art. VI: For the purpose of contributing to the security of Japan and the maintenance of international peace and security in the Far East, the United States of America is granted the use by its land, air and naval forces of facilities and areas in Japan.

So, the treaty is relevant to not only the security of Japan but also "international peace and security in the Far East." This means that it can be enacted, and the US forces in Japan can be mobilized for the "Far East" as well. What is the definition of "Far East"? According to the Japanese government, the areas that are covered include Japan and its surrounding area, as well as the Philippines and its northern area, which is explicitly mentioned to include (South) Korea and Taiwan (Nichibeianpo taisei Q&A, 1960).

The treaty is somewhat ambiguous as to what actions might be taken against an economic embargo or blockade, for example. However, war planners should be extra careful and prudent enough to be ready for a worst-case scenario. That is to say, it is not 100 percent certain that a limited economic blockade, for instance, is not going to escalate into a war. Thus, they must take that possibility into consideration, no matter how small it might be. They should and will presume that the treaty will very likely be enacted, and the US forces in Japan, if not the Japanese SDF itself as well, will also very likely intervene. Then, one can say that strategic ambiguity and clarity do not differ much. This aspect should be taken into consideration when examining the TRA and strategic ambiguity.[1] All this means is that Japan would most likely be attacked as well. It is almost certain that the US forces will seek support from Japan. The US forces in Japan consist of approximately 54,000 military personnel and 40 bases throughout Japan. This is obviously the cornerstone of US power in the Western Pacific and the Indo-Pacific. If China is to invade Taiwan and the United States decides to intervene militarily, the US would seek immediate access to these troops and bases to support Taiwan.

There is also the "prior consultation" pertaining to the operation of the treaty. This refers to an exchange of notes regarding the interpretation

---

[1] "Strategic ambiguity/clarity" and "*status quo*" are issues that are beyond the scope of this chapter, as they have been extensively discussed elsewhere.

of Article 6. This note was signed by then-Prime Minister Kishi Nobusuke and confirmed by then-US President Dwight Eisenhower in 1960. It stipulates that major changes in US deployment and equipment, as well as active combat operations that are undertaken from Japan (from US bases in Japan), will be subject to "prior consultation," excluding the supply, transit, and defense acts for the United States itself.[2] Of course, US combat operations for the defense of Japan, when Japan is under attack, i.e., in an Article 5 situation, are not subject to this prior consultation. This gave Japan the legal power to object to how US forces could be deployed in Japan and how they would operate. But it has never taken place at all because the United States has never requested it. The Japanese government has rationalized that there have been no major changes because the United States has never asked for a prior consultation. Despite this legal possibility, the fact that Japan's government has preferred to say nothing about it suggests (and it is generally assumed) that Japan would not refuse a US request. Japan's government has never made an explicit commitment to help defend Taiwan or to assist a possible US military response if a cross-strait conflict occurs. However, as the hub for US forces in the region, it will be difficult for Japan to deny a request for help.

6.4 Japan's Complicated Legal System and What Japan Can Do

6.4.1 *What has Japan been doing recently?*

Japan happens to be located very close to Taiwan; the closest Japanese island, Yonaguni, is only 110 km away. Japan has been trying to enhance its defense capabilities in the Nansei (Southwest) Islands near Taiwan. There had been no defense sites or facilities in this area until 2016, when Japan established a monitoring facility on Yonaguni Island. The US bases in Japan, those in Okinawa in particular, are assumed to be likely targets in a Taiwan contingency.

---

[2]The exact language is the following: "Major changes in the deployment into Japan of United States armed forces, major changes in their equipment, and the use of facilities and areas in Japan as bases for military combat operations to be undertaken from Japan other than those conducted under Article V of said Treaty, shall be the subjects of prior consultation with the government of Japan" (Exchanged Notes, 1960).

Let us briefly assess Japan's recent actions (Taichu Youjihe, 2023). First of all, Japan's Ground Self-Defense Force (GSDF) is to deploy rapid deployment units in the area so that they can quickly respond to a contingency. This is along the lines of US Marine Corps planning. Namely, the GSDF is to set up marine littoral regiments by 2025 to be able to rapidly dispatch and deal with emergency situations on isolated remote islands, such as the Nansei Islands. The 15th Brigade of the GSDF in Okinawa that covers the Nansei Islands will be upgraded to division level. As far as setting up garrisons is concerned, for example, the GSDF set up a garrison on Amami Ohshima Island as well as on Miyako Island in 2019 that house anti-surface and anti-air units. It also established a garrison on Ishigaki Island with similar capabilities in 2023. The effort includes making Japan's defense of bases robust by moving some facilities underground and also increasing its war-fighting capabilities, including hardening its supply lines. This is to ameliorate one of the most serious vulnerabilities that Japan has. All of these are on the Nansei Islands that are closest to Taiwan.

6.4.2 *Japan's official position and constitutional restrictions*

Japan does not have any formal diplomatic relations with Taiwan, only unofficial ties since it recognized the PRC in 1972. Japan's government has been reticent as to how it might respond to a possible Taiwan contingency. This includes not only how Japan would react to a Taiwan contingency but also what it might do to assist probable US military reactions, especially from US bases in Japan. While the 1979 TRA allows the United States to support Taiwan militarily, no such law exists for Japan, making Japan–ROC military collaboration extremely difficult.

We know that the Japanese public in general is inclined, somewhat cautiously, and there is the political will to take part in a possible Taiwan contingency. However, Japan's national defense laws are complicated. This complication would likely make on-the-ground decision-making too cumbersome and time-consuming, which would likely cause difficulty in implementation. No matter what some political leaders have been saying, Japan maintains, and will continue to maintain, its current official position on Taiwan. One crucial issue is what Japan would do to help the United States if and when the latter gets involved in a Taiwan contingency.

Let us take a brief look at Japan's overall national security system. First, it was only in 2015 that Japan made it possible to exercise the right of collective self-defense to some extent, by reinterpreting, though not amending, Article 9 of its Constitution. Article 51 of the UN Charter stipulates that "nothing in the present Charter shall impair the inherent right of individual or collective self-defence if an armed attack occurs against a Member of the United Nations." Japan, as a member state of the United Nations, should have the right of collective self-defense as an inherent right. However, Article 9 of the Japanese Constitution states the following:

> Aspiring sincerely to an international peace based on justice and order, the Japanese people forever renounce war as a sovereign right of the nation and the threat or use of force as means of settling international disputes.

> In order to accomplish the aim of the preceding paragraph, land, sea, and air forces, as well as other war potential, will never be maintained. The right of belligerency of the state will not be recognized.

The official interpretation, prior to the aforementioned reinterpretation, was that Japan as a sovereign state has an inherent right of collective self-defense, as the UN Charter says, but could not "exercise" it because its exercise exceeded the bare minimum necessary level of self-defense permitted under Article 9. Therefore, the exercise of the right of collective self-defense was totally prohibited until 2015. It should be noted that it is possible now only to some degree and not wholeheartedly. Japan distinguishes the use of arms (weapons) from that of force very clearly because Japan is explicitly prohibited from using force, except in self-defense, in Article 9. Therefore, Japan meticulously differentiates the use of force from the "use of arms (weapons)," which is confined to the realm of police actions.

In this sense, Japan's self-defense forces cannot be said to be a *bona fide* military. That's why there is the prefix "self-defense" attached. This forces Japan to carefully go through intricate procedures in order to make the use of force constitutional and acceptable to the public. In the event of a direct attack, of course, Japan can exercise the right of individual self-defense. It is also the case that what the SDF can do must be listed, not what it cannot do. That is, the SDF can do nothing unless a situation

110 *T. Takeuchi*

warrants a numerated, listed task in the list, which is called the "positive list" approach. Therefore, Japan needs a decision, or judgment, as to whether a particular situation fits with a listed task before it can mobilize the SDF, which would be time-consuming.

6.4.3 *Japan's complicated security laws*

Japan has basically five specific categories that pertain to its security in Taiwan contingencies. They are as follows: (1) "Critical Impact Situations," (2) "Emergency Response Situations," (3) "Anticipated Armed Attack Situations," (4) "Armed Attack Situations," and (5) "Survival-Threatening Situations." They are grouped into three broad categories: (a) "Important Influence Situations," which consist of (1) "Critical Impact Situations" and (2) "Emergency Response Situations"; (b) "Survival Threatening Situations," which stand alone; and (c) "Armed Attack Situations," which consist of (3) "Anticipated Armed Attack Situations" and (4) "Armed Attack Situations." It should also be noted that the geographical restrictions imposed on (a) "Important Influence Situations" were lifted. It is now possible for Japan to have a global reach, although it is inconceivable to exercise this on the other side of the world. The definitions are as follows:

(a) "Important Influence Situation": Situations that will have an important influence on Japan's peace and security, including situations that, if left without response, could lead to a direct armed attack on Japan.
(b) "Survival Threatening Situation": Situations in which an armed attack against a country that is in a close relationship with Japan occurs and, as a result, threatens Japan's survival and poses a clear danger of fundamentally overturning the Japanese people's right to life, liberty, and pursuit of happiness.
(c) "Armed Attack Situation": Situations in which an armed attack against Japan from outside occurs, or in which it is considered that there is an imminent and clear danger of an armed attack.

The right of collective self-defense pertains only to (b) above, "Survival-Threatening Situations." The exercise of the right of collective defense is limited because there are three conditions that must be met in order to make the exercise of the right of collective self-defense possible. These conditions are as follows:

(1) in a case where a nation with close ties to Japan comes under attack, and there is a clear threat to the Japanese state or could fundamentally threaten the Japanese people's constitutional right to life, liberty, and the pursuit of happiness;
(2) if there are no other appropriate measures to fulfill its duty to ensure Japan's existence and protect its people;
(3) when the use of force is limited to the bare minimum necessary.

Once again, in order for the SDF to use force in a "Survival-Threatening Situation," the above three conditions must be met. It is of course possible to use force in an "Armed Attack Situation" since this would be an exercise in individual self-defense. One more hurdle is that "prior authorization" of the Diet (Japan's parliament) is necessary, except in a presumably rare case that is so urgent and there is no time for the Diet to discuss it, in which case *ex post facto* approval is accepted. This prior-approval stipulation is to strictly adhere to the principle of civilian control. As one can easily see, it may cause a big problem in terms of timely reactions by the SDF. One might also add that Japan must convene its cabinet to decide and declare that a particular situation that is happening fits a particular legal category, etc. It does not have to be face-to-face anymore, but it will still take time to decide.

6.4.4 *Possible scenarios and a hitch*

There can be many possible scenarios should a Taiwan crisis happen. Here, it is assumed that there is an aggressive strike against Taiwan, excluding such situations as a disinformation strategy to destabilize Taiwan or an economic blockade. We mainly discuss a Taiwan crisis in the category of "Important Influence Situation" or "Survival-Threatening Situation," but a direct attack on Japan is also considered, which is an "Armed Attack Situation." What the SDF can do is summarized in Table 6.1 (Nakamura, 2023). Japan can do nothing if there is combat going on, when the situation is classified as an "Important Influence Situation." Even if there is no combat, Japan cannot do much to help Taiwan in this situation. Also, even if a situation is judged to be a

Table 6.1. Situational options available to the Japan SDF.

Situation / Response	Important influence situation		Survival-threatening situation	Armed attack situation
	No combat action at the scene	Combat action at the scene		
Protection of U.S. forces, equipment, etc.	O	×	O	O
Logistical support	O	×	O	O
Search and rescue	×	×	O	O
Right of collective defense			O	
Right of individual self-defense			×	O

"Survival-Threatening Situation," condition (1) mentioned above to enable the exercise of the right of collective self-defense should be noted, namely, "in a case where a nation with close ties to Japan comes under attack." Japan does not recognize Taiwan (or the ROC) as a sovereign state; therefore, the usual interpretation would be that condition (1) is not met. Then, Japan cannot help Taiwan, even in a dire situation.

There is a hitch, though, and this is indeed intentionally left opaque. There was a questionnaire in 2015 from a Diet member to the government on what this "other countries," etc., meant (Response to a Question, 2015). This questionnaire was obviously conducted with Taiwan in mind. The government replied that "[c]ountries with which Japan does not have diplomatic relations can be included, but it is difficult to answer this question because the meaning of 'regarded as countries' is not always clear." It is obvious that this was the government's desperate, hard-to-fathom scheme to leave some legal wiggle room for the possible involvement of Japan. However, from the viewpoint of decision-makers, this convoluted legal ambiguity is perplexing and makes them hesitate to decide in favor of involvement. The reason is that there is a possibility that one's decision can be judged to be illegal after the fact. One would possibly be tempted to play it safe and decide not to get involved. despite the political inclination to do something for Taiwan.

Is a Taiwan Crisis Also a Japan Crisis? Japan's Complicated Security Laws   113

If it is declared to be an "Important Influence Situation," as long as there is no combat on the scene, Japan can provide logistical support and help protect US forces and their armaments, etc. This is no doubt important in maintaining US forces' combat capabilities, especially in a drawn-out conflict. Because of Japan's geographical proximity, there is a good possibility that Japan would be directly entangled, which entails the exercise of individual self-defense, and Japan can help defend Taiwan if it is regarded as part of its own self-defense. In the likely scenario that US ships are targeted by China's anti-ship missiles, it is a combat scenario. It may be surprising, but Japan can do little to help the United States if it is only an "Important Influence Situation." In order for Japan to do something positive, at least a "Survival-Threatening Situation" must be declared.

When there is a perceived danger that Japan itself would be attacked, Japan can declare an "Anticipated Armed Attack Situation" and issue both a "defense convocation order" and a "standby order for deployment." When things get direr and Japan perceives an imminent danger that Japan itself is about to be attacked, then it can declare an "Armed Attack Situation" and order a "defense deployment." This "deployment order" is crucial because, without it, the SDF is allowed to use only arms (weapons), not force, just like a police force.

6.4.5 *Time-consuming*

Due to the elaborate and intricate procedures that Japan must go through, it is expected that the decision-making process would be time-consuming, and Japan's decision-makers, including the prime minister, would be hard-pressed to make decisions quickly enough, or they may procrastinate or be given a very short time to decide. This is in addition to the fact that Japan's general decision-making system is based on consensus, which in itself is time-consuming. Hence, it may be doubly time-consuming, making the situation on the ground increasingly harder to deal with as precious time passes. There may be a *fait accompli* by the time a decision is made. It takes time to implement the decision as well. Information gathering and processing capabilities are also a big concern. Since the decision-making procedures are complicated, the information provided to the decision-makers must be not only timely but also accurate and detailed. Otherwise, one cannot decide confidently and quickly whether a situation is,

114   T. Takeuchi

for instance, a "Survival-Threatening Situation" or an "Important Influence Situation." This part is very worrisome as well, because it is often said that Japan's intelligence-gathering capabilities are wanting: not good enough to provide accurate and timely information, let alone analysis.

6.5 Tabletop Exercises

6.5.1 *Explaining a tabletop exercise*

So far, we have examined Japan's legal system to deal with emergency situations. What would likely happen in a real situation? Fortunately, some tabletop exercises (TTXs), or war game simulations, have been conducted to simulate various scenarios and see what is likely to happen in possible situations. Their outcomes should give us some insights as to what kind of problems might arise and also how to streamline these cumbersome decision-making procedures to enable a timely and suitable decision (given the situation). This pseudo-real experience is very important because it is commonly assumed that Japan is not well prepared to deal with a Taiwan contingency.

Let us cite one TTX that was conducted by the Japan Forum for Strategic Studies in August 2022. This was a very well-documented and widely reported large-scale TTX, the outcome of which is basically in line with other TTXs. It is also noteworthy that many former defense officials, former SDF generals and admirals, and current lawmakers from the ruling LDP, including a former minister of defense who played the role of prime minister, took part in this TTX (Hōkoku-sho dai, n.d.; Japan Ministry of Defense, 2022, p. 193; Tabletop war games, 2023). The year in which the presumed incidents happened was set as 2027, which is often mentioned as a likely year for a PLA attack.[3] There were three scenarios: (1) rapid escalation from a gray zone situation; (2) Japanese nationals' transportation, evacuation, etc.; (3) PRC threat and use of nuclear weapons. China is assumed to have decided to "unite" Taiwan by force. It deliberately heightens the tensions in the South and East China seas and attacks the Senkaku Islands as a diversionary action.

---

[3] For example, this assertion was made by then-Admiral Philip Davidson (2021), the head of the US Indo-Pacific Command, at a hearing by the US Senate Armed Services Committee on March 9, 2021.

Is a Taiwan Crisis Also a Japan Crisis? Japan's Complicated Security Laws 115

What was expected to happen before the TTX was as follows: The Taiwan contingency would be declared a "Survival-Threatening Situation" and the Senkaku attack would be an "Armed Attack Situation." China knows that Japan must convene its cabinet to decide if a particular situation fits with a particular legal category, as was mentioned before. That is to say, this simultaneous attack makes timely decision-making harder in a situation where a quick decision and response are a must. Since scenarios (1) and (2) are presumed to happen simultaneously, the Japanese government faces a two-front situation, in which case Japan is most likely forced to focus on the defense of the Senkaku Islands over Taiwan. Then, China can go on blockading Taiwan, proceed to a surgical strike, and so forth, allowing the PLA to "unite" the island.

6.5.2 *How it went*

Only the first scenario is explained and discussed in this chapter. However, one must very briefly mention scenario (2) as well, because it will very likely happen simultaneously and thus be intertwined. It is reported in situation (2) that "incredibly it took two whole months for the government to formally categorize the two contingencies," not a day or two, not even a week or so. The reason is that, as was reported, the participants playing the role of political leaders were afraid that these designations would worsen the relationship with China and hence negatively affect the safety and evacuation of Japanese nationals in China (Takahashi, 2022). If the consideration of scenario (2) takes months to decide, it adversely affects what the government can realistically accomplish in scenario (1) as well because it is hard for Japan to do something tangible unless and until it designates the situation appropriately and orders a "defense mobilization," etc. The evacuation of around 110,000 Japanese nationals from China in a timely manner would be nearly impossible, even if there were some kind of agreement with the PRC to let them go. They may become pawns or hostages that Beijing can use for leverage against Tokyo.

As to situation (1) itself, the Japan cell of this TTX decided basically as follows: First of all, they faced a big problem as to how to recognize a situation. They hesitated to make a determination and took a considerable amount of time (it is not clear exactly how long it took) to come to an agreement, especially on how to designate the Taiwan situation.

In the end, they decided that the Senkaku situation was an "Armed Attack Situation" and the Taiwan contingency was a "Survival-Threatening Situation." This makes it possible to provide logistical support to US forces, which Japan did in the TTX. The United States participants, meanwhile, decided to apply Article 5 of the Japan–US Security Treaty (the right of collective self-defense). That is to say, the US will come to help defend Japan, including the Senkakus. All these designations and decisions were as expected.

Even if Japan decides to mobilize the SDF, how much support can Japan offer to US forces, especially in support of Taiwan? This is when the Senkakus are supposedly under attack, and thus Japan may be preoccupied with defending them. Also, there may be a legal issue: whether or not the US forces are judged to be operating for the defense of Japan or that of Taiwan. According to ex-Minister of Defense Morimoto Satoshi, "It's unclear whether the SDF could legally support US troops in defense of Taiwan in this situation" (*ibid.*). However, it is a two-front situation, and the US operations for Taiwan and for Japan would probably be closely intertwined and difficult to clearly separate them. China is fighting on two fronts, thus aiding Taiwan would most probably be judged as indirectly supporting Japan as well.

6.6 Concluding Remarks

It is clear that the vast majority of the people in Taiwan would opt for the *status quo*, although the on-the-ground *status quo* seems to have been changing incrementally in the face of Chinese aggression. We can see it through China's actions after the Pelosi visit. Prominent Japanese and US politicians have expressed strong support for Taiwan. This is in conjunction with the fairly strong public support for Taiwan, including military support, in the US, but not necessarily in Japan. The United States has a policy of strategic ambiguity. However, it also has the TRA, which enables it to provide arms and leaves the door open for military intervention in the case of a Taiwan contingency.

On the other hand, Japan does not have any clear policy with respect to a Taiwan contingency. Japan has very complicated security laws. The category that is in question in a Taiwan contingency is the "Survival-Threatening Situation," in which case it is possible to exercise Japan's limited right of collective self-defense. Whether or not this "Situation" can be applied to Taiwan is a tricky legal issue because it can only be applied in "an armed attack against a country that is in a close relationship with Japan." Is Taiwan such a country for Japan? Japan does not recognize Taiwan as a sovereign country. As was explained, the Japanese government issued a puzzling stance, out of desperation, in trying to find a legal way for Japan to be able to do something for Taiwan.

This murky legal situation aside, it is generally true that the Japanese government, and most of the Japanese people, think that Tokyo can simply declare a "Survival-Threatening Situation" to help defend Taiwan, as the TTX cited above shows. It tends to take too long to decide on an appropriate situation, and this is a big problem, especially if Japan itself is facing a crucial situation in which a timely decision must be made. The complicated and skewed, one might say, legal system is a high hurdle to overcome. Japan needs a simpler, more streamlined legal structure. In terms of the US forces in Japan, there is a prior consultation clause issue; however, it would not be a problem in real, practical situations because it is almost a foregone conclusion that Japan would say yes. The Security Treaty's Far East clause should be a stimulus for Japan to move in that direction as well.

Acknowledgments

This chapter is a result of the collaborative project "An Interdisciplinary Approach to Contemporary East Asia Studies" [21REN283] at St. Andrew's University Research Institute.

References

Davidson, P. S. (2021). Statement of Admiral Philip S. Davidson, US Navy Commander, US Indo-Pacific Command Before the Senate Armed Services Committee on US Indo-Pacific Command Posture.

Exchanged Notes, Regarding the Implementation of Article VI of Treaty of Mutual Cooperation and Security between Japan and the United States of America. (1960, January 19). Database of Japanese politics and international relations. Retrieved August 5, 2023, from: http://archive.today/2fl9P.

Gu, T. and Hwang, C.-M. (2022, August 5). China ends live-fire missile testing near Taiwan early amid protests from Japan, US. *RFA Mandarin*. Retrieved August 5, 2023, from: http://archive.today/vay2s.

Hōkoku-sho dai 2-kai seisaku shimyurēshon no seika gaiyō 'tettei kenshō: Taiwankaikyōkiki Nihon wa ikani sonaerubeki ka' [Report: Overview of the results of the second policy simulation 'Thorough Verification: Taiwan Strait Crisis How Japan Should Prepare'] (n.d.). Japan Forum for Strategic Studies HP' site. Retrieved August 5, 2023, from: http://archive.today/ttiex.

House, W. (2021). US-Japan Joint leaders' statement: 'US–Japan global partnership for a new era.' Washington, DC, April, 16. Retrieved August 5, 2023, from: http://archive.today/BusAF.

Hsieh, C. T. and Hsu, J. (2023, May 3). How America should support Taiwan. *The Japan Times*. Retrieved August 5, 2023, from: http://archive.today/EmvoS.

Ishida, K. (2021, November 4). *Taiwan Jin no 6-wari 'yūjinara Jieitai haken' Chūgoku gunki no chōhatsu uke seronchōsa* [60 percent of Taiwanese "Dispatch Self-Defense Forces in case of emergency" Opinion poll in response to provocation by Chinese military aircraft]. *Asahi Shimbun Newspaper*. Retrieved August 5, 2023, from: http://archive.today/0ZPz0.

Isoda, K. (2022, May 12). *Taiwan yūji, makikoma reru fuan 'ōini kanjiru' 44-pāsento Asahi Okinawa chōsa* [Anxiety about being involved in an emergency in Taiwan: 44% "feel a lot" Asahi Okinawa survey]. *Asahi Newspaper*. Retrieved August 5, 2023, from: http://archive.today/nS0kZ.

Japan Ministry of Defense (2022). Defense of Japan 2022. Retrieved from https://www.mod.go.jp/en/publ/w_paper/index.html.

Japan's 'sense of insecurity' is of its own making: Global times editorial (August 6, 2022). *Global Times*. Retrieved August 5, 2023, from: http://archive.today/bhBEx.

Johnson, J. (2021, July 6). Deputy PM says Japan must defend Taiwan with U.S. *The Japan Times*. Retrieved August 5, 2023, from: http://archive.today/f1Muj.

Johnson, J. (2022, May 23). Biden vows to defend Taiwan as Kishida pledges unprecedented hike in defense spending. *The Japan Times*. Retrieved August 5, 2023, from: http://archive.today/uJIYy.

Kishida, Biden reaffirm strong Japan-US alliance (2022, May 24). NHK World-Japan. Retrieved August 5, 2023, from: http://archive.today/zaCgE.

Lai, J. and Wu, H. (2022, August 5). China conducts 'precision missile strikes' in Taiwan Strait. *AP News*. Retrieved August 5, 2023, from: http://archive.today/dEazG.

Lung, Y. (2023, April 18). In Taiwan, friends are starting to turn against each other. *The New York Times*. Retrieved August 5, 2023, from: http://archive.today/PewOL.

Nakamura, S. (2023, March 30). The Japanese response to a Taiwan crisis — How to prepare and respond. *The Sasakawa Peace Foundation*. Retrieved August 5, 2023, from: http://archive.today/9Di57.

Nakazawa, K. (2022, August 24). *Shūkinpei gunji-i shuseki ga saika shita Nihon EEZ-nai no misairu chakudan* [Missile landing in the Japanese EEZ authorized by Chairman Xi Jinping of the Military Commission]. *Nihon Keizai Shimbun (Japan Economic Journal)*. Retrieved August 5, 2023, from: http://archive.today/ohXuU.

Nichibeianpo taisei Q&A [Q&A on Japan-U.S. Security Arrangements]. (1960, February 26). *Ministry of Foreign Affairs of Japan*. Retrieved August 5, 2023, from: http://archive.today/kCnWG.

"One country, two systems" rejected by majority: Survey (2019, March 23). *Taipei Times*. Retrieved August 5, 2023, from http://archive.today/yudgv.

Response to a Question from Counsellor Kenichi Mizuno (2015, March 21). *The Naikaku Sanshitsu, 189*(79). Retrieved August 5, 2023, from: https://www.sangiin.go.jp/japanese/joho1/kousei/syuisyo/189/toup/t189202.pdf.

Reynolds, I. and Nobuhiro, E. (2021, June 25). Japan sees China-Taiwan friction as threat to its security. *The Japan Times*. Retrieved August 5, 2023, from: http://archive.today/iIOS4.

Ryall, J. (2021, April 21). Japan troops won't get involved if China invades Taiwan, PM Yoshihide Suga says. *South China Morning Post*. Retrieved August 5, 2023, from: http://archive.today/HPh9h.

Sasaki, R. (2022, August 10). Japan's evolving approach to the Taiwan Strait. *The Diplomat*. Retrieved August 5, 2023, from: http://archive.today/EyHvP.

Smeltz, D. and Kafura, C. (2021, August 26). For first time, half of Americans favor defending Taiwan if China invades. *The Chicago Council on Global Affairs*. Retrieved August 5, 2023, from http://archive.today/KUj1F.

Smeltz, D. and Kafura, C. (2022, August 11). Americans favor aiding Taiwan against China. *The Chicago Council on Global Affairs*. Retrieved August 5, 2023, from: http://archive.today/7IzTj.

Tabletop war games reveal lack of security dialogue mechanism: Think tank. (2023, July 17). *Focus Taiwan*. Retrieved August 5, 2023, from: http://archive.today/DzpN1.

Taichu Youjihe Kyoten Seibi Kanryo [Setting up bases to deter China is now done] (2023, April 3). *Yomiuri Shimbun Newspaper*.

Taiwan contingency also one for Japan, Japan-U.S. alliance: Ex-Japan PM Abe. (2021, December 1). *Kyodo News*. Retrieved August 5, 2023, from: http://archive.today/Q0zMY.

Taiwan yūji, Nihon hakyū 'osoreru' 81-pāsento 'yōjin hōtai o' 55-pāsento [Taiwan Incident, Japan Affected: 81% "Concerned," 55% "Support Visits by High-Level Officials."] (2022, August 12). *Nikkei*. Retrieved August 5, 2023, from: http://archive.today/yD6Zn.

Takahashi, K. (2022, August 20). How would Japan respond to a Taiwan contingency? *The Diplomat*. Retrieved August 5, 2023, from: http://archive.today/59knQ.

© 2025 World Scientific Publishing Company
https://doi.org/10.1142/9789811298301_0007

Chapter 7

Placating China is a Losing Game: Regional Security at Risk Without Taiwan–Japan Mutual Defense

Dean Karalekas

On September 29, 2022, a 10-hour stand-off occurred between a Japanese patrol ship and vessels of the Republic of China (ROC) Coast Guard Administration. The incident was sparked when the patrol ship in question issued a warning to a research vessel attached to National Taiwan University, which was conducting marine research in a location 69 nautical miles from the Taiwanese port city of Hualien, insisting that it was operating within Japan's Exclusive Economic Zone (EEZ).

The Taiwanese vessel, *New Ocean Researcher*, radioed for assistance and was aided by an ROC Coast Guard patrol ship, whose captain maneuvered into position between the research vessel and the Japanese ship before demanding that they stop interfering with the science project. It was pointed out to the Japanese crew that the Taiwanese research vessel was operating within Taiwan's EEZ. The stand-off lasted for 10 hours, until the *New Ocean Researcher* left the area, allowing the Japanese Coast Guard ship to retreat with face (Chung, 2022).

Clearly, the Japanese felt that they were in the right, and that the Taiwanese ship was operating within Japan's 200 nautical mile EEZ; so they weren't going to back down. Likewise, the Taiwanese research vessel, and the ROC Coast Guard assets dispatched to aid it, were operating a stone's throw from port, and hence well within Taiwan's EEZ; they were not about to back down, either. Who was right? In this case, neither side was right; or more accurately, neither side was wrong.

Nor is the incident unique. There have been reports over the years of Japanese Coast Guard vessels sending Taiwanese fishing boats packing, especially near the disputed Diaoyutai/Senkaku Islands. These incidents highlight several problems besetting the ROC's relationship with Japan, one of which is the overlapping EEZs between the two countries (and more importantly, the lack of any consistent operating procedures for ascertaining what rights each side has within that area of overlap). Indeed, in the immediate aftermath of the stand-off, Taipei renewed calls for negotiations with Tokyo on finding ways to resolve the long-standing maritime disagreements that continue to hamper closer ties between the two countries (Souza and Karalekas, 2020).

From a more fundamental perspective, however, there is a lack of amity marring the Taiwan–Japan relationship that stands in the way of developing closer working ties on maritime security and other matters. Given the shared threat from an increasingly belligerent China, it would only seem natural that Taiwan and Japan would work closely together to shore up their mutual security vulnerabilities in order to meet this threat. Yet, this seems not to be the case, with both sides instead reverting to incidents of fundamental distrust as illustrated by the standoff described above. This chapter will briefly examine the history of the relationship between Taiwan and Japan with the aim of illustrating the people-to-people and cultural ties that have long existed, and argue for a paradigm of allyship that can be built upon this cultural framework. To do this, we must acknowledge the ambivalence that each side has toward the other, as well as examine the intricate nature of what is arguably the most consistent source of roadblocks to the further development of closer cooperation on maritime security issues: the dispute over sovereignty of the Diaoyutai/Senkaku islands.

Both countries are key links in the First Island Chain, and indeed almost form constituent parts of a common archipelago. As such, their political and cultural destinies are intricately intertwined, especially as the revanchist regime in Beijing threatens to annex Taiwan — an eventuality that, were it to come to fruition, would change the balance of power in Asia, pushing the United States out to the Second Island Chain, and giving Beijing control over much of the Pacific, including the sea lanes upon which Japan depends for its survival. This would put Japan in direct threat of either subjugation by the People's Republic of China (PRC), or a deadly war to stop the same.

It would be foolhardy to assume that the Chinese hunger for expansion, and what leaders in Zhongnanhai call the "road to national rejuvenation," would be sated by subsuming Taiwan into its political system. The same reasoning — that Taiwan, in ancient times, was subject to a previous regime in Beijing — has been made about Japanese territory; most particularly Okinawa. There are already Chinese scholars laying the historical groundwork for a Chinese claim over the Ryukyu Islands, arguing that the Kingdom of the Ryukyus had been a tributary state of Imperial China that was annexed by Japan in the late 1880s. Historians Zhang Haipeng and Li Guoqiang (2017) of the Chinese Academy of Social Sciences opined that, given this historical context, it may be time for the Chinese Communist Party (CCP) to "revisit this unresolved historical issue" (Haipeng and Guoqiang, 2017).

Indeed, in a demonstration of Beijing's ire following an August 2022 visit to Taiwan by then US House Speaker Nancy Pelosi, the People's Liberation Army (PLA) promptly launched a series of precision missile strikes around the island. Five of these missiles splashed down squarely within Japan's EEZ. In a public comment following the drills, the PLA announced that "all missiles hit the target accurately," confirming suspicions that these strikes were intentionally targeted at Japanese waters, and likely meant as a warning to Tokyo against supporting Taiwan (Shaffer, 2022).

It is clear, then, that Beijing's current expansionist tendencies do not, as a matter of principle, exclude Japanese territory; nor would they be placated by annexing Taiwan, but rather energized by such an eventuality. Japan's territorial integrity and national security are therefore integrally linked with that of Taiwan — especially with respect to Okinawa. And yet the governments on the two sides seem not to appreciate the urgency of this fact. The reasons for this go far beyond mere EEZ lines on a chart, and have their roots in the cultures of the two countries, and how the cultural interactions have led us to our current state of relations.

7.1 An Intertwined History

The peoples of Taiwan and Japan have a long history of close ties. These links go back to the prehistoric era, at least as far as the Ryukyu Islands are concerned. It is believed that Austronesian voyagers (who, according to the Out of Taiwan hypothesis, are the ones responsible for spreading the Austronesian language family throughout the Pacific) initially journeyed to Yonaguni, and thence to the Ryukyus, most likely from the northeast area of Taiwan. Indeed, in the complex Neolithic prehistory and the competing systems of mythology of the Ryukyu Islands, we see Austronesian influences in the south, with Jōmon dominating the central and northern Ryukyus. Of particular interest are the southern islands, such as Sakishima, which is believed to have been settled by Austronesians sailing out of Taiwan some 4,300 years ago, after which the islands became culturally isolated. Despite this Neolithic isolation, centuries of syncretism between Shintōism, Buddhism, Taoism, and Confucianism has made itself felt in Ryukyuan religious practice (Hudson, 2012; Huang, 2011).

Clues to this shared heritage — a heritage that goes back well before any Han Chinese migration to Taiwan — can be found in the commonality of certain mythological motifs. The Yonaguni origin legend of *Tidan-du-guru* mirrors almost exactly a myth of the Kavalan indigenous group of Yilan, on the northeast coast of Taiwan, situated a mere 110 km from Yonaguni. According to the Kavalan legend, modern humans came from a place to the south called Sunasai. Indeed, variations of this myth can be found throughout northern and eastern Taiwan, and the legend's distribution suggests possible ancient migration routes. If, as Huang (2011) suggests, Yonaguni forms part of this "Sunasai legend group," there may at the very least have been interaction between the Kavalan and the early Yonaguni islanders. They share other cultural characteristics as well, including a matriarchal society and detailed flood myths.

Fast-forward to the late 19th century, and we see the beginning of the period that most strongly cemented the Taiwanese kinship with Japan when the island, deemed unwanted territory, was ceded by the Qing Court to the Empire of Japan in 1895. This was accomplished via the stipulations of the Treaty of Shimonoseki, signed after the Chinese defeat in the First Sino-Japanese War. Within a generation, the inhabitants of Taiwan, who had previously followed Chinese customs and life patterns derived from their home provinces on the mainland — primarily Guangdong Province and Fujian Province — were now being educated to speak Japanese. Under the colonial government, the citizenry adopted largely Japanese lifestyles, wearing Japanese clothing; cooking Japanese cuisine; and reading Japanese novels. It is worth noting that it was during this era that the beginnings of a distinct Taiwanese identity began to take root: the people were not ethnically Japanese, but nor were they fully Chinese anymore, certainly not in any political sense, nor in terms of the new culture that they had developed (Roy, 2003).

7.2 Taiwanese Ambivalence about Japan

The refugees that arrived in Taiwan in 1949 fleeing the communist take-over of China were, by and large, the elites of Nationalist society: the ROC government established its seat in Taipei, but it was also the people, public property, universities, the military, and all the social institutions from Republican China that were being transplanted to the island redoubt, inevitably creating a rift between the ruling mainlander elites — mainlanders filled not just the government positions but also became the teachers (to inculcate the new cultural norms) and policemen (to enforce them) — and the subject population, many of whom would eventually come to miss their former affiliation with the Japanese.

Thus, we have a duality of consciousness in Taiwan with regards to Japan, wherein a certain segment of the population is antithetical to the amelioration of ties with Tokyo, as their ancestors (as well as their education and upbringing) considered the Japanese to be an enemy; and another segment of the population whose ancestors spoke Japanese, lived Japanese lives, and may even have been educated in Japan. Moreover, the latter do not share the almost Asia-wide antipathy for Japan that is a holdover from its wartime and colonial-era atrocities. This is because the Japanese administrators of Taiwan, while brutal, were also responsible for modernizing the island; building railroads, hospitals, schools, and generally paying far more attention to this, their "model colony," than the corrupt and incompetent imperial Mandarins had done during most of Qing rule over the island.

As a result, that portion of Taiwan society that loves Japan does so fervently, and in terms of the people-to-people relationships, that affection does not go unrequited. Speaking on the public perceptions between the two countries, Jeffrey Kingston, a professor in Asian studies at Temple University in Tokyo, noted that "People greatly admire Taiwan, they love Taiwan. One of the reasons they love Taiwan is no other country in the world loves Japan as much as the Taiwanese" (Hale, 2022).

7.3 Japanese Ambivalence about Taiwan

As discussed above, Taiwan's population is ambivalent about Japan. Likewise, there is in Japan an ambiguous position on the Taiwan question — one that is also driven by domestic politics. Even within the Liberal Democratic Party, which has dominated governance almost uninterrupted since the mid-1950s, conservative and reformist factions are in stark disagreement over what stance to take on the Taiwan Strait issue. Like the 2013 Japan–Taiwan Fishery agreement, much of the forward motion on Taiwan security has come at the behest of the Americans. This trend goes as far back as the 1952 Treaty of Taipei that formally ended the Second Sino-Japanese War and saw Japan recognize the ROC as the legitimate Chinese government, and continues with the "Taiwan Clause" of the 1969 US–Japan Joint Communiqué that codified Tokyo's acquiescence to the deployment of US military personnel stationed in Japan to respond to a PLA attack on Taiwan. For decades, the latter stood as the only official acknowledgment by the government of Japan that their national security is inextricably linked to Taiwan's security, and still, it had to be made as a *quid pro quo* with the United States, to secure a US promise to return Okinawa (Auer and Kotani, 2005; Lee, 2021).

Even in 1997, when the guidelines for the Japan–US security cooperation were being rewritten and a legal basis was being sought to allow the Japan Self-Defense Force to be deployed to aid the US military in "situations in areas surrounding Japan that have an important influence on Japanese security," Japanese leaders retreated to a politically ambiguous stance, refusing to clarify whether an attack on Taiwan constituted such a situation — or even whether the Taiwan Strait itself could be viewed as an "area surrounding Japan." It was not until the 2000s that this phrase began to be interpreted as a situational, rather than a strictly geographical, term (Inoue, 2022; Wang, 2000).

The situation has improved somewhat in recent years, with former Prime Minister Shinzo Abe having taken a more assertive stance against Chinese aggression, and the current Prime Minister, Fumio Kishida, having ancestral ties to Taiwan. Moreover, Japan's defense white paper of 2021 was the first iteration of this annual document to explicitly link Taiwan to the security of Japan. That of 2022 states outright that "The stability of the situation surrounding Taiwan is also critical for Japan's security and must be closely monitored with a sense of urgency." This represents an evolution from previous white papers, which were largely mum on the Taiwan issue. As an emboldened China is increasingly taken to saber-rattling under the dictator Xi Jinping, and the Russian invasion of Ukraine has illustrated the real face of war, unveiling the kind of death and depravity that would be taking place in Japan's backyard, some Japanese politicians and strategists have become less hesitant to speak frankly about the pivotal role Taiwan plays in Japan's security. Still, beyond such talking points, Japan has largely been reluctant to instantiate closer security relations with the island nation. It seems that these baby steps taken by the Japanese government toward a full recognition of the importance of security cooperation with Taiwan may, in the end, prove to be a day late and a dollar short.

7.4 The Diaoyutai/Senkaku Impediment

Complicating the prospects for amenable maritime cooperation between Taipei and Tokyo is the thorny issue of their competing claims of sovereignty over what the Japanese refer to as the Senkaku Islands, a group of five uninhabited islands and three rocks located north of the south-western end of the Ryukyu Islands in the East China Sea. In Taiwan, they are known as the Diaoyutai Islands; in China, as the Diaoyu Islands. They are claimed by the ROC, the PRC, and Japan, and though the Diaoyutai/Senkaku Islands lie just 102 nautical miles northeast of Keelung, Japan is in effective administrative control of them, and hence has the strongest claim.

Rather than employing the international community's rules and norms governing international law — the United Nations Convention on the Law of the Sea (UNCLOS), for example — China prefers the use of historical arguments to determine sovereignty. The Byzantine jurisdictional reasoning underpinning the argument behind the PRC's claim over these islands is complex, resting as it does upon the strength of the ROC claim that they fall under Taiwan administration. While the governments of the PRC and the ROC agree on little, they do agree on the proposition that the islands form part of Toucheng Township, in Taiwan's Yilan County. In other words: both sides agree that the Diaoyutai/Senkaku Islands belong to Taiwan: they only differ on the question of to whom Taiwan belongs (Valencia, 2014).

Until the late 1960s, neither Beijing nor Taipei had ever evinced any serious interest in claiming the Diaoyutai/Senkaku Islands, but then petroleum resources were discovered under the seabed there in a 1968 geological survey. When these results were published, first the ROC, and shortly thereafter the PRC, hastily launched territorial claims. Both claims were predicated on a historical-based argument alleging that the first, albeit vague, mention of the Diaoyu Islands can be found in an ancient Chinese document dating back to the 15th century. By the 17th century, Chinese texts began referring to the line between the Diaoyu Islands and the Ryukyus as the Black Water Trench, or *Heishuigou.*

In 1720, a Chinese official named Xu Baoguang was sent to Ryukyu by Beijing to confer robes of office upon the king of Ryukyu, then considered a vassal state of the Qing dynasty. Xu mentions the islands in his travelogue, in which he declares that Kume-jima, just south of the Black Water Trench, is the western demarcation line of the Ryukyuan Kingdom. This is interpreted to mean that the Diaoyutai/Senkaku Islands — and anything else situated to the west of Kume-jima — must therefore belong to China.

Japan has naturally been loath to lend any credence to this historical-based claim of Chinese ownership, especially because it is predicated on the former Ryukyuan Kingdom having been a tributary state of Imperial China. As mentioned above, Japanese leaders feared that this argument was a slippery slope and that an emboldened Beijing might stake a claim to Okinawa — a move that hawkish Chinese media and academics have already been pushing for since 2013. This tactic of "stealing history" would not be new for Beijing. The now-defunct Northeast Project by the Chinese Academy of Social Sciences was a naked attempt to appropriate aspects of the ancient history of an adjoining region (i.e., Korea), with the aim of establishing a dominant–subordinate relationship with the neighboring country, in this case through the distortion of Korean history and its incorporation into China's own (Smith, 2013; Nakayama, 2015; Perlez, 2013).

Japanese officials and academics are not sanguine about the Chinese claims because they see them as being founded upon a nonentity. They aver that the Ryukyus' tributary relationship to the Qing dynasty was chimerical, a fiction that was officially tolerated by Japan since 1655. Unbeknownst to the faraway Qing Emperor, the Ryukyuan kings had simultaneously been paying tribute to the Japanese Shōgun. Ironically, while the Qing court was happy to accept the Ryukyuan tribute in exchange for trade opportunities, and believed them to be loyal subjects, the kings themselves were chosen in Japan, at least until the Japanese Home Ministry assumed full jurisdiction over the islands in the mid-1870s, ending this tributary relationship. The Qing court dropped its claims over the Ryukyus in 1895, in the aforementioned Treaty of Shimonoseki. This, in fact, is why they are included in Japan's territories as enumerated in the 1952 San Francisco Peace Treaty (*Economy*, 2017; Zhang and Li, 2017).

The Japanese government erected sovereignty markers on the Diaoyutai/Senkaku Islands toward the end of the 19th century, an act which allowed Tokyo to officially incorporate them as national territory according to the laws governing *terra nullius* and the right to acquisition through occupation. In 1895, a Japanese businessman named Koga Tatsushirō opened a bonito processing facility on one of the Senkaku Islands, building a settlement there where 200-odd residents could live and work. The business proved unsuccessful, however, and the plant closed in 1940, since which time the islands have been uninhabited. At the end of World War II, US forces administered the islands until the early 1970s. In 1970, the Okinawa Legislative Assembly passed a resolution officially denoting the Diaoyutai/Senkaku Islands Japanese territory (Pan, 2007; Moteki, 2010).

The fact that the ROC even has a claim over the Diaoyutai/Senkaku Islands appears to be more trouble than it is worth. The PRC has demonstrated over the past several years that it is hungry to acquire territory, even going so far as to employ in the East China Sea many of the same tactics — using civil fishing-fleet militias, and salami-slicing techniques, for example — that it used to wrest control of the islands in the South China Sea. In contrast, Taipei has no desire to engage in such hostility-driven expansion, and there is no widespread support among the voter base in Taiwan for any such effort to take the islands by force from Japan, a fellow democracy. For this reason, Taipei has been silent on the issue, and doing its best to ignore the small number of hard-line factions demanding a tough stance. These voices are marginal and ineffectual and generally do not have the best interests of Taiwan at heart.

As an example, there is the case of the World Chinese Alliance in Defense of the Diaoyu Islands, an organization based in Taiwan. The president of this group, an activist named Huang Xilin, traveled to the Diaoyutai/Senkaku Islands in 2012 with a plan to raise the flag and demonstrate ROC sovereignty over the archipelago. Upon arrival, Huang unfurled the five-star red flag of the PRC. He later claimed in an interview that he had forgotten his ROC flag at home. While this misadventure may be comical, it is indicative of a wider trend in Taiwan: those persons pushing the government to aggressively press the ROC's claims in the East China Sea do not want what's best for Taiwan: they want what's best for China. The ROC government has no obligation to appease them. Rather, the government has an obligation to enact policies that will benefit the entire Taiwanese electorate (Zhang, 2015; Wang and Stamper, 2014).

One reason that the Diaoyutai/Senkaku Islands dispute still has a heartbeat in Taiwan is down to the personal convictions of its former leader, Ma Ying-jeou. After becoming ROC president in 2008, Ma quickly set to repairing the relationship with China, which had been strained by eight years of Beijing's refusal to engage in dialogue with Taipei. CCP leaders disapproved of the ruling Democratic Progressive Party from 2000 to 2008, as well as that party's efforts at cultural localization, which CCP leaders — and those of the Kuomintang (KMT) — viewed as de-Sinicization. To do this, Ma avoided disputes with the PRC over the ROC's sovereignty claims in the South China Sea while focusing more on the East China Sea disputes with Japan. Ma himself had a strong personal connection to the Diaoyutai/Senkaku Islands issue, going back to his days as a student activist in the 1970s (Atkinson 2010; Souza and Karalekas, 2015).

For example, Ma led a march consisting of students from National Taiwan University on June 17, 1971, delivering a list of Diaoyutai/Senkaku-related demands to the US and Japanese embassies. His *Baodiao* protest movement, dedicated to "defending the Diaoyu Islands," was only extracurricular: Ma's academic endeavors were related to the Diaoyutai/Senkaku issue as well, with the title of his dissertation at Harvard University being "Trouble Over Oily Waters: Legal Problems of Seabed Boundaries and Foreign Investments in the East China Sea." It comes as little surprise, then, that Ma's all-consuming interest in the Diaoyutai/Senkaku Islands had an oversized impact on his policymaking as president (Chen, 2018; Ogasawara, 2015).

This focus on the Diaoyutai/Senkaku issue was a double-edged sword. It led to one of Ma's most remarkable international triumphs when in 2012 he made a splash with his high-profile East China Sea Peace Initiative. The global media covered it extensively and, while Beijing ultimately quashed the effort, it gave Ma a reputation as a proactive, competent regional leader seeking peaceful coexistence and environmental sustainability. It also led to increased tensions with Japan when, in 2008, a private Taiwanese fishing boat, the *Lianhe Hao* — which was carrying 13 passengers, for reasons that were not made entirely clear at the time — collided with a Japanese Coast Guard vessel and sank. The coast guard sailors rescued the passengers and crew but held them on charges of territorial violations. Ma adopted a hardline stance with the Japanese government and demanded that Tokyo pay compensation for the sinking — more of a symbolic act designed to appear as a Japanese concession of ROC rights to the Diaoyutai/Senkaku Islands (MOFA, 2012; Souza and Karalekas, 2015; Valencia, 2014; Wang, 2010).

Perhaps Ma's greatest success was the April 2013 signing of a fisheries agreement with Japan on the topic of sharing resources in the waters surrounding the Diaoyutai/Senkaku Islands. Negotiations over this agreement had been intermittent for 17 long years, but the rise of China's belligerence in pressing its claims on the islands spurred Washington to put pressure on Taipei and Tokyo to finally sign the pact. It was widely hailed as a strategic success, and yet it has failed to usher in a more mature Taiwan–Japan security relationship (MOFA, 2013; Leng and Chang Liao, 2016).

Ma's stance on the Diaoyutai/Senkaku Islands could not be more different than that of his predecessor, former KMT leader and ROC president, Lee Teng-hui. As the nation's first directly elected president and a pivotal figure in Taiwan's democratization, Lee earned the nickname "Mr. Democracy" for his achievements in bringing the island's period of dictatorship and one-party rule to an end. This estranged him from the KMT party, as did the fact that he laid the foundations for the development of friendly Taipei–Tokyo relations, having grown up in Taiwan during Japanese rule and studied at Kyoto University. Long after having retired from politics, while on a 2015 visit to Japan, Lee was asked to whom he thought the Diaoyutai/Senkaku Islands belonged. "The Senkaku Islands belong to Japan, not Taiwan," Lee answered, pointing out that he had long expressed this view (Tiezzi, 2015).

7.5 Placating China: A Losing Game

Just as factions in Taiwan differ in their perspectives on Japan, views in Japan continue to be divided along the aforementioned two lines: one perspective that recognizes the extent of the threat posed by China and believes that Tokyo must engage in a formal security dialogue with Taipei; and the other perspective that seeks to avoid upsetting Beijing, and so parrots the fiction that Taiwan is an inalienable part of China, in line with the Japan–China Joint Statement of 1972, signed in a bygone era.

The problem with the latter view is that it assumes that Beijing's ire is authentic and not completely manufactured for geopolitical gain. Efforts to appease Beijing can all too easily be intentionally misconstrued and used as leverage by the CCP through the judicious and cynical

132   D. Karalekas

employment of a false sense of outrage. For proof, one need look no further than the Japanese government's 2012 purchase of several of the Diaoyutai/Senkaku islands.

Sparking this entire affair was Tokyo Governor Shintaro Ishihara, who has been described as a hawkish nationalist, and who announced that his office would negotiate the purchase of three of the uninhabited islands from their private owners, the Kurihara family. Ishihara intended to assert Japanese sovereignty over the archipelago in the face of increased Chinese activity there. It is worth remembering that a mere year and a half earlier, in September of 2010, China humiliated Japan after Chinese fishermen rammed two Japanese patrol boats near the islands, an incident that led to a diplomatic standoff in which China crippled Japan's high-tech industries by choking off their supply of rare-earth metals.

In order to placate China and prevent the right-wing governor from purchasing the islands and using them to stoke nationalist tendencies, which would undoubtedly anger Beijing, the administration of the then prime minister, Yoshihiko Noda, announced that his government would buy the islands instead, thereby forestalling any nationalistic provocations, and ensuring that Beijing is not upset. Situation averted; or so it was thought. Instead, Beijing responded to the news of the purchase with outrage, condemning it as a provocation and, according to one PLA general, calling for the islands to be used for military exercises. Even today, Beijing continues to cite the government's purchase of the islands as evidence of Japan's perfidy.

The lesson to be learned from this experience is clear: no amount of genuflecting will make Beijing happy, short of acquiescing to a complete CCP annexation of Taiwan, and whatever territory they set their eyes on next (see above, re: Okinawa). The inevitable conclusion, then, is to stop trying. If trying to placate China will not avert a war, then deterrence (by way of making a war unthinkable for planners in Beijing) is the only answer. For this to happen, the Japanese leadership must get off the fence and initiate an institutional security relationship with Taiwan. Taipei, for its part, must reciprocate.

Some small, mostly administrative, steps have been taken in this direction. In December 2021, Tokyo created a new office dedicated to handling issues relating to the East China Sea, including the Diaoyutai/Senkaku Islands and Taiwan. Sato Masahisa, acting chairman of the Liberal Democratic Party Diet Affairs Committee in the House of Councillors, in a recent interview called for a reduction of the level of ambiguity in the "strategic ambiguity" policy employed by Japan and the United States. He urged closer cooperation with Taiwan in such areas as infectious disease control, climate change, and disaster preparation and response, and noted the need to strengthen relations in the defense and security domain. While these are all positive steps, what are needed are practical measures with more heft (Takahashi, 2022).

7.6 Negotiating Security

The United States has worked hard since the Bush II administration to get Japan and South Korea to work together. If the same were to happen with Taiwan and Japan, it would be a perfect scenario. Just as the Americans forced Taipei and Tokyo to stop dithering on their long-stalled agreement on fishing rights in 2013, Washington must likewise pressure the two sides again to get serious about the worsening China threat, and to return to the negotiating table. As discussed previously, there is ambivalence on each side about the other — at least insofar as the officialdom in each nation is concerned. This ambivalence must be overcome for the good of the country and for the security of the region. To do otherwise would be tantamount to Nero fiddling while Rome burns.

From the Japanese perspective, Tokyo might consider asking the ROC to give up its claim to the Diaoyutai/Senkaku Islands. Geopolitically, this anachronistic claim is an albatross around the neck of Taiwan's leaders. It serves no purpose but to stand in the way of closer Taiwan–Japan ties, and only bolsters the spurious claim laid by China, and by the aforementioned crackpots who support China. Despite the difficulties of changing the constitution and other bureaucratic impediments, Taipei must find a way to drop its claim to the Diaoyutai/Senkakus, and the best way to accomplish this would be to retain the practical advantages (namely, the fishing rights) while jettisoning the geopolitical Gordian knot of the territorial claim. If Tokyo were to be content to guarantee access rights to Taiwanese fishermen, it could secure a way for Taipei to drop its territorial claim, and in doing so open the door to more substantial security cooperation.

From Taiwan's perspective, what is urgently needed is an institutionalized security relationship with Japan. This could take the form of a Japanese Taiwan Relations Act (TRA) patterned after that passed by the US Congress in 1979. This is exactly what a group of Japanese lawmakers called for in 2021, alongside a "2-plus-2 dialogue" between the foreign and defense ministers of Japan and Taiwan. It could alternatively begin with a mutual defense treaty. Tokyo has been on a signing spree lately, working on several such pacts in order to build up its alliances and secure its defense capabilities. Tokyo signed a bilateral security agreement with the United Kingdom in January 2023, after having inked a similar deal with Australia covering military, intelligence, and cybersecurity cooperation earlier in the previous year. Japan has also recently signed a defensive agreement with the Philippines. Clearly, Tokyo has been expanding its defense partnerships at an increased pace of late, but it makes little sense to leave Taipei out of the process, considering that Taiwan sits at the very center of the region's primary flashpoint. Whatever apprehensions Japanese voters might have with such a move would surely be overshadowed by the prospect of Taipei's willingness to drop its competing claim to the troublesome Diaoyutai/Senkaku Islands (Mizorogi and Kato, 2021).

7.7 Conclusion

In an effort to understand why amenable relations between the two neighbors seems so elusive, this chapter looked at the long history of close ties between the peoples of Taiwan and Japan — a relationship that goes back to prehistoric times, and a shared cultural inheritance that was cemented during the colonial era (1895–1945). Despite this long history, there is an ambivalence in each culture about the other, largely due to fear, on both sides, of upsetting a hypersensitive and querulous Beijing. This ambivalence is fed by the two sides' competing claims over the Diaoyutai/Senkaku Islands, leading to the sort of maritime standoffs described in the opening paragraphs. If leaders in the two countries can acquiesce to the fact that China cannot be placated, and hence stop trying, they will doubtless see the wisdom of working more closely together — through institutional mechanisms — to safeguard their mutual defense. There's an ancient saying, "the enemy of my enemy is my friend": the more Beijing acts like an enemy, the closer Taipei and Tokyo should become.

As the Taiwanese have learned, there is no distance one can go that will be enough to placate Beijing, short of a full and complete surrender. To paraphrase the American diplomat and historian George F. Kennan, the jealous and intolerant eye of Zhongnanhai can distinguish, in the end, only vassals and enemies, and the neighbors of China, if they do not wish to be one, must reconcile themselves to being the other.

References

Atkinson, J. (2010). China-Taiwan diplomatic competition and the Pacific Islands. *The Pacific Review, 23*(4), 407–427.

Auer, J. and Kotani, T. (2005). Reaffirming the "Taiwan Clause": Japan's national interest in the Taiwan strait and the US-Japan alliance. *NBR Analysis, 16*(1), 58.

Chen, M. (2018). Managing territorial nationalism in the East and South China Seas. In: A. Beckershoff and G. Schubert (eds.), *Assessing the Presidency of Ma Yi"ng-jiu in Taiwan: Hopeful Beginning, Hopeless End?* (pp. 317–333). New York: Routledge.

Chung, L. (2022, October 5). 10-hour stand-off between Taiwanese coastguard and Japanese patrol ship sparks call for talks. *South China Morning Post.* https://archive.ph/tqBVC.

Economy, E. C. (2017). History with Chinese characteristics: How China's imagined past shapes It's present. *Foreign Affairs, 96*(4), 141–148. Retrieved March 24, 2021 from http://www.jstor.org/stable/44823900.

Haipeng, Z. and Guoqiang, L. (2017). The treaty of Shimonoseki, the Diaoyu Islands and the Ryukyu issue. *International Critical Thought, 7*(1), 93–108.

Hale, E. (2022, October 16). Despite tough words, Japan might not enter a Taiwan War. *Voice of America News.* Retrieved from http://archive.today/HFtA3.

Huang, C.-H. (2011). Ethno-cultural connections among the Islands around Yonaguni-jima: The network of the "East Taiwan Sea." *Ogasawara Research, 37,* 7–24.

Hudson, M. J. (2012). Austronesian'and 'Jōmon'identities in the Neolithic of the Ryukyu Islands. *Documenta Praehistorica, 39,* 257–262.

Inoue, M. (2022, July). Political ambiguity: Japan's stance on the Taiwan strait. *East Asia Forum Quarterly 14*(3), 15–16.

Lee, K. (2021). From victory to defeat: The Chinese Mission in Japan, 1946–1952. Doctoral dissertation, University of Cambridge.

Leng, T.-K. and Chang Liao, N.-C. (2016). Hedging, strategic partnership, and Taiwan's relations with Japan under the Ma Ying-Jeou administration. *Pacific Focus, 31*(3), 357–382.

Ministry of Foreign Affairs (MOFA) of Republic of China (ROC) (2012). The Republic of China's Sovereignty claims over the Diaoyutai Islands and the East China Sea peace initiative. Catalog Card No.: MOFA-EN-FO-102-016-I-1. Ac.

Ministry of Foreign Affairs (MOFA) of Republic of China (ROC) (2013). *Republic of China (Taiwan) Signs Fisheries Agreement with Japan.* Taipei: Press Release.

Mizorogi, T. and Kato, M. (2021). Japan Lawmakers Want "Taiwan Relations Act" of their own. *Nikkei Asia.* Retrieved from https://archive.vn/oLYvo.

Moteki, H. (2010). The Senkaku Islands constitute an intrinsic part of Japan. Society for Dissemination of Historical Fact. Retrieved from https://www.sdh-fact.com/CL02_1/79_S4.pdf.

Nakayama, T. (2015). An English translation of Xu Baoguang's Poems on the eight views of the Ryukyu Kingdom. *The Meio University Bulletin, 20*, 135–139.

Ogasawara, Y. (2015). Ma Ying-Jeou's doctoral thesis and Its impact on the Japan–Taiwan fisheries negotiations. *Journal of Contemporary East Asia Studies, 4*(2), 67–92.

Pan, Z. (2007). Sino-Japanese dispute over the Diaoyutai/Senkaku Islands: The pending controversy from the Chinese perspective. *Journal of Chinese Political Science, 12*(1), 71–92.

Perlez, J. (2013, June 13). Calls grow in China to press claim for Okinawa. *The New York Times*. Retrieved from http://archive.today/ZHEkI.

Roy, D. (2003). *Taiwan: A Political History*. Ithaca: Cornell UP.

Shaffer, S. (2022, September 15). Why Japan needs to talk to Taiwan. *Foreign Policy Research Institute*. Retrieved from http://archive.today/JGfV1.

Smith, P. J. (2013). The Senkaku/Diaoyu Island controversy: A crisis postponed. *Naval War College Review, 66*(2), 27–44.

Souza, M. D. and Karalekas, D. (2015). Domestic politics and personal beliefs in Taiwan's territorial claims. *Panorama of Global Security Environment 2015–2016*, pp. 409–420.

Souza, M. D. and Karalekas, D. (2020, July 20). Confronting Japan to defend against China: Senkaku as a case study in Taiwan's politics. *Global Security Review*. Retrieved from http://archive.today/UoQor.

Takahashi, I. (2022, November 9). Sato Masahisa: No time to waste on Japan-Taiwan defense cooperation. *Nippon.com*. http://archive.today/xo6KQ.

Tiezzi, S. (2015, July 30). Taiwan's former president causes controversy in Japan. *The Diplomat*. Retrieved from http://archive.today/wq67r.

Valencia, M. J. (2014). The East China Sea disputes: History, status, and ways forward. *Asian Perspective, 38*(2), 183–218.

Wang, K.-H. (2010). The ROC's maritime claims and practices with special reference to the South China Sea. *Ocean Development & International Law, 41*(3), 237–252.

Wang, Q. K. (2000). Japan's Balancing Act in the Taiwan Strait. *Security Dialogue, 31*(3), 337–342.

Wang, V. W.-C. and Stamper, G. (2014). Taiwan's policy toward the Diaoyu/Senkaku Islands dispute and the implications for the US. *Education About Asia, 19*(2), 45.

Zhang, H. and Li, G. (2017). The treaty of Shimonoseki, the Diaoyu Islands and the Ryukyu issue. *International Critical Thought, 7*(1), 93–108.

Zhang, K. (2015). 'Patriots' with different characteristics: Deconstructing the Chinese anti-Japan protests in 2012. MIT Political Science Department Research Paper No. 2015–2018.

© 2025 World Scientific Publishing Company
https://doi.org/10.1142/9789811298301_0008

Chapter 8

Unprecedented Danger: Japanese Visions of Taiwan's Ordeal and the Role of Deterrence

Alexandre Calvo

A look at a map suffices to see that Japanese national security requires that Taiwan not be held by hostile forces, or Finlandized. Thus, no discussion of Taiwan's defense is complete without an examination of Tokyo's policies, morale, and capabilities. Furthermore, that examination cannot take place in isolation, but rather within the context of the broader network of formal and informal security arrangements found in the region, a network which while being led by Washington, features an increasingly significant role for other capitals such as Tokyo, as America's relative power continues to stagnate. Taiwan is also a key factor in Japan's foreign and defense policies since it facilitates a more nuanced view of the country's contemporary history and colonial past.

8.1 Unprecedented Danger

Why are Chinese designs on Taiwan considered to be an unprecedented danger to Japanese national security? The reason is two-fold: geographical and historical. They are a danger because Taiwan sits close to Japan and astride many vital Sea Lines of Communication (SLOCs), connecting the country to much of the outside world. That danger is unprecedented because, barring the closing stages of the Second World War, this is the first time in centuries that Japan has faced the real possibility that a hostile power may be able to effectively isolate it. The fact that this threat is materializing during a period of so-called peacetime is no consolation to Japanese policymakers, since peace is much more than the absence of open conventional military conflict, and Beijing leaders have proven adept at advancing their territorial designs in areas such as the South China Sea without crossing that line. East Asia, and more generally the Indo-Pacific, are not at peace.

While most people in industrialized countries take the Internet for granted, we should not forget that, despite the growing potential for satellite provision, it remains very much reliant on submarine cables. The incident at Taiwan's Matsu Island, in which two undersea Internet cables were severed by Chinese vessels (a fishing boat and a cargo ship) in February 2023, serves as a reminder of this vulnerability, such cables having suffered 27 similar incidents (the cause not always having been ascertained) in the previous five years (Wu and Lai, 2023). While the nature of the February 2023 incident remains unclear, it may well have been a warning, or operational test, and its significance was rightly stressed by some participants in the Taiwan Studies Summer School 2023 at the School of Oriental and African Studies. A look at undersea cables serving Japan shows that very few connect the country to Russia; a sizeable number do so to America through the Pacific; but an equally significant portion do so with China and with Southeast Asia, and of the latter, many rely on nodes in or close to Taiwan, or traverse nearby waters (Submarine Cable Map, 2023; Submarine Networks, 2023).

The maritime industry often similarly fails to attract the attention it deserves, but as an island nation devoid of most natural resources and closely integrated into the world economy, Japan cannot afford to be even potentially cut off from its SLOCs and, as noted, many sit astride nearby Taiwan, echoing General MacArthur's immortal words describing the island as "unsinkable carrier-tender" vital to US national security (Manchester, 1978, p. 676). Such words, similar to those already used in war-time Japan (不沈空母 or "unsinkable aircraft carrier"), which also described Formosa as "圖南の飛び石" (a stepping stone toward the South) (Ts'ai, 2009, p. 173), are equally applicable from the perspective of present-day Japan.

This is why we noted that a look at a map sufficed to see that Japanese national security required that Taiwan not be held by hostile forces or

Finlandized. The challenge for Tokyo is how to achieve this in a new domestic and international setting: no longer as a colonial power (as it was in 1895–1945) or a *de facto* US protectorate (post-WWII), but in a middle-of-the-road scenario: that of a sovereign country closely allied to America and other maritime democracies and playing a leading role in the Indo-Pacific. This intermediate position between colonial master and US protectorate implies many challenges for Tokyo, as well as many opportunities, and both objectively overlapping national interests and good mutual perceptions may facilitate a task that is nevertheless fraught with danger.

8.2 The Japanese Constitution, Collective Self-Defense, and Taiwan

To examine Japanese policy toward Taiwan it is first necessary to look at its constitutional, legal, and treaty framework. A central aspect of this examination is the issue of whether Japan would consider an attack (including a cyberattack), blockade, or attempt at landing, on the island as a trigger for its concept of collective self-defense, and the restrictions, if any, on potential assistance, both to Republic of China (ROC) forces and to US and allied counterparts.

Even today, Japan's post-war constitution, also known as the "MacArthur Constitution," is mislabeled as a "Pacifist" constitution, forcing many analysts to approach the issue of the defense of Taiwan with little if any reference to Japan. However, while a key aspect of Japan's occupation and reform under Proconsul MacArthur was demilitarization and an end to any capacity to singlehandedly deploy offensive forces, the constitution, while never formally amended, has been reinterpreted almost from day one. Step by step, in a gradual but relentless fashion beginning during the occupation and the Korean War, Japan has granted its military more powers to act as an instrument of foreign policy and national security. Also from day one, the issue of how to defend Japan has been intimately linked with that of how to defend Taiwan, and although MacArthur was forced by President Harry Truman to withdraw his earlier quoted address to the Veterans of Foreign Wars where he referred to Formosa as "unsinkable carrier-tender" and essential to the US defensive perimeter in the Pacific, his assessment was *de facto* accepted by both Washington and Tokyo (Manchester, 1978, p. 676). What has basically been changing is the balance between US and Japanese capabilities and responsibilities, as Japan gradually recovered its sovereignty, experienced an economic miracle, and rearmed. The recent decision to double its defense spending to 2 percent of gross domestic product (GDP) by 2027, coupled with former prime minister Shinzo Abe's legacy in reinforcing Japan's domestic legislation so that, among other goals, it can better assist Taiwan if attacked, comprise the latest developments in this regard. Furthermore, they are proof that, despite his untimely death, Abe's ideas live on and continue shaping developments in the Indo-Pacific, including Japan's Taiwan policy.

While references to the island in Japanese official statements and documents are often traditionally indirect or must be guessed at by the reader, it is clear that Japan's "three new national security documents" [the National Security Strategy (NSS), the National Defense Strategy (NDS), and the Defense Buildup Program] published in December 2022 have been drafted with the island in mind. Lieutenant General Wallace "Chip" Gregson (USMC, ret.), a former US Assistant Secretary of Defense, Asian and Pacific Security Affairs, rightly noted that this triad "serves Taiwan well," adding that "Taiwan is now no longer stranded in an anomalous 'special' status, separated somehow from the Japanese archipelago," a logical but welcome development (Gregson, 2023).

Thus, we can say that the necessary legal and administrative framework to allow Japan to make a meaningful contribution to Taiwan's national security is very much in place and, more precisely, that the Constitution is no bar to it. The concept of collective self-defense is a key development here, marking a gradual but significant departure from the traditional view that Japan could only use force to defend itself but not to defend an ally (Takasaku and Michishita, 2014, p. 9).

Where Japan's position, in line with that of most of its allies, is still not fully satisfactory for Taiwan is in its failure to acknowledge the island's right to self-determination as the foundation stone of defense commitments. The 2022 National Security Strategy of Japan (Cabinet Secretariat, 2022) openly admits that "Japan's basic position regarding Taiwan remains unchanged" and describes bilateral relations as "a nongovernmental working relationship based on the Japan–China Joint Communiqué in 1972." Although words of praise for the island follow, to wit: "Taiwan is an extremely important partner and a precious friend of Japan, with whom Japan shares fundamental values, including democracy, and has close economic and personal ties," it could be argued that a logical next step would be to acknowledge the Taiwanese right to decide their own future and form of government in accordance with international law. Instead, a wish is expressed, to the effect that "cross-strait issues are expected to be resolved peacefully," and although this makes it clear that force is not acceptable, one could say it is not very realistic, given that Beijing has made it abundantly clear on myriad occasions, by both word and deed, that it reserves the right to use force to annex Taiwan. Ultimately, it is a position that rests on the hope and assumption that, as China opens up to the world and integrates into the global economy, it will come to accept that the final status of Taiwan cannot be settled by force. However, it should by now be clear that this is not realistic and that Beijing's policy of the four modernizations and rapprochement with the West have not brought about a liberal, let alone democratic, country, but rather a stronger one with the same disregard for Taiwan, yet with much stronger military — and in particular naval and maritime — means to threaten the island.

Thus, while it is unlikely to see this Japanese policy amended in the short term, it is likely to come under close scrutiny, sooner or later. To claim that relations with Taiwan are based on an agreement with Beijing is dangerous and promotes miscalculations. It lessens the credibility of promises to use force to defend the island since, at the same time, it is treated as a Chinese internal "or cross-strait" affair. A critical re-examination requires two factors: a similar debate in other maritime democracies, and substantial progress in economic decoupling from China.

A logical evolution, but one unlikely to be taken by Japan on its own, would be to acknowledge Taiwan's right to self-determination, while ceasing and desisting from using terms such as "cross-strait," which dangerously support China's view that Taiwan is an object, not a subject. Many commentators see such a step as a dangerous provocation, but it could be argued that current Japanese policy is even more dangerous, because it seems to try to square two fundamentally opposed tenets: that Taiwan is part of China, but that the People's Republic of China (PRC) should not use force to terminate the island's *de facto* sovereignty. Germany's renunciation of any designs on Austria could be seen as an alternative template to secure peace in East Asia.

To conclude this section, we need to remember that this brief examination of Japan's constitutional and defense regulations cannot take place in isolation, but rather within the context of a broader network of formal and informal security arrangements found in the region. While the security alliance with Washington remains the cornerstone of Japan's national defense policy, the country has also reached agreements and deepened coordination with other actors in recent years, ranging from regional partners such as India and the Philippines; countries returning to the Pacific like the United Kingdom; and a former colony, the Republic of Korea (ROK). Also noteworthy is closer coordination with NATO, although the opening of an office in Tokyo seems to have been postponed. For Taiwan, this is significant for many reasons. First of all, Japan is well positioned to act as a catalyst for greater involvement and coordination among maritime democracies in supporting the island. Second, since it is simply not possible to defend Japan without defending Taiwan, Tokyo's growing range of bilateral defense coordination agreements indirectly promotes greater attention to the island. Third, in the case of the Philippines, by aiding Manila build up its capacities to deal with Beijing's subconventional and combined non-lethal maritime warfare — through among other means the provision and funding through official development funds of coastguard cutters, coupled with training and joining bilateral and multilateral exercises — Tokyo has helped relieve pressure on Taipei.

Every Chinese ship, be it naval, coastguard, or maritime militia, deployed against Filipino forces, is one less ship available to harass Taiwan. Should the Philippines give in to Chinese pressure, this would deal a double blow to Taiwan, releasing additional Chinese units and facilitating the island's envelopment and blockade. Tokyo is well aware of this, and while it is not openly admitted in defense documents and other official statements, it underlies defense coordination with Manila. Domain awareness, and in particular the provision of air defense radars, is another key aspect of Japanese assistance to the Philippines and again a move that will very much benefit Taiwan. Tokyo is transferring four air surveillance radar units (three fixed, one mobile), manufactured by Mitsubishi Electric Corp., and since October 4, 2022, has been training Philippine Air Force (PAF) personnel in their operation (Japanese Ministry of Defense, 2022). This air defense system will greatly increase Manila's ability to monitor Chinese activities on Taiwan's Southern flank, and although not officially stated, the resulting data are likely to make their way to Taipei. Japan is simultaneously reinforcing its Southwestern flank, not just deploying additional troops in Okinawa but improving its surveillance assets there, and we can therefore say that Tokyo is helping guard both of Taiwan's flanks and ensuring that Taipei has the necessary intelligence on developments there.

Lastly, where Japan has failed, despite well-meaning and logical steps by the then prime minister, Abe, is in seeking to drive a strategic wedge between Russia and China; a move that, had it been successful, would have also benefited Taiwan.

8.3 Japanese Capabilities, Morale, Public Finances, and Industrial Base

Japan's Taiwan policy and security and defense coordination with the island depend not just on the policies, interests, and legislation examined up to this point, but also on the country's military (in a broad sense; including both hardware and personnel) capabilities, morale, public finances, and industrial base.

It is beyond the scope of this chapter to examine all of Japan's security and defense capabilities that may be deployed in support of Taiwan, and instead, we shall briefly examine a few; namely, space surveillance and Internet provision, undersea cable repair, and submarine construction.

Concerning space, recent years have seen Japan move to reinforce its presence in this new defense realm, taking steps such as the establishment in 2020 of the Space Operations Squadron at the Fuchu Air Base in Tokyo [the Self-Defense Forces (SDF)'s first space unit], followed by a second squadron based at Hofu Kita Air Base in Yamaguchi Prefecture, with a total of 200 personnel in the SDF space program and closer cooperation with the civilian Japan Aerospace Exploration Agency (JAXA) (Narisawa, 2023). At the same time, Taiwan is yet to launch any military satellites, despite efforts to develop a space program taking advantage of the island's strong industrial base in areas such as semiconductors and steps forward such as the October 2023 launch of its second domestically developed satellite, the meteorological satellite 獵風者 (meaning Wind Hunter)/Triton (FORMOSAT-7R) (Wang, 2023; Taiwan Space Agency, 2022).

While some coordination with Japan has already taken place, for example in the design and construction of FORMOSAT-5, and the provision by Taiwan of instruments for some Japanese research satellites, we could well see further work in this area, motivated at least in part from one of the lessons learned from the war in Ukraine. It has not gone unnoticed in Tokyo and Taipei that among the first targets to be attacked by Russia was Ukraine's Internet infrastructure, and that the quick provision of

Starlink services operated by SpaceX negated its impact and significantly bolstered Kiev's ability to resist and counterstrike. As a result, both capitals have realized they need access to similar capabilities in order to ensure continued access to the Internet in times of open conflict. In the case of Taiwan, we have already explained the island's vulnerability to attacks on undersea cables and the recent incident in Matsu.

Where Japan and Taiwan seem to differ is in the role of what is, to date, the sole provider of such services: SpaceX. Taiwan has announced plans for setting up a state-backed Low Earth Orbit (LEO) company, a spinoff from the Taiwan Space Agency, bringing together private partners with the purpose of deploying its own constellation (Hille, 2023). Japan's SDF, conversely, have been conducting tests with Starlink, starting in March 2023, with the goal of improving their communication capabilities, and may conclude an agreement with another company by the end of the year. This is the first time that the SDF have employed privately owned LEO satellites (Japan gives spaceX, 2023).

What has received much attention among the Taiwanese national security community and defense reporters, and could force a rethink of Japanese plans and push Taipei and Tokyo to work together on an alternative, is the fear that Starlink may not be available in the event of an attempted Chinese blockade or invasion of Taiwan due to its ultimate owner's conflicts of interest. It is actually surprising that, while NASA is forbidden by legislation from cooperating with its Chinese counterparts (a logical decision and a harbinger of things to come, as the US and other maritime democracies seek to gradually decouple from Beijing and limit the extent to which China can rearm on the back of foreign advanced technology and capital), NASA works closely with companies belonging to conglomerates heavily involved in China and thus is at grave risk of being compromised or forced into collaboration. Manufacturing cars in China and providing communication services to the Taiwanese and Japanese military may be a difficult balancing act to pull off, and Taipei and Tokyo may well conclude that, absent US action to solve this conundrum, they may well be better served by developing an alternative, perhaps together with other interested parties sharing the same concerns.

In the realm of the seabed, Japan is one of the most advanced countries in terms of fiber-optic cable repair capabilities, with at least four civilian ships, plus the SDF's secretive cable-laying ship JS *Muroto*, whose missions are seldom publicized but which conducts yearly drills with the US Navy. Furthermore, two Japanese companies [Nippon

Electric Company (NEC)'s subsidiary Ocean Cable and Communication (OCC) and Fujitsu] are among the top submarine cable manufacturers worldwide (Gresh and Nakamura, 2023).

This constitutes an excellent foundation to become a leading power in the defense of subsea infrastructure, as well as in the waters around Taiwan. Another way in which Japan may aid the island is by reinforcing and hardening its own cable infrastructure, including an increase in the number of landing stations, something already announced.

Altogether, it may amount to a particularly meaningful contribution, given that China is not just resorting to cutting undersea Internet cables serving Taiwan but trying to become a major player in the industry and following a policy of demanding permission from companies laying cables through its EEZ (in contravention of UNCLOS) and more generally the whole of the South China Sea (as was recently made clear in the case of the Southeast Asia-Japan Cable 2 connecting Japan, Taiwan, Hong Kong, Singapore) (Everington, 2023).

Having said that, we should bear in mind that any Japanese contribution to Taiwanese national security — whether on the seabed or in any other domain, including those discussed elsewhere in this chapter — should be framed in terms of mutual self-interest. Thus, statements like that by Eli Huang, a special assistant to former ROC Deputy Defense Minister Lin Chong-pin, labeling Taiwan's submarine fiber-optic cables as the island's "Achilles' heel" (Huang, 2017) should be expanded, in the sense that they are not just Taiwan's Achilles' heel but also Japan's. Thus, the plans announced by both governments in 2023 to reinforce their undersea cable infrastructure should ideally be bilaterally coordinated and part of a wider Indo-Pacific Strategy by maritime democracies.

Still in the underwater domain, another area where Japan–Taiwan defense coordination shows significant potential is submarine construction. Taiwan currently operates only two largely obsolete diesel submarines, with a third training boat. Taipei is facing grave difficulties importing further conventionally powered boats from European manufacturers and is likewise unable to procure them from their US counterparts since American yards no longer produce them. In 2016 the island launched the Indigenous Defense Submarine (IDS) program, also known as the "Hai Chang Program." Aimed at the construction of eight boats, it involves a number of domestic actors but also reportedly relies on different foreign technologies and components (Dotson, 2023). While exact details remain outside the public domain, Japan's role is clearly significant. And while rumors of a sale of *Soryu*-class attack submarines never materialized, Tokyo seems to be extensively cooperating with Taipei, in terms of technologies, components, and personnel, and the resulting design bears some similarities with the aforementioned Japanese class of boat. Some observers have expressed doubts as to the deterrent impact of this program, given the characteristics of the Taiwan Strait, but such voices seem to assume that, faced with aggression, an island democracy must play by the aggressor's rulebook rather than choosing the most suitable time and place to strike back.

Japan's ability to cooperate with Taiwan also depends on the always difficult-to-assess triad of morale, public finances, and industrial base. Morale is a concept that is very difficult to quantify, but an essential one given the presumably prolonged nature of any open warfare phase of the current conflict, assuming a continued US and allied decision not to fight China on its own territory, coupled with a nuclear policy of no-first-use, as well as no use of tactical nuclear weapons against conventional forces. Of course, none of this is set in stone, but it is beyond this chapter's remit to examine alternative scenarios. Therefore, once the first opening salvoes are fired, Taiwan is in for a long war. Three questions then arise concerning Japan. First, whether the Japanese public would support their government in the face of Chinese threats, a risk of escalation, and an extension of the conflict, as well as the human and financial costs to be expected. While observers more familiar with the country may doubt it, those with a more nuanced view may come to different conclusions, while acknowledging that more work on economic decoupling is necessary to ensure this. Furthermore, what matters is not absolute but relative resilience, and China, by virtue of its greater ethnic and social complexity, plus non-consensual government, may turn out to be more fragile than Taiwan and Japan after all. Second, Japan's public finances remain weak, with a growing national debt and no expectations of a significant improvement. While the debt is basically denominated in yen, rises in interest rates could challenge the government's ability to service it, putting a dent in the ability to deliver the promised increases in defense spending to 2 percent of GDP and the capacity to sustain the costs of open conflict, likely to be substantial even in scenarios in which Japan plays just a supporting role. It is difficult not to conclude that an improvement in Japan's economy and public accounts would make a substantial contribution to its capacity to cooperate with Taiwan. Third, concerning Japan's substantial industrial base, the war in Ukraine has served as a timely reminder of the high tempo of consumption that characterizes modern war. Not just of ammunition, but of every kind of supply, from medical stores to fuel. If we add to this the lessons from COVID-19, with countries around the world begging China for supplies because they had forgotten the downside of industrial offshoring, we see how important it is to ensure the ability to sustainably mass-produce the sinews of war. Thus, Tokyo's challenge is two-fold: to ensure the necessary industrial capacity, and to guarantee that it does not involve China-based or connected manufacturing.

8.4 Japan and the Doctrinal Debate on Taiwan: Non-lethal Force at Sea, Unconventional Warfare, Porcupine Strategy, and Deterrence

The debate on how best Taiwan can defend itself involves a discussion on a number of concepts, the most significant being non-lethal force at sea, asymmetrical/unconventional warfare, conventional war, porcupine strategy, and deterrence (both conventional and non-conventional). We need to look at them through Japanese eyes in the context of Chinese designs on Taiwan, examining how they fit or not with current and prospective Japanese interests, policies, and capabilities, and with existing or planned coordination between Taipei and Tokyo.

Bilateral defense coordination has traditionally been geared toward conventional warfare, for example, in the submarine-building program discussed earlier; however, both Taiwan and Japan face a wider spectrum of challenges, including the employment by China of non-lethal force at sea, with its maritime militia of fishing vessels ramming ships. While this needs to be taken into account in joint planning and training, at a capacity-building level, industrialized Taiwan does not seem to need Japanese assistance in the way the Philippines, for example, does.

Concerning the so-called "porcupine" strategy, of hardening military targets and seeking to respond to a conventional Chinese strategy, rather than engaging in an arms race, a wide range of observers have recommended that Taipei follow this route. However, in and of itself, it threatens to fatalistically accept a war of attrition fought only on Taiwanese soil and impose a horrific cost on the island's population. Perhaps the fact that many of these observers have no family there may have subconsciously influenced their thinking. Since, to a lesser extent, this has also been advocated for Japan, there may be room for greater exchanges and debates

148　*A. Calvo*

between the two nations, in search for an alternative or at least some nuance. This may take the form of developing effective deterrents, such as weapons systems able to inflict unacceptable damage to an aggressor's territory and population so as to be able to make it think twice before going to war. A deterrent need not match that of the enemy: it suffices to threaten it with destruction, which, if taken to an extreme, is known in nuclear doctrine as MAD, or mutually assured destruction. Neither Taiwan nor Japan have openly incorporated such thinking into their defense doctrines, either at the conventional or nuclear levels, but by seeking to acquire an enemy base strike capability (while stressing it does not amount to preemption, but to counterstrike), Tokyo may have taken a timid step forward in that direction. Right now, the possibility of either country developing a deterrent, conventional or nuclear, remains not just controversial and taboo, but unrealistic. However, should their strategic position continue to deteriorate, their leaders may reach the conclusion that it is time to start thinking the unthinkable.

8.5　Lessons from Ukraine: A Wakeup Call for Tokyo and Taipei?

The current war in the Ukraine offers a number of useful lessons for both Taiwan and Japan, some of which already seem to be prompting action in both countries. An example, which we have already discussed, is the perceived need to secure Internet access through Low Earth Orbit satellite constellations. We have also discussed the demands of prolonged conflict in terms of treasure and ammunition. In this sense, the war has turned out to benefit maritime democracies in the Indo-Pacific, serving as a warning, while it is an obstacle to Beijing's attempt to disguise its rearmament and irredentism under the guise of a "peaceful ascent," in a reminder that the myth of a careful, patient, wise PRC able to outsmart rivals by thinking long term is just that; a myth. Furthermore, it shows that Beijing has no true allies, but simply partners of convenience who end up doing whatever they deem fit, without the slightest degree of strategic cooperation.

It is of course also important not to read too much into wars halfway around the globe, resulting from their own historical and political causes. Having said that, a sure lesson that both Japan and Taiwan would do well to bear in mind is the speed with which threats can turn into hostile actions, and the risk that ambiguity may contribute to miscalculation and aggression. In other words, if Beijing says, as it repeatedly does, that it reserves the right to use force against Taiwan, this is no empty bluff, but evidence that it could happen at any time. There is no point in estimating that the necessary forces for an attempted invasion are still not there, because an attempted landing is only one of many ways in which a shooting war can start, with a blockade being another. Coordination in submarine construction is a major step for Japan to contribute to this scenario, since submarines can be used both to fight a blockade and to impose a counterblockade, but at a higher, political level, Tokyo's ambiguity on which scenarios, if any, would prompt military assistance to Taiwan or even direct intervention remain a major factor promoting a potential Chinese miscalculation. It would be unfair to single out Tokyo for such criticism, since the same can be said about the United States and any other regional actor, but such a policy only emboldens those in Beijing who may be tempted to believe that they can attack Taiwan without risking a wider war. It is the same mistake that we can observe when looking back at wars such as the Second World War in Europe, Korea, and the Falklands. In all three cases, invaders not only sincerely believed but also had good objective reasons to do so that their actions would elicit no meaningful response, other than empty token gestures and diplomatic protests. We can only speculate on what could have happened if it had been made clear, in a credible fashion beforehand, that force would be met by force. In the case of Taiwan, we should be able to at least openly discuss the pros and cons of such alternatives to strategic ambiguity, and we should expect a growing number of voices to take part in such a debate in Taiwan, Japan, and their partner and ally countries, in the coming years.

8.6 Summing Up: The Fate of Taiwan and Japan are Intertwined

It is difficult not to conclude that Taiwan–Japan relations are among the most important in the Indo-Pacific, and a key to both countries' national security. They are expected to keep growing stronger in the face of shared threats and challenges, as does coordination at a wider regional level, and bilaterally among concerned actors such as the Philippines. To sum it up: Taiwan needs a proactive Japan ready to assist on the beaches and the landing grounds, while Japan is simply indefensible in a scenario in which Taiwan is in hostile hands, meaning there is no room for backtracking.

There is, furthermore, another subtler reason why Taiwan and Japan need each other, namely, the contribution of memories of the island's Japanese colonial period to their respective self-image and identity. This is of course a sensitive topic, and one not prone to generalizations and simplistic positions. Having said that, while Imperial Japan did not occupy the island with the local population in mind, and as any such era has its dark moments, the Japanese record in Taiwan is overall rather positive, and saw the island's economy, public health, and standards of living progress significantly, with direct access to the Japanese market and under an indirect gold standard, while remaining shielded from the turmoil that engulfed China at the time. Taiwan shows the better side of Japan's colonial period, and was the best fit for its desire to be seen as the Britain of the East and another force for good. For the Taiwanese, the era serves as a reminder that they are not simply a piece of China; that Beijing's historical claims are not credible; that their status is yet to be determined; that they have long been a different society from that across the strait; and that they have nothing to gain and much to lose under Beijing's rule. For the Japanese, memories of their rule on Taiwan can support efforts to balance regular attacks on their recent history, including abuse of PoWs and civilians, exploitation of comfort women, and other war crimes, seeking a middle-ground between uncritical acceptance of such views and wholesale rejection of their past and an orthodox defense of Imperial Japan's actions. Both extremes would damage the country's national defense and its contribution to that of neighboring Taiwan. A Japan humbled by past mistakes and automatically associating the use of force with the pursuit of illegitimate goals would find it very difficult to summon the necessary courage to resist aggression, while a Japan unable to critically reexamine its past and bent on rejecting even the slightest criticism from other countries would be one challenged to keep working on the vital bilateral and multilateral alliances making up the web of maritime democracies in the Indo-Pacific; maritime democracies condemned to hang together, lest they hang separately.

To sum this all up, the challenge for Japan is to secure a more positive historical image while acknowledging more openly the mistakes and abuses of its past. At the same time, the challenge for Taiwan is to seek a historical consensus that, while respectful of the plurality of views found in any democracy, is strong enough to underpin a national security policy based on diverse citizens sharing the same trench (Calvo, 2015). In seeking both goals, Japan and Taiwan need each other. After all, despite all the military hardware, training, and agreements, at the end of the day, citizens in any democracy will demand to know why they are fighting, and the ability or otherwise to answer that question will turn out to be a key factor in determining whether those democracies shall prevail or go under.

References

Cabinet Secretariat (2022, December). National security strategy of Japan. Retrieved from https://www.cas.go.jp/jp/siryou/221216anzenhoshou/nss-e. pdf.

Calvo, A. (2015, February 27). Taiwan in Japan's historical narrative. *China Policy Institute Blog, University of Nottingham.*

Dotson, J. (2023, June 14). Taiwan's indigenous submarine program announces milestone goals for 2023. *Global Taiwan Brief.* Retrieved from http:// archive.today/vsYEK.

Everington, K. (2023, March 15). China obstructs new subsea cable to Taiwan. *Taiwan News.* Retrieved from http://archive.today/xZvx7.

Gregson, W. (2023, January 11). Japan's new national security posture and Taiwan's security: Japan's constitution is not a suicide pact. *Global Taiwan Brief.* Retrieved from http://archive.today/erTWc.

Gresh, G. and Nakamura, H. (2023, May 18). Japan: New lord of the Subsea? *The Diplomat.* Retrieved from http://archive.today/Y4CDL.

Hille, K. (2023, January 6). Taiwan plans domestic satellite champion to resist any China attack. *The Financial Times.* Retrieved from http://archive. today/d3A76.

Huang, E. (2017, December 3). Taiwan's Achilles' Heel in a conflict with China is not what you Think. *The National Interest.* Retrieved from http://archive. today/gMp5K.

Japan gives spaceX's starlink satellite constellation trial run (2023, June 25). *The Japan News.* Retrieved from http://archive.today/MSb3t.

Japanese Ministry of Defense (防衛省・自衛隊). (2022, October 3). アイリピンへの警戒管制レーダーの移転について. Retrieved from http://archive. today/8gSJt.

Manchester, W. (1978). *American Caesar.* New York: Dell Publishing.

Narisawa, K. (2023, June 28). SDF beefing up activities in space to protect Japan's satellites. *The Asahi Shimbun.* Retrieved from http://archive.today/ nKyC9.

Submarine Cable Map (2023, August 23). TeleGeography. Retrieved from https://www.submarinecablemap.com/multiselect/country?ids=japan, taiwan.

Submarine Cable Networks (2023, August 23). Submarine networks. Retrieved from https://www.submarinenetworks.com/en/.

Taiwan Space Agency (2022, July 20). Taiwan-made TRITON satellite fully Assembled, expected to be ready for use by end of 2022. *Latest News.* Retrieved from http://archive.today/tF19R.

Takasaku, M. and Michishita, N. (高作正博・道下徳成), イラストでわかる集団的自衛権, 2014. Tokyo: Eiwa Mook.

Ts'ai, H. (2009). Taiwan in Japan's Empire Building: An Institutional Approach to Colonial Engineering. New York: Routledge.

Wang, A. (2023, July 14). Taiwan flags space ambition with domestically developed weather satellite. *Reuters.* Retrieved from http://archive.today/1upn2.

Wu, H. and Lai, J. (2023, April 18). Taiwan suspects Chinese ships cut islands' internet cables. *AP News.* Retrieved from http://archive.today/LAjI8.

© 2025 World Scientific Publishing Company
https://doi.org/10.1142/9789811298301_0009

Chapter 9

Air Superiority: The Critical Element for Denying a PLA Invasion of Taiwan

Sadamasa Oue

Japanese Prime Minister Yoshihide Suga and US President Joe Biden issued a joint statement titled "Japan–US Global Partnership for A New Era" on April 16, 2021, in which the two leaders made the historical statement: "We underscore the importance of peace and stability across the Taiwan Strait and encourage the peaceful resolution of cross-strait issues" (The White House, 2021). This is a manifest expression of the shared goal of Japan and the United States to prevent war and maintain the *status quo* across the Taiwan Strait. Now, the critical question is how to deter a more bellicose China, combined with effective use and orchestration of diplomatic, informational, and economic strategies in close cooperation with Japan, the United States, and regional allies. Most important is that Taiwan develop a viable strategy to defend itself against the overwhelming military forces of China's People's Liberation Army (PLA). Pondering the specific risks of a Chinese attack on Taiwan, Admiral Philip Davidson, former head of the Indo-Pacific Command, told senators at the Senate Armed Service Committee on March 9, 2021 that "the threat is manifest during this decade, in fact in the next six years" (Senate Armed Services Committee, 2021). Therefore, Taipei needs to rapidly develop and share its defense strategy and plans with Washington, as the United States is its sole security guarantor, as well as with Tokyo, as Japan is a proximate neighbor that will inevitably become entangled in such a conflict. This

153

way, the three nations can more effectively align their respective defense efforts and jointly enhance deterrence vis-à-vis China.

Regarding Beijing's intentions, the supreme leader of the People's Republic of China (PRC), Xi Jinping, declared in a January 2, 2019 speech marking the 40th anniversary of the Message to Compatriots in Taiwan, "We make no promise to renounce the use of force and reserve the option of taking all necessary means." The Chinese people's affairs should be decided by the Chinese people, Xi said, warning that the Taiwan question concerns China's core interests and the natural and national bond of the Chinese people ("Full text," 2019). With this intent in mind, Xi has undertaken structural reforms to reshape the PLA in order to construct a military capable of power projection and conducting complex joint operations, including those that would be involved in a Taiwan contingency. We do not know how effectively the PLA has achieved this reform goal, or whether or not they have acquired the required capabilities, but recent PLA activities around Taiwan, as well as remarks by Chinese Communist Party (CCP) and PLA leaders, reveal increasing confidence about achieving their objective if they decide to act (Oue, 2019). In fact, the PLA is developing capabilities to provide options for the PRC to dissuade, deter, or, if ordered, defeat third-party intervention during a large-scale theater campaign such as a military invasion of the Republic of China (ROC), or Taiwan. The PLA's anti-access/area-denial (A2/AD) capabilities are currently the most robust within the First Island Chain, and the PRC aims to strengthen these capabilities to reach farther into the Pacific Ocean. A serious challenge is the almost certain delay in support from US forces for several weeks, if not months. Worse, recent wargames jointly conducted by the Pentagon and RAND Corporation have shown that a military clash between the United States and China over Taiwan would likely result in a US defeat (Davis, 2020). Thus, the Biden administration must develop the capability to mobilize allies' cooperation, particularly Japan, in the event of a Taiwan contingency.

With the backdrop of the Biden administration's more intense competition with China and China's growing belligerent domestic support for unification, the PLA may believe that only by directly conquering and controlling the island can China realize its goal of national unification. To prevent Xi Jinping from taking a chance during his tenure, Taiwan must present a robust military strategy that would raise the costs and increase the risk of invasion, making Xi's calculus more difficult and less confident. This chapter proposes an active denial strategy (ADS) as the most appropriate option for Taiwan under the present operational circumstances, and air superiority is a critical element to implementing this.

9.1 The PLA's War Plan and Military Balance

9.1.1 *Joint Island Attack Campaign*

According to the PLA field manual, "Only by militarily occupying the island can we fundamentally conquer the separatist force's natural living space, and totally end the long military standoff across the strait" (Easton, 2017). The PLA has a range of options to compel annexation of Taiwan, including an air and maritime blockade, limited force or coercive options, and either a full-scale or limited invasion of Taiwan proper. Nevertheless, the military option is risky. The political risks and costs are high, and the CCP cannot afford failure or an armistice once the campaign is undertaken. In such a case, Taiwan could immediately declare independence — a move that would more than likely be supported by international condemnation against the PRC. Accordingly, as the field manual articulates, Taiwan should expect and prepare for a full-scale PLA invasion.

After his intensive study of PLA documents, Ian Easton, a researcher with the Project 2049 Institute, concluded that the Joint Island Attack Campaign (JIAC) is the PLA's conceptual war plan that is updated regularly and examined in exercises and training. The JIAC is a high-intensity, full-scale joint operation involving missile and air raids, air and maritime blockades, amphibious and airborne landings, and inland warfare. Easton analyzes the JIAC and suggests it has three phases of operations. If diplomatic, economic, and informational strategies fail, the first phase would constitute a blockade and bombing campaign to obtain uncontested control over the air and sea across the Taiwan Strait. The PLA's missions include executing mass missile raids behind the screen of electronic and cyber attacks; securing air superiority; neutralizing the ROC naval fleet; blockading major ports; and bombing Taiwan. The second phase is an amphibious landing to capture beaches, ports, and airfields near Taipei and other targeted cities. Missions would include positioning invasion forces to attack Kinmen, Matsu, and Penghu; embarking amphibious troops; clearing mines and beach obstacles; conducting surprise assaults on targeted beaches, seaports, and airstrips; and landing multiple amphibious divisions in two major waves of attack. The third phase is to engage in combat on the island itself to occupy Taiwan and control the surviving local population. The missions include securing footholds on Taiwan; building up major landing zones and offloading a large occupying force; capturing strategic terrain and military bases inland; capturing Taipei and other major cities; instituting martial law; and clearing the mountains of guerrilla defenders. As such, the JIAC would be a complex joint operation relying on coordinated, interlocking campaigns for logistics, air, and naval support, as well as information operations and electromagnetic warfare. Moreover, the PLA must consider the intervention of US forces that would significantly, if not decisively, enhance an already fortified Taiwan defense. Beijing has been keenly aware of the necessity to overcome these challenges.

China continues to build capabilities that would contribute to a full-scale invasion, including significant increases in the numbers of ballistic and cruise missiles, new-generation fighters, and amphibious assault ships. The PLA might be able to hold US forces back beyond the first island chain and defend critical assets on the Chinese mainland using integrated air and missile defense systems. "A 25-year campaign of ship-building and weapons procurement, begun in direct response to the humiliation of 1996, has provided the PLA Navy (PLAN) a fleet of 360 ships compared with America's 297" ("China's growing military," 2021).

Moreover, Chairman Xi, accompanied by two vice chairs of the Central Military Commission, attended a ceremony to commission three large warships on April 23, 2021, including a destroyer, a helicopter-carrier, and a ballistic-missile submarine. Considering the accelerated acquisition of weapons suitable for an amphibious operation, coupled with the structural reforms making the PLA capable of conducting complex joint operations, it would seem that Xi intends to keep his word that he will not pass on the responsibility of dealing with the cross-strait split to the next generation ("Full text," 2019). Therefore, Taiwan should prepare for a full-scale invasion as described in the JIAC.

9.1.2 *Military balance of air and missile power*

Is the threat that China's conventional air and missile forces pose to the ROC Air Force (ROCAF) and Navy manageable? This is an important question, because if the conclusion is wrong, Taiwan's exposure to Chinese bombardment and missile attacks at the outset of war would be far higher and more decisive, and this would allow the PLA to freely and arbitrarily conduct subsequent amphibious and airborne landing operations. This vulnerability — which depends on whether Chinese precision strikes will be effective against Taiwan's defenses — will remain a critical factor in Taiwan's ability to deter or withstand Chinese use of force. Therefore, determining the correct military balance of the PLA and the ROC military is a major focus of this chapter.

China's multi-decade military buildup and modernization have resulted in serious disparities of military capabilities across the strait, and the gap is growing. The PLA's conventional precision strike forces include over 600 short-range ballistic missiles (SRBMs), more than 150 medium-range ballistic missiles (MRBMs), 200 intermediate-range ballistic missiles (IRBMs), more than 300 land-attack cruise missiles (LACMs), ground attack munitions, anti-radiation UAVs, and artillery-delivered high-precision munitions (Commission, 2020). China's fourth- and fifth-generation fighters number over 1,000 in total, whereas Taiwan operates only 300 fourth-generation fighters. The recently announced sale of 66 F-16Vs to Taiwan, although meaningful, will not significantly change the military balance. Furthermore, the PLA Air Force (PLAAF) Eastern Theater Command (ETC) has recently been given higher priority in receiving the PLAAF's most advanced tactical aircraft, such as the advanced Shenyang J-16 multi-role aircraft and the new low-observable Chengdu J-20A design. This reflects the PLA's belief that airpower will be a key factor in maritime or amphibious operations across the Taiwan Strait. For air defense, the PLA deploys S-300 and S-400 surface-to-air missiles (SAMs) along the Chinese coastline. The S-400 consists of radar with 400 km coverage and several types of missiles with a range from 40 km to 400 km, posing a significant threat to the ROCAF counterattack forces beyond the strait ("The Military Balance," 2021).

Although the total force capabilities of the PLA are capable of overwhelming those of the ROC military, Beijing must determine the allocation of forces to JIAC and strategic reserves for other contingencies. The ETC likely executes operational control over national defense matters related to Taiwan and Japan, including contingencies in and around the Taiwan Strait and the Senkaku/Diaoyutai Islands. In 2019, the ETC focused on a series of training exercises to improve joint operations and combat readiness, organizing exercises and drills consisting of long-distance training and mobilization, aerial combat, and live-fire training (Commission, 2020). The PLA units located within the ETC include three group armies, a naval fleet, two marine brigades, two air force bases, and one missile base. The area of responsibility of the

Southern Theater Command (STC) covers mainland and maritime Southeast Asia, including the South China Sea. This geographic area implies that the STC is responsible for securing the South China Sea, supporting the ETC in any invasion of Taiwan, responding to territorial disputes, and assuring the security of Sea Lines of Communication (SLOCs), seen as vital to China's global ambitions. Considering the primary role of the ETC, and the supporting one of the STC, the PLA will likely employ most of its forces and military infrastructure in the ETC as well as some forces and air bases close to Taiwan in the STC as an augmentation or reserve force in waging the JIAC.

The ROCAF currently operates 55 Mirage 2000s, 87 F-5Es, 143 F-16A/Bs, and 127 F-CK-1s, of which approximately 300 are fourth-generation fighters. Taiwan developed and operates several types of ballistic and cruise missiles, including the following: Hsiung Feng I and II anti-ship missile systems, Hsiung Feng III, which is a medium-range supersonic missile capable of destroying both land-based targets and naval targets, and Hsiung Feng IIE, a surface-to-surface cruise missile system with a range of 1,000 km (620 miles), putting the Yangtze River and Pearl River deltas within reach. The air-to-ground cruise missile Wan Chien is believed to have a range of up to 200 km and is capable of striking airfields near the Chinese coast. Moreover, the supersonic land-attack missile Yun Feng is said to be Taiwan's most powerful weapon. It has a range of at least 1,500 km, making it capable of striking targets in China's heartland, including Beijing, Tianjin in the north, Shanghai in the east, and the Three Gorges Dam in central China (Chung, 2020). The Yun Feng is outfitted with a ramjet engine and can carry a semi-armor-piercing high-explosive fragmentation warhead. These surface-to-surface missiles (SSMs) and air-to-surface missiles (ASMs) would play a decisive role in the active defense of the ROCAF, degrading the PLA's air capabilities so as to prevent the PLA from assuming air superiority. Although the numbers of missiles and their deployments are highly classified, employing these assets in conjunction with fighter aircraft will be critical if Taiwan is to develop and execute a winning strategy against the JIAC.

Regarding Taiwan's air defense, the Patriot Advanced Capability (PAC)-3 guided air and missile defense system provides a long-range, all-altitude, all-weather air defense system to counter tactical ballistic missiles, cruise missiles, and advanced aircraft. The American company, Lockheed Martin, was recently awarded a US$620 million contract to upgrade more than 440 PAC-3 missiles for Taiwan to reinforce the island's arsenal (Liu *et al.*, 2020). In addition, the Avenger Air Defense System is a self-propelled surface-to-air missile system that offers mobile, short-range air defense protection for ground units against cruise missiles, unmanned aerial vehicles, low-flying fixed-wing aircraft, and helicopters. Taiwan also deploys a series of indigenously developed Tien Kung I–III surface-to-air anti-ballistic missile and anti-aircraft defense systems. The Tien Kung III's firing range has been boosted from about 45 km to about 70 km, allowing it to intercept the PLA's guided missiles. The Tien Chien I–II series of short-range infrared-guided air-to-air missiles are equipped with fire-and-forget, radar-slave capabilities. The Tien Chien I is also the surface-to-air missile used in the Antelope tactical ground-to-air anti-aircraft defense system (Chung, 2020).

As any invasion of Taiwan would most likely begin with an exchange of missile salvo attacks followed by air raids, how to deploy and employ these missiles and war planes will determine subsequent operations on both sides.

9.2 Defense Strategy for Taiwan: Active Denial

9.2.1 *Options for deterrence and defense*

Heginbotham and Samuels (2018) argue that deterrence theories generally differentiate between two types of deterrent strategies: punishment and denial. The punishment approach relies on the ability to inflict unacceptable losses on an attacker's most valued assets, often in his home country, whereas denial seeks to deny an attacker the benefits of conquest, either through defeating his attack in set-piece battles — what they call "forward defense" — or through prolonged, active resistance — also called "active denial" (Heginbotham and Samuels, 2018). Considering the huge imbalance of power favoring the PRC, and hence the asymmetric nature of any prospective cross-strait war, the punishment option does not appear to be a feasible defense strategy for Taiwan to pursue. The only meaningful military strategy for Taiwan is therefore a denial strategy, in conjunction with extended nuclear deterrence by the United States.

To decide which denial strategy is more appropriate for Taiwan, several variables need to be assessed, including the relative strength of the antagonists (namely, the PLA), the potential benefits of exogenous factors on one side or the other, and the level and intensity of threatened conflict. The Heginbotham and Samuels (2018) theory explains that forward defense is well suited to deterrence when the practicing side (Taiwan) has the capacity to deploy military forces that are superior to those that a potential aggressor might bring to bear in an attack. Obviously, this is not the case in Taiwan. Regarding exogenous forces and events, forward defense relies on the likelihood of victory in a rapid set of force-on-force clashes to deter the enemy, and is not, therefore, heavily dependent on robust exogenous forces.

Active denial, on the contrary, is best suited for circumstances in which it is reasonably believed that exogenous factors will work against an attacker over time. Once Beijing decides to invade Taiwan to force unification, the PLA must seek as rapid a conquest as possible before US forces have the opportunity to intervene, whereas the ROC military must prolong the battle as long as possible, to provide enough time for US forces to arrive and change the outcome of the conflict. Finally, the political risks associated with armed aggression borne by Xi Jinping are so enormous that he cannot afford to risk failure by using half-hearted operations. Time would not be on his side. For Taiwan, the war would be a matter of survival. Accordingly, the active denial strategy is the only rational choice for Taipei, and it must prepare to meet a full-scale Joint Island Attack Campaign.

One might argue that Beijing could employ a salami-slice strategy to occupy Taiwan's remote islands, such as Taiping Island and the Pratas Islands, to achieve a *fait accompli*. In fact, even if the ROC military were to adopt a forward defense strategy, those remote islands would be difficult to defend due to their geographic features. Moreover, the PLA could use these small campaigns to reduce the ROC's air and naval forces by attrition, paving the way for a full-scale invasion against Taiwan proper. Should such an invasion take place, Taiwan must have a diplomatic strategy to mobilize international support to retake the islands so that it nullifies the *fait accompli* with non-military measures. In any case, China will not achieve its ultimate goal of unification with salami-slicing attacks alone.

9.2.2 *Implementing an active denial strategy*

Deterrence is likely to hold when a potential aggressor sees little prospects for a short, reasonably predictable victory. Even when the defender is unable to muster clearly superior forces capable of prevailing quickly in force-on-force encounters, that defender may devise a strategy to ensure

Air Superiority: The Critical Element for Denying a PLA Invasion of Taiwan 161

prolonged resistance and heightened risk to the aggressor. Thus, the denial strategy maintains a force that can continue to fight until exogenous conditions tip the balance (i.e., a US military intervention). Such a strategy would not require an immediate decisive engagement, which would place friendly forces at risk of annihilation.

It is not clear whether China has the capacity to invade and conquer Taiwan. The PLA military leadership, as well as the Chinese public at large, appear confident, although a 2020 report released by the ROC Ministry of National Defense (MND) concludes that the PLA still lacks the landing vehicles and logistics required to launch an invasion into Taiwan via the Taiwan Strait (Tu and Xie, 2020). Nevertheless, Chinese conventional military capabilities exceed Taiwan's in all categories. Without the United States to provide reinforcements, Taiwan does not have the capacity to defeat a full-scale PLA attack. Moreover, China has the means to attack US Forces stationed in Japan, and as far as Guam (roughly 3,500 km from China). By employing attacks with cruise and ballistic missiles, together with a growing force of traditional air and naval assets, Beijing could try to achieve quick victory over Taiwan while using its A2/AD strategy to keep US forces from intervening.

The most serious threat to Taiwan is China's large and sophisticated force of ballistic and cruise missiles that could target air bases and other critical infrastructure. These systems are highly accurate and could close runways and destroy air defenses, opening the door to follow-on attacks by Chinese aircraft. Taiwan needs to efficiently and effectively deploy air and missile defense assets including the Patriot PAC3 and Tien Kung III, to maintain the ability to survive, fight, and ultimately dispel invading forces.

Therefore, the most important characteristic of the active denial strategy is a resilient force posture. To achieve this, Taipei should enhance the survivability of its military elements, even at the expense of such inland combat capability as the M1A2T Abrams tanks. A combination of measures should be applied to improve resiliency, including dispersion of key assets across an expanded basing structure; mobility and deception; improved recovery capabilities; and balanced active and passive defenses. Conversely, an active denial strategy should not be construed as exclusively a reactive defense. Taiwan should adopt quick counterattack strategies whenever appropriate to strike PLA air power at their bases, and sea power in the strait, making the adversary's assessment and judgment difficult. Furthermore, the ROC military's counterattacks, even if sporadic, would demonstrate Taiwan's will to keep fighting, while appealing to the United States and the international community for assistance.

The key objective of an active denial strategy is to gain sufficient time to make the most use of exogenous factors that might work against China during a protracted conflict. The first and foremost question is the prospect of US intervention. Some ROC military officers admit it will take at least a couple of months for US forces to come and swing the balance in favor of Taiwan. So, the longer the fight can be delayed, the better Taiwan's chances will be. Any time earned could allow US forces to disrupt China's SLOCs, known as the "Malacca Dilemma." Beijing has only a limited capacity to mitigate this vulnerability. Above all, Xi Jinping must also be concerned with the possibility of domestic instability, which would emerge if the war does not end quickly. A protracted war would introduce all kinds of uncertainties.

In summary, the ROC military's mission priorities would be, first, defending key assets that enable the government and military to continue functioning; second, disrupting the PLA's amphibious operations to buy time for US intervention; and third, counterattacking to deny and halt the PLA invading forces before US reinforcements could arrive and shift the overall balance of forces.

9.3 Active Denial Strategy and Air Superiority

9.3.1 *A prerequisite to other operations*

The PLA must establish air superiority to obtain uncontested control over the airspace across the Taiwan Strait to pave the way for its amphibious operation. China may also dispatch airborne Special Operation Forces (SOFs) by airdropping them directly into Taipei, attacking Taiwan's political leaders and government functions. However, as the majority of invading forces would arrive by amphibious means, the commander in charge would have to secure control of the skies while a fleet crosses the strait and unloads soldiers onto a Taiwan beachhead.

From the perspective of the ROC military, too, air coverage is necessary to conduct battle in the littoral zones to destroy the enemies' vessels at sea and destroy landing forces arriving onshore as well as infiltrating coastal areas. As long as the ROCAF can secure air superiority, even if limited with respect to time and place, it could confuse and degrade the

PLA's landing forces. The ROCAF should maintain at least the capability to interdict airborne landing SOFs and prevent the PLA from accomplishing swift occupation of the political capital in Taipei. In short, securing air superiority is a prerequisite for Taiwan's active denial strategy. As such, air superiority will likely be a dominant factor for the success or failure of the first phase of the JIAC for the PLA, and the active denial strategy of the ROC military.

9.3.2 *Force protection and counter air operations*

The active denial strategy has three objectives throughout its implementation. First, it aims to make the PLA's strategic calculation more difficult. The denser the fog of war becomes, the more uncertainty and chances for error there will be in the PLA's decision-making process. Although China deploys more than 1,200 SRBMs, the PLA commanding authority needs to plan how many missiles should be launched in the first wave, against which targets, how many launch waves should follow, and how many missiles must be stored as a strategic reserve. As missiles are expendable and finite, Taiwan may let the PLA use them against useless targets by using mobility, deception, camouflage, concealment, bombing resistance, jamming, and diversifying and dispersing its forces. A precision attack needs precise targeting information. Taiwan must have robust strategies to deny the PLA accurate targeting information. It will also be useful to disrupt the PLA's ISR capability to assess the extent of battle damage caused by missile attacks and air raids, as an insufficient damage assessment would necessitate another round of attack, extending operations and wasting valuable, finite munitions.

Second, a critical requirement of the strategy will be to protect and preserve critical assets to maintain air superiority at decisive nodes of the JIAC, including F-16s, E-2Ts, and essential base functions such as runways and refueling capabilities. The MND's 2019 National Defense Report lists up to eight measures for force protection. The ROC military fully understands the importance of minimizing damage and sustaining combat capability to conduct follow-up operations. Those protection measures include; (1) using designs for tunnel shelters, underground facilities, and mobility to construct a force protection capability and to strengthen multiple force backups and battlefield-survival capabilities; (2) refining rapid runway and taxiway repair capacities, reinforcing political and military command-and-control centers, constructing hardened aircraft shelters in air force bases, and establishing backup centers or mobile command-and-control systems; and (3) enhancing mobilized air surveillance and defense capabilities to react to adversarial air and missile threats (MND, 2019).

It is also necessary to set up early warning systems to detect initial missile salvo attacks so that as many vulnerable fighters as possible are capable of taking off in a flash scramble manner and are able to escape from these attacks. Those fighters may land on the highway if runways are not available due to battle damage. The annual Han Kuang Exercise is designed to validate these emergency combat quick turnaround operations. If no place can be found for landing, their ultimate destination may be Yonaguni Airport, the nearest airport in Japanese territory with a 2,000 m runway. Another critical operation for force protection is Integrated Air and Missile Defense employing PAC-3, Tien Kung I–III, and point defense missiles and artillery. Taiwan should develop a list of its most valuable assets to be protected from missile and air raids and deploy SAM systems accordingly. Rules of engagement must be crafted to effectively intercept the most harmful threat, while preventing duplicate attacks on the same targets. Some of the air defense assets should be preserved to interdict the PLA's airborne landing operation.

The third objective is to disrupt the PLA's operations and reduce its offensive capabilities by conducting counter air operations against high-value targets right from the beginning of the JIAC. Once the ROC military has weathered the initial missile attacks, it must strike back against PLA air bases and other high-value targets with Hsiung Feng IIE/III and Yun Feng missiles. The PLA ETC has only a few air bases across the strait from Taiwan, while many are located beyond 600 km from Taipei. Effective attacks on exposed airbases will hinder and reduce the aerial bombing that will follow the missile attacks. Probably, the best targets against which to launch these SSMs would be fighters, bombers, and other aircraft on the parking ramp during turnaround operations (i.e., refueling, reloading munitions, and quick maintenance). Regarding F-16s and other fighters, these should be employed for defensive air operations to secure air superiority. As the PLA's air defense, with its S-300 and S-400 missile systems, has a wide range of shooting coverage, the ROC military must refrain from using fighter airplanes for these counter air operations, to avoid any attrition from the enemy's air defenses. As this scenario indicates, the utility of long-range missiles such as the Hsiung Feng IIE/III and Yun Feng would be very high. While the inventory of these missiles is highly classified, the ROC military should do a target analysis on the PLA's order of battle and acquire and store the appropriate numbers for future use.

9.3.3 *Securing air superiority*

The PLA's JIAC is not a simultaneous but a phased approach strategy. This means that unless the previous phase has been completed successfully, the next operation would not be undertaken. The PLA's most important goal in the initial phase is to obtain uncontested control over the airspace across the Taiwan Strait. Only once the PLA achieves air superiority can a successful amphibious landing on Taiwan's beaches proceed. As China's landing vessels are at their most vulnerable while crossing the strait, Taiwan's surface-to-ship missile force must be capable of destroying them in the littoral zone and on the landing beaches, as emphasized in the Overall Defense Concept (ODC). However, we should expect SSM units to be targeted by PLAAF and PLAN attack aircraft. If so, Taiwan would lose any chance of repelling an invasion force at sea, unless the Taiwan air force counters and intercepts such an air-power escort.

If the PLA achieves air superiority over the island, moreover, it could launch an airborne and SOF landing operation with the aim of quickly seizing control of Taipei's political center followed by heavily armed troops. The PLA commanders, however, will have to make some tough targeting decisions, unless they have confidence in their air control. Do they launch more bombing and missile attacks, or should they move on to the amphibious and/or airborne landing? They also must assess how many of Taiwan's fighters survived, what bases are still functional, and what air and missile defense systems are still in place. Therefore, disrupting the PLA's situational awareness is as important as determining appropriate force protection measures. At the critical juncture of PLA's JIAC, Taiwan must employ air power to deny the invasion forces coming from the sea and the air, while continuing to defend and preserve air force capabilities. If done effectively and efficiently, this air superiority strategy will increase the fog of war, degrade the enemy's intelligence gathering capabilities, and reduce the enemy's confidence in their strategy.

9.3.4 *Force posture for active denial strategy*

Before the crisis, Taiwan must acquire, deploy, maintain, and exercise the force structure and weapon systems needed for an active denial strategy. ROC soldiers, sailors, and airmen should be trained, and doctrines, standing operating procedures, and rules of engagement should also be developed accordingly. Priority will be force protection, air and missile defense, counter air, and offensive missile capability. Indigenous missile production must be expedited, too. While fortification of the island is being pursued, Taiwan must continuously refine its active denial strategy and create uncertainty in the PLA's ability to accurately assess Taiwan's strategy and capability to defend itself. In addition, one cannot overlook Taiwan's commercial capabilities including construction, transportation, and communications needed for mobilization to complement damage repair tasks on airbases. Finally, one must not forget strategies to mobilize civil defense forces designed to minimize civilian casualties and motivate the public to resist and support national defense.

American Foreign Military Sales (FMS) have played an important role in enhancing the ROC military's capacities as well as broadcasting the US commitment to the defense of Taiwan. The administration of former US President Donald Trump increased FMS contracts to Taiwan in terms of both quantity and quality, most notably 66 F-16C/D block 70 multirole fighters in August 2019. The contract includes 75 F-110 engines, 75 Link-16 systems, 75 AN/APG-83 fire control radars, and 120 AN/ALE-50 towed decoy systems (Lubold and Youssef, 2020). It should take a while for the ROCAF to receive all 66 F-16s together with the other systems and deploy them as operationally ready forces. Nevertheless, they will significantly enhance the ROC military's capability to secure air superiority, assuring the implementation of an active denial strategy. Furthermore, the most recent FMS case includes MQ-9 Reaper drones, land-based Harpoon anti-ship missiles, a High-Mobility Artillery Rocket System with 64 ATACMS missiles, long-range AGM-84H/K SLAM-ER cruise missiles, and external sensor pods for F-16 jets that allow the real-time transmission of imagery and data (Stone and Zengerle, 2020). These weapon systems are designed to attack coastal targets on land as well as at sea, supporting counter air and air interdiction operations.

From Taiwan's perspective, Taipei must keep an active and robust dialogue open with Washington about the ROC active denial military strategy (ADS) for its own defense and what Taiwan can expect the United States to do in supporting that strategy. Some criticize the ineffective use of scarce budgetary resources for expensive weapons such as M1At Abrams main battle tanks, amphibious assault ships, and indigenous diesel submarines (Hunzeker and Davis, 2020). These weapons, despite their high-profile capabilities, may not be ideally suited for Taiwan's ADS posture to endure a prolonged, high-intensity war, as discussed in this chapter.

Taiwan must maintain a fine balance in investing precious limited resources to support today's operational capabilities and the future force structure it needs. Faced with the Chinese threat of JIAC, Taipei should strengthen operational readiness including full storage of logistics supplies, missiles, and munitions, fulfilling all vacant posts, and preparing all weapon systems and equipment needed to support a robust air superiority capability that underpins an effective active denial strategy. According to the author's own experience in the Japan Air Self-Defense Force, FMS procurement distributes less and less budget into domestic defense industries, weakening Taiwan's own production and advanced technology capacities.

In any case, as proposed by the former US national security adviser, Robert O'Brien, Taiwan needs to turn itself into a "porcupine" to make it clear to China that the risks of attempting to invade Taiwan are not worth it, and the United States must agree on what sort of "spines" that porcupine should present (Stone and Zengerle, 2020). In addition, as important as weapon systems are for Taiwan's ADS posture, Taipei should request that the United States provide invisible yet critical support, such as early warning of PLA missile launches and air raids, battle damage assessment of PLA targets, and information warfare capabilities.

9.4 Policy Implications of the Overall Defense Concept

9.4.1 *Insufficient force protection measures*

The ROC Ministry of National Defense has developed an ODC consisting of force protection elements, waging a decisive battle in the littoral zone, and the destruction of the enemy on the beachhead. The 2019 Defense Report suggests that force protection is the key to determining the combat strength needed for extended operations. The ROC military may employ tactics involving mobility, concealment, dispersion, deception, and camouflage. Escort operations and sophisticated cyber warfare strategies will be used, as well as employing a swift and effective damage control capability to contain initial destruction caused by the enemy, and effectively support follow-on operations. This idea is consistent with the ADS proposed in this paper. Force deployment and protective measures should be implemented accordingly. Moreover, soldiers need to be trained to persevere in an enemy offensive throughout the campaign, particularly at the beginning of salvo attacks by missile forces. Reserve forces as well as civilian capabilities should be developed for such purposes as repairing damaged air base infrastructure. Recent reports have criticized the ROC military's insufficient logistics support, ineffective use of reserves, and lack of mobilization capabilities, and these problems must be urgently addressed (Feng, 2020).

9.4.2 *Forward defense vs. active denial in coastal campaign*

The ODC emphasizes Decisive Battle in the Littoral Zone and the Destruction of the Enemy at the Landing Beach as decisive campaign elements to employ the integrated capabilities of three service branches, and to give the PLA no place to land its troops. Without a doubt, amphibious landing operations are the most vulnerable moment for an invading army, providing the ROC military with an opportunity to fight force-on-force by adopting a forward defense strategy. Should Taiwan choose a forward defense strategy, the ROC military needs to employ all forces at its disposal, in particular fighter attack aircraft armed with anti-ship missiles to destroy as many enemy vessels as possible. As such air interdiction operations would inevitably expose participating ROCAF aircraft to threats of SAMs and air-to-air combat, attrition could be too high to maintain air superiority in the following operations. Therefore, the ROC military should conduct coastal defense according to an active denial strategy by mainly employing surface-to-ship missiles to destroy vessels while using fighters armed with air-to-air missiles to ensure air cover and minimize attrition. In this regard, it is good news that the most recent robust FMS sales package meets the capabilities needed for an active denial strategy.

9.4.3 *Tenacious resistance necessary*

The ODC does not explain how to fight if the PLA successfully captures a bridgehead to support a deeper invasion on the island. It would be at this critical moment that ADS would make a difference to conduct persevering operations and buy time. Military leaders need to educate Taiwan citizens about the importance of public resistance and to get rid of the sense of fatalism among so many in Taiwan. Recent polls suggest that half of all respondents believe that Taiwan will ultimately unify with China due to increasing PLA military threats (Taiwan National Security Survey, 2020). The United States must be able to count on Taiwan's resolution before it decides to wage a war against China to defend Taiwan. As for Taiwan, it must convince the United States that it is prepared to defend itself. It must have the desired capabilities, appropriate level of readiness and force structure, and correct military strategy that is strongly supported by Taiwan's people.

9.5 Conclusion

There is widespread recognition in Taiwan, as well as in Japan and the United States, that war with China would be a catastrophe, particularly as the military balance of power shifts in China's favor and Taiwan is increasingly economically dependent on China. The most desirable future for the three states is to continue to deter China from undertaking an invasion because of a miscalculation and/or overconfidence. Taiwan should take the lead in uniting Japan and the United States in efforts to send a strong strategic message to China. Taiwan's adoption of an active denial strategy supported by a robust air superiority capability will be a strong demonstration of such a message.

Acknowledgments

This chapter is a result of the collaborative project "An Interdisciplinary Approach to Contemporary East Asia Studies" [21REN283] at St. Andrew's University Research Institute.

References

China's growing military confidence puts Taiwan at risk (2021, May 1). *The Economist*. Retrieved from http://archive.today/t09H8.

Chung, L. (2020, July 11). The Taiwan missile tech aimed at keeping a PLA attack at bay. South China Morning Post. Retrieved from http://archive.today/Y7OJW.

Commission (2020). Military and security developments involving the People's Republic of China 2020: Annual Report to Congress. US-China Economic and Security Review Commission. Retrieved from https://media.defense.gov/2020/Sep/01/2002488689/-1/-1/1/2020-DOD-CHINA-MILITARY-POWER-REPORT-FINAL.PDF.

Davis, D. L. (2020, August 6). Can America successfully repel a Chinese invasion of Taiwan? *The National Interest*. Retrieved from http://archive.today/ttgnX.

Easton, I. (2017). The Chinese invasion threat: Taiwan's defense and American strategy in Asia. Project 2049 Institute.

Feng, J. (2020, October 30). Taiwan ex-general says Taiwan soldiers lack weapons: 'Are they supposed to fight with brooms?' *Newsweek*. Retrieved from http://archive.today/RKchf.

Full text: 2019 New Year Speech by President Xi Jinping (2018, December 31). *CGTN*. Retrieved from https://america.cgtn.com/2018/12/31/full-text-2019-new-year-speech-by-president-xi-jinping.

Heginbotham, E. and Samuels, R. J. (2018). Active denial: Redesigning Japan's response to China's military challenge. *International Security*, 42(4), 128–169. Retrieved from http://dx.doi.org/10.1162/isec_a_00313.

Hunzeker, M. and Davis, B. (2020, August 10). The defense reforms Taiwan needs. *Defense One*. Retrieved from https://www.defenseone.com/ideas/2020/08/defense-reforms-taiwan-needs/167558/.

Liu, X., Guo Y., and Du, Q. (2020, July 10). US arms sales to Taiwan more 'symbolic' than of military value: Expert. *Global Times*. Retrieved from https://www.globaltimes.cn/content/1194154.shtml.

Lubold, G. and Youssef, N. A. (2020, September 16). US set to sell Taiwan $7 billion in arms. *Wall Street Journal*. Retrieved from http://archive.today/PtT4J.

MND (2019). 2019 National defense report of Taiwan. Ministry of National Defense of the Republic of China. Retrieved from https://www.ustaiwandefense.com/tdnswp/wp-content/uploads/2020/02/Taiwan-National-Defense-Report-2019.pdf.

Oue, S. (2019, April 12). Taiwan kaikyō no rankiryū chūkan-sen shinpan ga maneku Nakadai funsō no kiki [Risks of the China-Taiwan Conflict Caused by the Turbulence of the Median Line in the Taiwan Strait]. *Mainichi Shimbun*. Retrieved from https://mainichi.jp/premier/politics/articles/20190411/pol/00m/010/003000c.

Senate Armed Services Committee (2021, March 9). Hearing to receive testimony on United State IndoPacific command in review of the defense authorization request for fiscal year 2022 and the future years defense program. Retrieved from https://www.armed-services.senate.gov/imo/media/doc/21-10_03-09-2021.pdf.

Stone, M. and Zengerle, P. (2020, September 16). Exclusive: US pushes arms sales surge to Taiwan, needling China — Sources. *Reuters*. Retrieved from https://www.reuters.com/article/us-usa-taiwan-arms-exclusive/exclusive-u-s-pushes-arms-sales-surge-to-taiwan-needling-china-sources-idUSK BN2671M4.

Taiwan National Security Survey (2020, October). Duke University and National Chengchi University. Retrieved from https://sites.duke.edu/pass/taiwan-national-security-survey/.

The Military Balance 2021 (2021, February). International institute for strategic studies. Retrieved from https://www.iiss.org/publications/the-military-balance/the-military-balance-2021.

The White House, Office of the Press Secretary (2021). US-Japan joint leaders' statement: "US — Japan global partnership for a new era" [Press release]. Retrieved from http://archive.today/BusAF.

Tu, A. and Xie, D. (2020, September 1). China not ready for full assault: Report. *Taipei Times*. Retrieved from https://www.taipeitimes.com/News/front/archives/2020/09/01/2003742623.

© 2025 World Scientific Publishing Company
https://doi.org/10.1142/9789811298301_0010

Chapter 10

Prescribing Taiwan's Submarine and Mine Acquisition Policy: A Japanese Perspective

Masahiro Matsumura

In late September 2023, the Republic of China Navy (ROCN) finally unveiled its first domestically made conventional submarine. With a displacement of approximately 2,500 tons and a length of 70 m, or 230 feet, the boat will be delivered to the navy by the end of 2024 after several tests, and commissioned into service in early 2025. The ROCN plans to build an additional seven subs of the same class. The first boat cost US$1.54 billion, including the initial cost of installations, equipment, and necessary services, which is about three times as expensive as the most advanced Japanese conventional submarine of comparable size. This raises serious questions about its cost-effectiveness and opportunity cost. Also, it remains to be seen if the subs are combat effective[1] due to the longtime technical inabilities and technological risks involved[2] (Wong, 2023; Chau, 2023; Yeo, 2023). This chapter will attempt some in-depth

---

[1] For example, the case of the Australian homegrown *Collins*-class subs, which are similar in size and requirements, are known to be severely ridden with technical problems, making it sub-optimal in combat readiness (Wroe, 2012).

[2] It is well known that Taiwan seriously lacks the production capabilities of not only effective ultra-high tensile steel, major parts and subsystems, especially weapon systems, but also system integration technologies. Certainly, parts and subsystems can be imported, but

discussion on these important but often overlooked aspects, especially in Taiwan, in pursuit of remedial policy proposals. An early draft of this chapter was presented at an online workshop co-organized by St. Andrew's University and National Chengchi University, held in December 2021. The current author of this chapter is highly confident that the line of discussion and policy proposals at that time remain sufficiently valid and appropriate.

10.1 The Strategic Context

With China's nakedly invasive neo-colonialism and quest for hegemony ever intensifying, Taiwan once again finds itself the focal point of threats to the peace and security of the western Asia-Pacific region. Due to the huge disparity in military and economic power across the Taiwan Strait, the Republic of China (ROC) on Taiwan is deepening its already heavy reliance on its sole security guarantor, the United States, while expectations are growing that Japan, a major US ally, might decide to serve as a supplement and/or complement to that deterrent. That possibility is more important now than ever, as US power and commitment to the region are appearing less and less reliable, given that its position of regional hegemony is suffering a significant decline, notwithstanding the rhetoric in support of Taiwan from the administration of US President Joe Biden heating up, surpassing even that of the previous Trump administration, which was particularly hawkish on China. Unfortunately, Japan alone is unable to fill that gap, as it lacks adequate power-projection capabilities and remains hamstrung by heavy constitutional constraints on the overseas deployment of its military assets.

Speaking on the topic of a US–Japan global partnership for a new era, the then Japanese prime minister, Yoshihide Suga, issued a joint statement with Biden on April 16, 2021, in which the two leaders vowed to stand together in the event of a possible Chinese aggression against Taiwan. Both countries were under heavy domestic political and fiscal constraints, however, as well as dealing with the ongoing COVID-19 pandemic at the time, and so specific defense and military measures had yet to be taken (The White House, 2021).

---

cannot be easily integrated, including for controlling the sound volume of the acoustic signature that influences the stealthiness of the boat.

Thus, Taiwan urgently needs to beef up its self-defense capability to survive a possible Chinese aggression until the US military is able to intervene with the support of the Japan–US alliance. It goes without saying that Taiwan is not and will never be able to reverse its utterly unfavorable military power imbalance *vis-à-vis* the People's Republic of China (PRC), and yet it is essential that Taipei maximize its defensive capabilities through cost-effective armaments despite its limited resources.

From the Japanese perspective, Taipei has proven unable to push itself forward through the use of cost-effective armaments, and it is unlikely that decision makers will change the current line on arms acquisition policy. The intention of this chapter is to spur discussion of this important issue, particularly within Taiwan's defense establishment and among external stakeholders. To that end, this chapter will examine the political obstacles and offer specific policy proposals with respect to naval armaments, with a focus on submarine and mine acquisitions, which present themselves as feasible, cost-effective acquisitions.

10.2 Political Obstacles

Due to the huge cross-strait disparity in military and economic power, Taiwan can never be a meaningful player in international power politics, and will remain a pawn therein. Taiwan alone is simply not able to reverse the military and economic imbalance that has developed across the Taiwan Strait, and thus it relies totally on the United States to act as security guarantor and to defend the island from invasion by the People's Liberation Army (PLA). Despite high-sounding diplomatic rhetoric such as the aforementioned joint statement, the strength of America's commitment to the region and its hold on hegemony are increasingly tenuous. It would seem therefore that Taiwan has two alternatives (The White House, 2021; Matsumura, 2020b).

The first is to stress that Washington make a solid commitment to the defense of Taiwan, regardless of the state of affairs, and sufficient military power to back up that commitment (Zhang, 2020). Such a politically rational stance would help assuage the Taiwanese electorate's anxiety and accrue political support for the administration of ROC President Tsai Ing-wen. The other would be to appease China while procrastinating on unification, with the aim of negotiating for favorable terms on some form of autonomy. This second tack will become unavoidable if the first approach is judged to be unsustainable (Su, 2015, 2017, 2018a, 2018b; Mendis and Liu, 2020).

Since the outbreak of the Wuhan pneumonia in early 2020, the PRC has ramped up its saber-rattling against Taiwan, perhaps to distract from its culpability for the worldwide pandemic. It does so by threatening to unleash its historically unprecedented military might against its democratic neighbor — a neighbor that had earned media plaudits and international respect for its successful handling of the outbreak. Given China's highly aggressive stance of late, the ROC armed forces need to ensure high survivability against the salvos of China's massive ballistic and cruise missiles targeting its bases and military facilities, as well as the weapons platforms and vehicles therein. This missile assault would be followed by massive, repetitive, and continual air raids by PLA aircraft. Despite annual military exercises to practice the use of highways as runways in the event of a full-scale attack, a significant portion of ROC military aircraft remain highly vulnerable to those salvos and raids, except for several squadrons of air superiority fighters housed in classified underground air stations in Taiwan's mountainous areas. Taiwan's small submarine fleet, consisting of two medium-sized and two larger boats, will not be fully effective for combat missions in the shallow Taiwan Strait, where the average water depth is only around 60 m. Major surface combatant vehicles, such as those homeported at the Suao Naval Base in northeastern Taiwan, will have to stay there in wartime, given that the ROC Navy lacks a sufficient anti-submarine warfare (ASW) capability ("Taiwan Submarine Capabilities," 2021).

Thus, to defend Taiwan and mount an effective counterattack against China's invasion forces, Taipei needs to swiftly acquire and deploy cost-effective low- to medium-tech weapons systems within the limits of its existing fiscal and human resources, which makes medium- to long-term acquisition of expensive high-tech platforms an unjustifiable expense.[3] In reality, however, Taipei appears to have continuously placed an emphasis on acquisition of expensive, high-tech weapons platforms. Specifically, Taipei remains eager to develop not only full-sized submarines, but also light combat aircraft and major surface combatant vessels, among others,

---

[3] The Trump administration's arms export plan of 2019 *vis-à-vis* Taiwan follows this logic in part, given that it includes 108 major battle tanks (M1A2 Abrams) and 250 manportable surface-to-air missiles (FIM-92 Stingers) ("Gunji-Warudo Chuugoku no Yuutsu," 2019).

as shown by official announcements of the government's acquisition plans and R&D policy (Liu, 2020).

In the protracted but stable state of the cross-strait confrontation, Taiwan's current platform-centered acquisition policy may be partly effective in mitigating the effects of the Chinese Communist Party's (CCP) psychological warfare, aimed at intimidating Taiwan's population. But this policy is untenable under the current heightened risk of PLA invasion[4] because it demands the immediate beefing up of Taiwan's defense capabilities. This lack of policy rationality begs the question of whether Taiwan should pursue a different approach, such as one predicated on political rationality in light of the need to attain popular support, or will industrial concerns take precedence over national security interests (Matsumura, 2020a).[5]

A case can be made against the utility of Taiwan's acquisition of large-displacement submarines, and that as a cost-effective arms acquisition policy alternative, the defense budget would be better spent on the acquisition and deployment of mines, as well as on larger numbers of smaller boats, even midget submarines.

10.3 Policy Alternatives

10.3.1 *Little operational need*

In 2017, the ROC government launched a plan for the indigenous development of conventional large-displacement submarines. The move was made out of irritation and impatience, because the country has long been prevented from acquiring a foreign-made submarine. As a maritime middle power, Taiwan has long been eager to field an effective submarine force, as a small but indispensable component of its overall naval power. Even a single submarine in a specific area of operation will exert a significant deterrence effect due its stealthy nature, making it an effective semi-strategic weapon against China (Matsumura, 2017; Jin, 2019, p. 11).

---

[4]Given the dynamics of its demographic onus, China will most likely follow a long-term path to a geriatric peace but demonstrate a mid-term bellicosity for regime survival that involves using a small war as diplomatic instrument (Matsumura, 2014).

[5]Luttwak points out South Korea's failed acquisition of M47 Patton tanks due to its priority on economic and commercial interests (Luttwak, 2020, p. 140).

178 M. Matsumura

Looking closely, however, large-displacement submarines would hardly meet Taiwan's operational and tactical needs. The planned boat will be approximately 70 m long, with a beam of 8 m and a height of 18 m, and be between 2,000 and 3,000 tons in displacement (Wang, 2019). A boat that size would not have the spatial maneuverability to operate well in the shallow Taiwan Strait, whose average depth is around 60 m, and half of which is less than 50 m deep. There is also the problem of significant diffuse reflection of sonar waves, which are essential for blind underwater navigation. Moreover, Taipei has little operational need to control the deep open seas of the western Pacific, because China's amphibious assault forces will surely attempt to establish a beachhead on the island's west coast, which is not only closer but is topologically more suitable than its rocky east coast for landing and disembarkation. Given its limited military power, the ROC should rather concentrate almost exclusively on the defense of the island's west coast, leaving the sea control of the wider maritime theater of operation facing the Pacific, as well as its southbound and northbound Sea Lines of Communication (SLOCs), to the US Navy and, to a lesser extent, to the Japan Maritime Self-Defense Force.

10.3.2 *Inadequate technological capabilities*

For several decades, leaders in Taipei have tried in vain to purchase foreign-made submarines, because the necessary engineering, production, and system-integration expertise to build them domestically did not exist in Taiwan (Fumitani, 2015). This is evidenced by the surplus nature of Taiwan's extant sub fleet: a pair of vintage US-made World War II-era submarines and two Dutch boats built in the early 1980s. The ROC government has long been unable to find a willing submarine exporter due to the severe international isolation imposed on the country since its diplomatic derecognition by an overwhelming majority of the nations of the world. After Washington switched recognition to Beijing in 1979, members of the US Congress agreed to continue to act as Taiwan's security guarantor and to preserve the cross-strait *status quo*. To that end, Congress passed the Taiwan Relations Act, institutionalizing this relationship and vowing to supply Taiwan with defensive weapons — a designation that effectively excludes submarines. All other sub-exporting countries have followed suit for fear of diplomatic, trade, and other retaliation by China.

Given China's rapidly growing military power, including its submarine fleet, Washington has been aware of the need to strengthen Taiwan's ability to repel PLA forces in a Chinese invasion long enough for the US military to come to the rescue. In 2001, the then US president, George W. Bush, agreed to sell eight diesel-electric submarines to Taiwan. Thereafter, however, the United States and its major allies became increasingly economically interdependent on China, and needed to enlist Beijing's help on international security concerns. As a result, subsequent US administrations have dishonored the 2001 agreement by effectively ignoring Taiwan's high-profile requests for submarines.

In April 2018, Washington approved a license for the necessary technology transfers in aid of Taiwan's domestic submarine plan,[6] through which US defense contractors could help Taiwan construct its own submarines. The United States is no longer able to export large-displacement conventional submarines because it no longer manufactures them, having shut down its production lines several decades ago.[7] Today, America only produces nuclear submarines that carry a backup diesel engine, but it has already lost the engineering expertise needed for conventional submarine building. Re-establishing an obsolete production line using old design drawings and other records would not only be costly, it would be a practical impossibility. The only help the United States can offer Taiwan is in the area of in-service subsystems and relevant portions of system integration, not for total system integration. Moreover, the United States lacks Air-Independent Propulsion and related system integration technologies, the net result being that Taipei will have no choice but to rely on at least one major active conventional submarine exporter in addition to the United States.

As the US relationship with China has shifted from one of strategic partnership to an open rivalry over regional hegemony, Washington's long-time behavior of restraining Taiwan from acquiring combat-ready submarines has shifted to a policy of proactive technology assistance, playing the role of intermediary between Taiwan and various sub exporters. In September 2018, it was reported that retired experts from two Japanese submarine manufacturers — Mitsubishi Heavy Industries (MIH) and

---

[6] This includes a combat management system, sonar systems, modern periscopes, and weapon systems in addition to the Mk-48 advanced heavyweight torpedo that was approved in June 2017 (Yeo, 2018).

[7] The last US *Barbel*-class conventional sub was decommissioned in 1990.

Kawasaki Heavy Industries (KHI) — had been invited to Taiwan for engineer training and a feasibility study (Strong, 2018). In March 2020, some 30 contracted engineering consultants from Germany, Italy, the United Kingdom, the United States, Japan, and South Korea arrived to take part in various parts of Taiwan's homegrown submarine project (Yang, 2020). The move affected an air of cooperation among private corporations and individuals, though it was made possible by at least tacit government approval, and possibly by positive government endorsement, given the discretion that export control authorities have to block military technology transfers. This collective approach may help collaborating countries and corporations buttress against China's pressure and retaliation.

Yet, the prospects for the project are bleak because Taipei chose a South Korean sub builder, Daewoo Shipbuilding & Marine Engineering Co., Ltd, (DSME) to lead the project. Many South Korean engineering advisers reportedly attended the groundbreaking ceremony in November 2020 at the CSBC Corporation shipyard in Kaohsiung ("Taiwan no 'Kokusan-Sensuikan'," 2021). This suggests that other engineers were either largely excluded, or they played mere secondary adviser roles. Certainly, DSME has given Indonesia a license to build improved *Chang Bogo*-class subs, which is a South Korean license-built version of the German Type 209-1200 class, and the company's engineers recently helped Jakarta to complete local building of a 1,400-ton diesel submarine capable of sailing more than 50 days submerged (Vavasseur, 2021). But South Korean submarines are notorious for their poor performance, including serious lack of stealth and low battery performance during submerged operations ("Kankoku no 'Sukuigatai' Sensuikan-Jijyou," 2015; Okada, 2016; Min, 2020). There also exist significant diplomatic risks, in that China may exert strong pressure on the South Korean government and DSME to stop assisting Taiwan with its sub-building project.[8]

10.3.3 *Fiscal constraints and low cost-effectiveness*

Even though conditions in the international political situation and the defense industry may have improved in Taiwan's favor, homegrown subs

---

[8]Local Taiwanese media reported that all the South Korean submarine engineers in Kaohsiung were abruptly returning in small groups to their country, presumably due to Chinese pressure (Huang, 2021).

Prescribing Taiwan's Submarine and Mine Acquisition Policy   181

may prove to be inadequate in terms of stealth and combat effectiveness, leaving the ROC Navy with suboptimal capabilities and significant cost overruns. The former involves the risk of being unable to achieve the required warfighting capabilities or field an effective force structure, while the latter problem presents a significant opportunity cost for the acquisition of alternative cost-effective weapons. Given that NT$493 billion (US$1.77 billion) has been budgeted for the very first submarine to be built ("Taiwan, Hatsu no 'Jimae'," 2020), eight submarines in total will cost about US$16 billion and consume a significant portion of Taiwan's overall defense budget ("Taiwan's submarine-building plan," 2021).

If this proves to be the case, and Taiwan's first domestically produced submarine is found to significantly underperform the requirements placed on it, there will be a strong temptation to cancel subsequent boats in the ambitious submarine project in favor of a focus on the swift acquisition and deployment of more cost-effective weapons, especially as by then Taiwan's time will be rapidly running out before the growing Chinese threat becomes a reality.[9] It is therefore important to begin a discussion of alternative cost-effective naval weapons that can be swiftly deployed to build up Taiwan's defensive capabilities against a PLA invasion.

10.4 Weapons Systems Alternatives

10.4.1 *Small submarines*

Given the above constraints and limitations, Taiwan can acquire a dozen small submarines, and possibly two medium-sized submarines with a standard displacement of 450–900 tons, to replace the ROC Navy's Dutch-made *Zwaardvis*-class boats. Such submarines only need to submerge to 100 m below sea level, and no more than 200 m, making them most suitable for littoral operations in the shallow Taiwan Strait and its immediate vicinity to guard against a possible full amphibious invasion from China. Of course, this would exclude missions to the western Pacific and the seas along the eastern coast of Taiwan. These operational constraints mean that Taiwan's need for submarines could be satisfied by

---

[9]US Admiral Philip Davidson stated that China could invade Taiwan within the next six years, in his estimation. He made the comments at his nomination hearing on March 9, 2021 as the 25th Commander of the US Navy Indo-Pacific Command at the US Senate Armed Services Committee (Davidson, 2021).

acquiring highly reliable boats made to the technological standards of the 1960s and 1970s, particularly given China's notoriously poor ASW capability (Murray, 2014, pp. 24–26).

As discussed earlier, Taiwan needs to give up its aspiration for a limited blue water submarine warfare capability and instead seek to field a sufficient littoral/cross-strait submarine warfare capability, while relegating control over the wider sea areas to the US–Japan alliance. It may be possible for Taipei to secure technology transfers from a major sub-exporting country to achieve this limited purpose, as it would not technically change the cross-strait *status quo* or break the rules governing transfers of anything more than defensive weapons to Taiwan. This conflicts with the policy decision of the current Tsai administration to build large diesel submarines between 2,500 and 3,000 tons in displacement, which could provoke Beijing into exerting political pressure on South Korea, to say nothing of the technological and fiscal risks and opportunity costs involved. Apparently, the South Korean government, and DSME in particular, have taken significant risks by overtly ignoring the restriction on changing the cross-strait *status quo*, which could possibly result in the production of an underperforming first sub and, at worst, termination of Taiwan's sub-building project altogether.

When and if the current ambitious sub plan fails, Taipei will have to recalibrate the project toward a lower-budget effort to field small subs with modest technical requirements to meet strict operational needs, minimizing the fiscal opportunity cost. The country can rely on Japan, as the only active builder of advanced conventional submarines that has a stake in Taiwan's security, while buttressing its sole security guarantor, the United States, through a robust bilateral alliance. A relatively low level of technology transfer and technical cooperation on small submarines may be feasible, given the US–China rivalry over hegemony. The US and Japanese governments have already taken an unprecedented step by acquiescing to the informal involvement of Japan's two major submarine builders, MIH and KHI, in the ongoing Taiwan submarine project (Strong, 2018; Yang, 2020).

This support could take a step forward if Japan were to share with Taiwan the design blueprints and other records of its small, outdated, homegrown submarines, such as the *Hayashio* and *Natsushio* classes. The channel for such information-sharing would be circuitous but feasible, taking advantage first of the information security agreement between Tokyo and Washington, and then between Washington and Taipei. When necessary, Tokyo and Taipei could conclude a bilateral agreement that would enable direct military technology transfer, emulating the Protection

Prescribing Taiwan's Submarine and Mine Acquisition Policy 183

of Information Agreement of 1981 between the American Institute in Taiwan and the Taipei Economic and Cultural Representative Office in the United States. Although such technical cooperation alone would never enable the actual construction of submarines with high reliability and effectiveness, it would surely facilitate the advancement of Taiwan's domestic sub-building expertise.[10]

10.4.2 *Minelaying subs and AUV/UUV*

Despite Taiwan's obsession with having large, torpedo-armed, conventional submarines, naval mines would make a cost-effective alternative[11] for deterring a PLA invasion, particularly because China lacks the necessary mine-sweeping capabilities (Hyodo, 2015, pp. 92–93). Bottom mines can be easily laid by submarines, Autonomous/Unmanned Underwater Vehicles (AUV/UUV), aircraft, and even specially outfitted fishing boats. These negative-buoyancy mines — indeed, even just knowledge of their presence — can impede and possibly prevent an attempt by enemy vessels to engage in invasion operations across the Taiwan Strait. More specifically, laying multiple-influence bottom mines on China's continental seabed off the mainland coast, especially around major naval and trade ports for blockade, will be most effective.[12]

Moreover, those mines, once in place, will impede and possibly stall China's international trade because they will disrupt its major SLOCs. This disruption will most likely be protracted, due to the serious dearth of China's mine-sweeping capability, and further compounded if it employs mines as a countermeasure against ROC naval vessels.[13]

This means that China would not be able to rely on the overwhelming number of foreign-flag commercial ships, such as container ships, bulk

---

[10]Considering Taiwan's strong industrial aspirations, this chapter excludes the option in which Japan may produce and lease outdated medium-sized submarines to the United States and then sublet them to Taiwan. A recent similar case includes Russia's lease of a nuclear attack submarine to India (Raghuvanshi, 2019).

[11]A single MK-48 torpedo costs US$2.5 million, and US$3.5 million for a Mk-48 ADCAP, while a single Italian Manta multiple-influence bottom mine can be purchased for US$25,000 (Sherman, 1998; Tossavainen, 2017).

[12]It is generally known that Taiwan lacks the capability to lay moored contact mines in the deeper waters of its western flank.

[13]China has been attempting to strengthen its mine warfare capability for decades (Erickson *et al.*, 2009).

cargo ships, and oil tankers, in addition to a minority of Chinese flag ships, nor to continue importing enough oil and natural gas from the Persian Gulf area, as well as foreign machinery, that are essential for the continued operation of China's industrial manufacturing sector. Beijing may see its ship insurance premiums skyrocket until those mines are thoroughly eliminated. China, currently the world's largest trading nation in goods, will inevitably face serious economic debilitation as that trade is curtailed, even a little. All of these factors would lead to interrupting China's economic growth, lowering social stability, and putting the very survival of the CCP regime in jeopardy. China's desire to annex the island presents an existential threat to Taiwan, and so the ROC armed forces must be prepared to attack the PRC's Achilles' heel without mercy, even if it portends a negative impact at home due to Taiwan's precarious economic dependency on China.

To achieve the limited purpose described above, it would be most cost-effective for Taiwan to possess midget submarines outfitted with mine racks on their hulls, or use torpedo tubes, to lay a series of mines. For example, Taiwan can emulate the North Korean *Yono*-class submarine, with a displacement of 130 tons, which is significantly cheaper and technologically easier to build. Taiwan can even opt for a dual-use solution, retrofitting sightseeing or pleasure submarines that are already widely available on the market for as little as US$80,000, and often made of fiber-reinforced plastics, that can easily dive 100 m below sea level, and sometimes up to 300 m. These are hypothetically capable of carrying mines if equipped with mine racks on their hulls, and would be most suitable for short-distance missions to lay mines in the Taiwan Strait. Needless to say, Taiwan can swiftly achieve acquisition and deployment of such dual-use submarines because, by definition, there are no major political or legal obstacles to their exportation to Taiwan (Hyodo, 2017, pp. 137–140).

To cope with the increased risk of a Chinese invasion, it is high time that Taiwan take a cost-effective arms-acquisition approach. This policy initiative can begin with submarines and underwater mines.

Acknowledgments

This chapter is a result of the collaborative project "An Interdisciplinary Approach to Contemporary East Asia Studies" [21REN283] at St. Andrew's University Research Institute.

References

Chau, T. (2023, September 19). Taiwan submarine dream surfaces as China tensions rise. *Nikkei Asia*. Retrieved from https://asia.nikkei.com/Spotlight/Asia-Insight/Taiwan-submarine-dream-surfaces-as-China-tensions-rise.

Davidson, P. S. (2021, March 9). Statement before the Senate armed services committee on US Navy Indo-Pacific Command Post. Retrieved from https://www.armed-services.senate.gov/imo/media/doc/Davidson_03-09-21.pdf.

Erickson, A. S., Murray, W. S., and Goldstein, L. J. (2009). Chinese mine warfare: A PLA Navy 'Assassin's Mace' capability. China Maritime Studies Institute, US Naval War College.

Fumitani, K. (2015, November). Tairiku-Chuugoku ni Taikou!? Shikashi Gijyutsu-ryoku mo Kenzou-Nouryoku mo Kakusa ha Otona to Kodomo [*To counter China with a huge capability gap vis-à-vis China? Taiwan decided for homegrown submarines*]. *Gunjikenkyu* [Japan Military Review], *50*(11), pp. 220–231.

Gunji-Warudo Chuugoku no Yuutsu — Taiwan heno Bei-Heiki-Baikyaku gai Imi surumono [*Military Issue: PRC's depression about what US arms transfer to Taiwan means*]. (2019, July 23). Sankei Shimbun. Retrieved from https://www.sankei.com/west/news/190722/wst1907220021-n1.html.

Hyodo, N. (2015). *Konnanni Yowai Chuugoku-Jinmin-Kaihogun* [*PLA's Weaknesses*]. Tokyo: Kodansha.

Hyodo, N. (2017). *Nihon No Buki De Horobiru Chuuka-Jinmin-Kyowakoku* [*Ending China with Japanese Arms*]. Tokyo: Kodansha.

Huang, Y.-J. (2021, April 15). Qianshui Guozao Hanji Gongchengshi Zaoshiya Jiang Fanguo: Haijun, Bufangbian Gongkai Shuoming [*South Korean engineers for domestic submarine building will soon return to their country under pressure*]. Up Media. Retrieved from https://www.upmedia.mg/news_info.php?SerialNo=110903.

Jin, Z. (2019, August 1). Woguo Haijyun-Qianjian-Budui Fazhan zhi Licheng [*The historical process of the development of our country's naval submarine fleet*]. *Haijun Xueshu Shuangyuekan* (Navy Academic Bimonthly), *53*(4), pp. 6–19.

Kankoku no 'Sukuigatai' Sensuikan-Jijyou: Sosei-Ranzou de Shutsugeki, Kaigunhei ha 'Semai Kannai ha Iya' to Nimmu wo Keien [*The helpless state of South Korean submarines: Sub are inoperable due to sacrifice of quality to quantity, and seamen are unwilling to be on board due to narrow living space*]. (2015, December 30). Sankei Shimbun. Retrieved from https://www.sankei.com/west/news/151230/wst1512300006-n1.html.

Liu, F.-K. (2020). Taiwan's security policy since the cold war era: A review of external military assistance and the development of indigenous defence industry. *History of Global Arms Transfer, 9*, 3–25.

Luttwak, E. N. (2020). *Rutowattsku No Nihon-Kaizo-Ron* [*Rejuvenating Japan: A National Strategy*] (2nd edn.). Tokyo: Asuka Shinsho.

Matsumura, M. (2014, December). China's demographic Onus and its implications for the Japan–US alliance: The increasing need for deterring China's aggression against the Senkaku Islands. *Jebat: Malaysian Journal of History, Politics & Strategic Studies, 41*(2), pp. 1–22.

Matsumura, M. (2017, September 25). Homegrown subs plan misfires. *Taipei Times*. Retrieved from http://www.taipeitimes.com/News/editorials/archives/2017/09/25/2003679086.

Matsumura, M. (2020a, September 23). Security key amid political swings. *Taipei Times*. Retrieved from http://archive.today/0SBHt.

Matsumura, M. (2020b, March). The Backgrounds and constraints of Tsai's landslide victory: No way out of the continuing trilemma of orthodoxy, internal and external legitimacy. *Issues & Studies: A Journal of Asian Pacific Studies, Quarterly in Japanese, 49*(3), pp. 1–36.

Mendis, P. and Liu, F.-K. (2020, May 17). The early casualties of the TAIPEI act in the post-coronavirus world. The National Interest. Retrieved from http://archive.today/WQrsk.

Min, G.-R. (2020, June 11). Daebeob "hyeondaejung-gong-eob, jamsuham bullyang chaeg-im…jeongbue 58eog-won baesanghaeya" [*Supreme Law "Hyundai Heavy Industries, responsible for submarine defects… to compensate the government of 5.8 billion won"*]. *Yonhap News Agency*. Retrieved from https://www.yna.co.kr/view/AKR20200611098200004.

Murray, W. S. (2014). Underwater TELs and China's antisubmarine warfare: Evolving strength and calculated weakness. In: P. Dutton, A. S. Erickson, and R. Martinson (eds.), *China's Near Seas Combat Capabilities (China Maritime Study, Number 11)* (pp. 17–30). Newport, RI: Naval War College China Maritime Studies Institute.

Okada, T. (2016, March 22). Kaiji-Sensuikan 'Jinryu' no Seinou ga Urayamashii, Kankoku ha Ketsukan darake, Chuugokuha Kopi [*Envy of the high performance of JMSDF submarine, Jinryu, in contrast to South Korean subs full of defects and Chinese subs as dead copies of Russian subs*]. SankeiBiz.

Raghuvanshi, V. (2019, March 8). India signs $3 billion contract with Russia for lease of a nuclear submarine. *Defense News*. Retrieved from http://archive.today/DiPQp.

Sherman, R. (1998, December 12). MK-48 Torpedo. Federation of American Scientists. Retrieved from https://fas.org/man/dod-101/sys/ship/weaps/mk-48.htm.

Strong, M. (2018, August 21). Experts from Japanese companies Mitsubishi, Kawasaki to join Taiwan submarine project. *Taiwan News*. Retrieved from https://www.taiwannews.com.tw/en/news/3511598.

Su, C. (2015, November 1). Cong daxiao sanjiaokan 'weichi xianzhuang' ['maintaining the *status quo*' from perspectives of big and small triangles]. *Lianhe bao* [*United Daily News*].

Su, C. (2017, July 27). Meiguo zai shuailuo ma? [Is the US declining?]. *Zhongguo Shibao* [*China Times*].

Su, C. (2018a, September 2–3). Zhongguo duitai dongwu de kenengxing 'shang xia' (The possibility of Communist China's military attack on Taiwan 'part I & II'). *Lianhe bao* [*United Daily News*].

Su, C. (2018b, October 7–8). Meiguo hui lai jiu ma? 'shang xia' [Will the US come to the rescue? 'Part I & II']. *Lianhe bao* [*United Daily News*].

Taiwan, Hatsu no 'Jimae'-Sensuikan wo Chatsukou, Chugoku wa Hanpatsu [China opposes the ground-breaking of Taiwan's first homegrown submarine], (2020, November 24), Nihon Keizai Shimbun [*Nikkei*]. Retrieved from https://www.nikkei.com/article/DGXMZO66567820U0A121C2FF 1000/.

Taiwan no 'Kokusan-Sensuikan' wa Kankoku-Shudou: Nihon no Gijyutsusha ha 'Kaya no Soto' ni [South Korea will lead Taiwan's homegrown sub project, with Japanese engineers left out in the cold]. (2021, February). Sentaku.

Taiwan submarine capabilities (2021, February 17). Nuclear Threat Initiative. Retrieved from http://archive.today/SjFTq.

Taiwan's submarine-building plan (2021, January). *Strategic Comments*, *27*(1). doi:10.1080/13567888.2021.1880214.

The White House, Office of the Press Secretary (2021). US-Japan joint leaders' statement: "US — Japan global partnership for a new era" [Press release]. Retrieved from http://archive.today/BusAF.

Tossavainen, T. (2017, August 17). Mine countermeasures needed for submarine access. US Naval Institute Blog. Retrieved from http://archive.today/ hvEWn.

Vavasseur, X. (2021, March 17). First Indonesian-built submarine handed over to TNI AL. *Naval News*. Retrieved from http://archive.today/1WTFw.

Wang, C. (2019, May 9). Qián jiàn zhuānyòng chǎngfáng dòngtǔ zǒngtǒng: Guó zào shì wéiyī de lù [Groundbreaking of the special plant for submarine President: National construction is the only way]. *Central News Agency*. Retrieved from //www.cna.com.tw/news/firstnews/201905090054. aspx.

Wong, T. (2023, September 28). Haikun: Taiwan unveils new submarine to fend off China. *BBC*. Retrieved from https://www.bbc.com/news/world-asia-66932808.

Wroe, D. (2012, December 129). Our sub fleet world's worst: Report. *Syndney Morning Herald*. Retrieved from https://www.smh.com.au/politics/federal/our-sub-fleet-worlds-worst-report-20121212-2b97g.html.

Yang, S. (2020, March 18). Taiwan's indigenous submarine project enters rough waters amid coronavirus restrictions. *Taiwan News*. Retrieved from https://www.taiwannews.com.tw/en/news/3899467.

Yeo, M. (2018, April 9). US State department OKs license for submarine tech sales to Taiwan. *Defense News*. Retrieved from http://archive.today/JGV3v.

Yeo, M. (2023, September 29). Taiwan launches its first homemade submarine. *Defense News*. Retrieved from https://www.defensenews.com/global/asia-pacific/2023/09/29/taiwan-launches-its-first-homemade-submarine/.

Zhang, X. (2020, March). Meiguo keneng xisheng taiwan ma? [Might the U.S. sacrifice Taiwan?]. *Mingzhi* [*Taiwan People Monthly*], 48.

© 2025 World Scientific Publishing Company
https://doi.org/10.1142/9789811298301_0011

Chapter 11

Evaluating Taiwan's Defense Strategy in a Time of Uncertainty: Diversified Challenges and Dilemma of Responses

Hon-Min Yau

Since 2016, when Tsai Ing-wen of the Democratic Progressive Party was elected president of the Republic of China (ROC), the People's Liberation Army (PLA) has increased its activities around the Taiwan Strait with frequent military exercises and aggressive air incursions. In October 2020, at the beginning of Tsai's second term in office, the then ROC Minister of National Defense Yen De-fa reported to the Legislative Yuan that the PLA had conducted 1,710 air sorties and 1,029 naval vessel sorties into Taiwan's Air Defense Identification Zone (ADIZ), which is the most median line crossings in 30 years (*Focus Taiwan*, 2020). Traditionally, both the ROC (Taiwan) and the People's Republic of China (PRC, or China) had each restrained their respective military aircraft from approaching the median line of the Taiwan Strait, which is an implicit boundary line put in place to reduce the possibility of unwanted armed contact and military escalation. However, on September 21, 2020, a spokesman for China's Ministry of Foreign Affairs, Wang Wenbin, directly discredited the median line's validity and claimed that such a tacit understanding never existed [Ministry of Foreign Affairs (China), 2020b]. Since that point of time, many PLA military activities have intentionally entered the airspace on the east side of the median line.

The frequency of the PLA's naval and air intrusions to the adjacent areas of Taiwan was substantially increased along with the numerous high-profile international visits to Taiwan since 2020, first by the speaker of the Czech Senate, Milos Vystrčil (Ministry of Foreign Affairs, 2020a), and then by the US Under Secretary of State for Economic Growth, Energy, and the US Environment, Keith Krach (Office of the President, 2020). What is even more noteworthy is that the PLA dramatically escalated the regional situation by conducting multiple military drills after then US House Speaker Nancy Pelosi's visit to Taiwan in August 2022 (Reuters, 2022), and the incident was crowned as the Fourth Taiwan Strait Crisis. More military drills followed in April 2023 after President Tsai's meeting with the then US House Speaker Kevin McCarthy in California (Shepherd and Chiang, 2023), and even after the transit of ROC Vice President Lai Ching-te through New York during his state trip to Paraguay (*Focus Taiwan*, 2023b). On September 17, 2023 alone, the PLA Air Force (PLAAF) dispatched Su-30s, J-10s, KJ-500s, and Y-20s, conducting military drills in a total of 103 sorties at the south end of the Taiwan Strait around the Pratas Islands (Ministry of National Defense, 2023).

Given these developments, some security observers have asserted that the intention of the PLA's intensified military activity is political (*Global Times*, 2020), and Taiwanese anti-war scholars have even insisted that these military activities are protests against numerous international political leaders' visits to Taiwan and high-profile Taiwanese officials' trips abroad since 2020 (*Focus Taiwan*, 2023a). Conversely, due to President Tsai's second term and her administration's US-leaning security strategy, others have interpreted China's moves as being the results of PRC leader Xi Jinping's growing political ambitions and reflective of the widespread hawkish military sentiment among the Chinese public. Both of these factors have been pushing Beijing authorities to consider using military means to deal with Taiwan (Easton, 2020; Madjar, 2020). Under such circumstances, this chapter investigates these security developments within the new context and identifies the national, regional, and international implications for the Indo-Pacific region.

11.1 A Recess of Liberal Order and Looming Military Threat

The fact is that even at the beginning of the intensifying Sino-US competition, since 2016, Taiwan has still been among the top three import partners of China in terms of cross-border trade (howmuch.net, 2020). Traditionally, international trade and global norms are two essential elements that are seen by the liberal school of thought in International Relations (IR) as being able to reduce conflict, due to the increased cost of war and the possibility of an improved understanding among the international actors involved (Barnett and Finnemore, 2004; McDonald, 2004). Following this logic, invading Taiwan would be like attacking China's own commercial supply chain, which would be an unwise decision for Beijing, especially during the economic downturn caused by the COVID-19 pandemic since 2020 and increased Sino-US technology and economic competition, which has been ongoing since 2016. Moreover, since 2020, China has been putting down the protest movement in Hong Kong and engaging in repetitive territorial clashes in the East China Sea, the South China Sea, and along the China–India border (*Al Jazeera*, 2020). Nevertheless, with the presence of China as the obvious crouching military tiger in Asia, conflicts in the Taiwan Strait seem to be approaching.

However, one of the missing elements from the above arguments of the liberal school is a democratic institution (Pevehouse, 2005; Russett and Pevehouse, 2011), which is the essential component that constrains a country's leader through accountability. The Chinese Communist Party (CCP) under Xi's leadership since 2012 has become an extremely authoritarian regime. The oxymoron is that communism in China is a deviation from Western Marxism, and not an indigenous school derived from Chinese culture. However, the CCP has meticulously encouraged its propagandistic institutions to indoctrinate the Chinese public with party dogma, and it has skillfully linked its political legitimacy to the survival of Chinese tradition. There is no democratic mechanism for power transition in China: As stated in Article 1 of its Constitution, "Leadership by the Communist Party of China is the defining feature of socialism with Chinese characteristics" (National People's Congress, 1982). According to this constitutional article, the Chinese state is a puppet of the CCP, and there are no real national interests, only the CCP's interests. The most important of these is the CCP's survival. What is more worrisome is that after Xi Jinping's third term since 2023, China moved to a further centralized political system, with the originally one-party regime now a one-man state. As exemplified by the unfortunate occurrence of Vladimir Putin's Russo-Ukraine War in 2022, Xi Jinping's political survival will outweigh all the other matters.

Hence, to maintain Xi's legitimacy and hold on power in China, the CCP under Xi has shifted away from the original Communist slogan of "Workers of the world, unite," which reflects an internationalist worldview, to focus on "the rejuvenation of the Chinese nation," a purely nationalist mantra (Chinese Communist Party, 2013). Nevertheless, Xi portrays himself as the vanguard of China's "core interests" to lead the Chinese people. Among the growing list of China's expanding core interests, the top priority for Xi and the CCP is territorial integrity. In this regard, the CCP is traditionally taking extreme actions in accordance with this nationalist narrative (Hughes, 2006). In a future cross-strait conflict, China under Xi Jinping would likely appeal to domestic nationalist sentiment and demonize any democratically established administration in Taiwan as a foreign proxy attempting to secede from "One China."

Finally, since Joe Biden took office as the president of the United States in 2021, he has largely adopted a policy of maintaining the course of action set by the previous administration, which included placing sanctions on Chinese business entities and tech competition. However, US policy during the tenure of US President Donald Trump unintentionally undermined global norms by withdrawing from many international institutions. Hence, Biden has been working very hard to build his own alliances by working with US friends and enhancing initiatives such as the Quadrilateral Security Dialogue (The Quad) including Japan, Australia, and India; and AUKUS, an enhanced trilateral security partnership between Australia, the UK, and the US. In addition, he has also clearly expressed steadfast support for Taiwan's defense four times by 2023 (Kine, 2022). Sooner or later, the American "decoupling" economic strategy will encourage US-reliant businesses to move out of China and reduce cross-border trade. In the foreseeable future, if armed conflict in the Taiwan Strait is not imminent, the possibility of such an armed conflict will undoubtedly increase, along with a retreat of the liberal international order accompanied by a waning of the constraining power of cross-strait trade and investments.

11.2 From Security Dilemma to Security Challenge

In retrospect, the median line that bisects the Taiwan Strait was imposed by the United States as a means of conflict management and to prevent a cross-strait Security Dilemma. It has been noted that after Chiang

Kai-Shek's retreat to Taiwan in 1949, the ROC military still maintained a posture of "retaking the mainland," while the PRC sought to "liberate Taiwan." After China committed multiple military aggressions in the early 1950s against Taiwan, Washington signed a military alliance pact with Taipei in 1954, the Mutual Defense Treaty between the United States of America and the Republic of China, to deter Beijing from military hostility. Though the United States did not want Chiang Kai-Shek to interpret the treaty as an invitation to retake China, it was believed that the median line was defined as a demarcation line for the US military's conflict management in the region. During the 1950s, Taiwan had a superior air force, and China often perceived ROC military aircraft activities along China's coastal region as acts of provocation. A Security Dilemma exists when one party cannot make itself more secure without making another state believe it is less secure. Hence, the United States only guaranteed security protection of Taiwan to the east of the median line at the time (Cheng, 2019). The same conception could also be noted in 1979 when the United States switched its diplomatic ties from Taiwan to China. At that time, the Taiwan Relations Act only authorized the sale of defensive weaponry, limiting both their range and firepower. In addition, the US 1972 Shanghai Communiqué with China also reaffirmed Washington's "interest in a peaceful settlement of the Taiwan question." The United States's hope was to limit the military buildup across the Taiwan Strait. Since then, both Taiwan and China have scaled back their military activities from the median line, and there has been less chance of misinterpretation and miscalculation, and the opportunity for armed conflict has been reduced.

Today, the security environment in the region is dissimilar. China's military spending is 15 times that of the ROC, and it has arguably the world's third-largest military, after the United States and Russia (US DoD, 2020). Along with the continuous buildup of its military muscle, the CCP has never renounced the option of using force against Taiwan [Taiwan Affairs Office (China), 2019]. Hence, the cross-strait security environment could arguably be located in a more offensive realist trajectory. From this perspective, a theoretical application of the Security Dilemma would naturally lead to the conclusion that war in the region is inevitable and rational (Mearsheimer, 2001, pp. 35–36). Under this course of development, the first objective of China's growing military presence in the Taiwan Strait would be a combination of political and military warfare, including salami-slicing tactics, to reduce Taiwan's options for a military defense.

China has already eroded Taiwan's defense of depth in the sky over the Taiwan Strait. With hindsight, China expanded its military presence on the west side of the median line from its coastal line after the 1996 Missile Crisis, covering the airspace zone over the Taiwan-controlled offshore islands, such as the Matsu Islands, Kinmen, and the Wuqiu Islands. In 2018, as a further indignity, China unilaterally established an air route for civilian flights — designated M503 — uncomfortably close to the median line. In addition to raising the risk of a shooting war, the civilian traffic that flies this route gives cover to the Shaanxi Y-8 military transport planes Beijing occasionally sneaks through, likely to conduct electronic surveillance and test Taiwan's monitoring capabilities (Alert 5, 2018; *Liberty Times*, 2020). In 2019, the ROC Air Force (ROCAF) concluded that the PLAAF had already successfully established six patterns of long-haul training routes around Taiwan proper, based on the PLA's frequent intrusions into ROC airspace (ROCAF Facebook, 2019). China means to conduct military training in the actual field of operations, and some military observers suspect that the PLA's intention is also to execute intelligence preparation of the battlefield around the Taiwan Strait in advance of a future conflict (Chang, 2020). In 2020, the PLA not only conducted joint military drills around the Taiwan-owned Pratas islands, but also dispatched multiple fighter jets over the median line (Chan, 2020). China's masterful expansion has gradually revised the old cross-strait *status quo*. Renowned IR scholar Ken Booth once stated that a Security Dilemma could be divided into a dilemma of interpretations and a dilemma of responses (Booth and Wheeler, 2007, pp. 4–5). As China's looming military threat with hostile intentions could not be misinterpreted by Taiwan and the international community, the old "security dilemma" in the Taiwan Strait is now considered a "security challenge" to Taiwan. With China's constant increase both in its military capacity and its intentions, there is, in fact, no "dilemma of interpretations" for Taiwan, as these PLA activities will undoubtedly become severe security challenges. In other words, the next big question surrounds Taiwan's "dilemma of responses:" namely, how should ROC policymakers react?

11.3 A Porcupine Strategy

Faced with this kind of regional development, when Joe Biden took office in 2021, he seemed to have adopted a policy of "porcupine strategy" to enhance Taiwan's capabilities (Detsch, 2021). However, the porcupine strategy is not a new proposal for Taiwan, as it is a continuation of the strategy of the Trump administration to harden the island's ability to defend itself. In fact, in October and November 2020, the US Defense Security Cooperation Agency (DSCA) approved two batches of arms sales to Taiwan, and the package included Harpoon Coastal Defense Systems (HCDS), High Mobility Artillery Rocket Systems (HIMARS), AGM-84H Standoff Land Attack Missile Expanded Response (SLAM-ER) Missiles, MS-110 Recce Pods for F-16 fighters, and MQ-9B remotely piloted aircraft.[1] According to Reuters, the United States intends to buttress Taiwan's defenses to make it difficult for China to attack (Stone and Zengerle, 2020). This concept was also explained by Trump's National Security Adviser Robert O'Brien, in a speech at the University of Nevada in Las Vegas on October 7, 2020 (Brunnstrom, 2020). As O'Brien succinctly noted, the ROC needs to "turn themselves into a porcupine" militarily, observing that "Lions [China] generally don't like to eat porcupines."

Nevertheless, academically speaking, the porcupine analogy truly has a longer historical origin. It was first discussed to describe Switzerland's successful defense against Hitler's potential invasion during the Second World War. For the usage of the term in East Asia, it was first used in relation to the Taiwan Strait by William S. Murray (2008) in his article "Revisiting Taiwan's Defense Strategy." In particular, his article argues, first, that the precision strike capabilities of the PLA's ballistic and conventional missiles will deny the ROC Air Force and Navy access to their airbases and ports. Second, Taiwan's acquisition of offensive weapons has been costly, and they are limited in range, and although they could be a means to provoke China, Murray argued that there would never be enough of them to deter a PLA invasion. Third, Taiwan should concentrate its resources on building up a standing military on the island, with a specific focus on mobile, short-range, and defensive missiles. Fourth, such a porcupine strategy is defensive by nature and should not provoke China, although it could likely discourage China from invading Taiwan. Finally, such a policy would provide enough time for the United States to deliberate a potential intervention and execute it.

Analysts have noted high similarities between the arms sale approval by the DSCA in 2020 before Trump left office and the purchasing package

---

[1] Details can be found at https://www.dsca.mil/press-media/major-arms-sales.

suggested by Murray's article (2008, pp. 16–17). Given the resurgence of interest in investigating the utility of such a porcupine strategy from both the Trump and Biden administrations and prior, the next section will revisit Murray's observations and arguments and assess their utility in the current cross-strait context.

11.4 Reflections on the Porcupine Strategy

In the study of military strategy, three critical aspects, quality, quantity, and context, are often considered in the calculation of competing parties. Although Murray's academic investigation of a porcupine strategy has made a contribution in covering the considerations of qualitative and quantitative factors in the region, the arguments seem to overlook some contextual factors.

First, Murray's (2008) arguments are based on the assumption that there is a security dilemma, not a security challenge, across the Taiwan Strait: "Offensive counterstrike weapons, furthermore, are potentially destabilizing," Murray states, noting that, "This shift in [a porcupine] strategy might also be less provocative to the PRC than Taiwan's current policy of offensive defense" (p. 4). In his assumption, Taiwan's military reduction to a purely defensive posture has the potential to contribute to regional peace. Nevertheless, China by 2022 is different from China in 2008. In 2008, Beijing prioritized the development of the Chinese economy before becoming consumed with "the status of a great country," and there were globalization concerns dulling the temptation to go to war over Taiwan. Furthermore, since 2016, China has been involved in many disagreements with the United States, including over intellectual property rights, the trade deficit, human rights, cyberattacks, and technology competition, and it also claims the objective of regaining its historical international status. While the CCP under the current General Secretary, Xi Jinping, seems determined to achieve "the rejuvenation of the Chinese nation" by the second of "Two Centenaries" (The Central Commission for Discipline Inspection, 2018), this Chinese "lion" seems hungry enough to eat the food on the plate, even if it is a Taiwanese "porcupine," to follow O'Brien's analogy. Scholars such as John F. Copper (2006) and John J. Mearsheimer (2018) predict that a conflict in the Taiwan Strait is very probable.

Second, Murray's (2008) strategy as enunciated in his article is based on a single scenario and static tactic of China's island invasion, and his porcupine strategy is not only strategically defensive but also tactically passive (p. 3). His arguments are based on the scenario of an island invasion, which starts with bombardment and proceeds to amphibious attacks, wherein a blockade is an extension of failed amphibious attacks. Yet, for Taiwan, staying on the defensive means accepting a passive role in the conflict (Murray, 2008, pp. 17–18), and ceding to China the time and place to take action. As Taiwan's military force capacity was only built on inflexible assumptions about a Chinese invasion of the island, this renders the ROC military powerless to respond to unexpected scenarios. Currently, both the RAND Corporation and the ROC Ministry of National Defense believe that the PLA could take the following four possible stand-alone options to create military leverage over Taiwan: military exercises, a joint fire strike, a blockade, and an island-landing campaign (Easton *et al.*, 2017, p. 3; MND, 2017; MND, 2018). Scholars argue that the first three options would only allow China to achieve limited objectives, instead of unifying Taiwan; hence, they see that Murray's main assumption is generally correct, as China could only take over Taiwan through an amphibious invasion (Yang, 2009).

Nevertheless, by 2023, China has conducted various types of air and naval operations around Taiwan posing threats other than the actual triphibious invasions. The previous thought from Murray's original arguments overlook the fact that China's available options are actually based on its relative military power in comparison with Taiwan's. If the ROC were to give up offensive assets to resist China's coercive diplomacy, as suggested by Murray's porcupine strategy, that might continue to amplify the effect of the first three options and eventually become encouragement for China to undertake more airspace intrusions, naval intrusions with its aircraft carriers, or joint fire strikes, and even an air/sea blockade. On the one hand, the utility of a joint airstrike is similar to a strategic bombing operation, which means undermining the public's will to resist by creating Shock and Awe effects. However, the US failure in Afghanistan by 2021 and the continuous Ukrainian will to fight against Russian invaders show conflicting pictures of the physiological leverages during wartime. Hence, Murray's argument presupposes that strategic bombing is voided when such an argument is still disputable among scholars (Smith, 1977). On the other hand, if China were to use its military force below the armed conflict threshold in scenarios of blockades or air/naval intrusions, Taiwan would be incapable of responding if there were no symmetric capability. In both situations, the ROC military might not suffer any substantial damage on the island, but the Taiwanese public's will to resist, as well as military morale, could easily be crippled.

Third, the success of deterrence through a porcupine strategy is far from assured. Assessments from military observers often conclude that, once the PLA fires the first shot, China would be looking for a quick and decisive endgame, as is often claimed by China's state-controlled broadcaster: "the first battle [with Taiwan] would be the last battle" (Ellis, 2020; Ou and Huang, 2018, p. 56). Under Xi's leadership, China has evolved from an authoritarian regime into one closer to totalitarianism, and the CCP may worry less about the body bag syndrome. This situation might offer the CCP more damage-tolerant capabilities than most democratic societies. As such, the unbearable and "unacceptably high costs and risks" (p. 31) to China incurred by Taiwan's fortification, as specified by Murray (2008), may, instead, become a necessary evil for Xi in regard to achieving his "historical mission" (Terrill, 2016). Besides deploying more missiles, Murray (2008, p. 4) also suggested in his porcupine strategy that Taiwan should harden its infrastructure and store critical supplies. The dilemma is that these methods of force mobility, camouflage, deception, operational redundancy, rapid repair, and blast mitigation may already be implemented, but these measures would be useful for Taiwan's defense only if their details were kept secret. Yet, if China has no way to perceive just how Taiwan is fortifying its infrastructure, how will it influence the Chinese leadership's cost–benefit analysis? (Jervis et al., 1989). As the effectiveness and visibility of one's fortifications are hard to measure, when the CCP is making a trade-off between the survival of the party and the human cost, the extent to which Murray's porcupine strategy could deter such a politically motivated military action is debatable.

Fourth, Murray (2008, p. 15) also recognizes that the precondition for the porcupine strategy's success is based on the general public's willingness to resist. When Taiwan can only fight a war of attrition at its own front door, it is questionable how long a porcupine strategy could help Taiwan hold out, if not physically then psychologically. Not only are China's military and resources disproportionately more abundant than Taiwan's, but war history has already taught us how devastating the psychological effect can be for military resistance. World War I taught us that the German military was mostly capable when the German empire surrendered to the Triple-Entente powers' long-term blockade. One of the crucial factors for British success in the Battle of Britain during World War II was the constant resupply of the Royal Air Force to resist the

German air bombing campaign. Likewise, without Western allies' supply of financial and material resources, the confidence and capability of Ukrainian resistance to Russian aggression will be quite questionable. Hence, for a resource-constrained Taiwan, a porcupine strategy, ironically, would be based on the premise that Taiwan can maintain and mobilize its public willingness to defend itself with a sufficient replenishment of its arsenal.

Finally, some research argues that air control and sea control are not required for one country's effective defense (Yang, 2009), as suggested in Murray's porcupine strategy (Murray, 2008, p. 30). Hence, Taiwan could better allocate this funding to building more mobile missile platforms to support an air- and sea-denial mission. However, land-launched anti-ship missiles will likely be confined in range due to the limitations of the terrain from which they can be launched. Their accuracy and effectiveness would also be limited in the absence of sufficient knowledge of the target locations, namely, the adequate ability of target acquisitions. In addition, this line of argument further ignores the fact that the defender (Taiwan) may not need to have air control and naval control, but an attacker (China) certainly needs them to effect a successful amphibious operation. This is why past military research emphasizes the PLA's need to destroy Taiwan's air force and navy right at the beginning of the operation (Shlapak *et al.*, 2000, p. xvi). Suppose Taiwan's air force and navy are engaging with the PLA in a game of hide-and-seek: In that case, it would certainly influence the PLA's confidence in initiating an amphibious operation, and further prolong the conflict.

11.5 Misconception of Taiwan Strait Contingencies

Murray's porcupine strategy also reflects a common misconception about the Taiwan Strait situation by international security observers. People generally believe that, since there is no way for Taiwan to counterbalance China's immense military power, Taipei can only hope to sustain the island's defense long enough for the potential arrival of US forces (Taylor, 2020). Certainly Taiwan, like Ukraine during wartime, would welcome every bit of support it can get in its David-and-Goliath fight. However, Taiwan also needs to be careful in terms of offsetting the certain harm that will be incurred by China's certain military threat, with the uncertain expectation of rescue and support by any ally. As such, Taiwan also needs to look forward to extending the conflict in the dimensions of both time and space, even under its own endeavor, but for other more important reasons.

First, with the consideration of *Jus ad bellum*, neither Taiwan nor China would want to fire the first shot in a Taiwan Strait conflict. Although Taiwan's statehood is contested in the international community, and China does not recognize Taiwan's sovereignty, the UN elaborated in its "Definition of Aggression" in Resolution 3314 that parties involved in a conflict are referred to as "states," which is a term that is "used without prejudice to questions of recognition or to whether a State is a member of the United Nations" (UN General Assembly, 1974). In addition, Taiwan is not a member of the United Nations, but China is. Hence, Articles 2–3 regarding the maintenance of international peace and security and Articles 2–4 regarding the use of force in territorial integrity and political independence in the UN Charter still have the power to affect China's decision-making. Hence, prolonging the duration of a cross-strait conflict would not only allow more opportunities for foreign military aid to arrive, but it would also offer more opportunities for international intervention, in terms of both diplomatic and material aid.

Second, during the 1996 missile crisis, the then chief of general staff of the ROC military, Luo Ben-li, believed that China's economic center was in the Southeast of its territory, and Taiwan would not be able to change the PLA's course of action without having an impact on regions beyond just the Taiwan Strait (Qi, 2006, p. 110). As of 2023, Taiwan's aircraft and navy vessels are unable to suppress the PLA's military within China's coastline, but offensive standoff weapons (Chung, 2020), like the HF-2E, Wan-Chien, and Yun-Feng missiles, offer Taiwan the capability to extend its military operations to deep within the Chinese heartland. However, Taiwan should strictly maintain its stance of not targeting any countervalue targets, as this is internationally and morally forbidden, but should instead focus on counterforce targets such as the PLA bases and the military installations to deny, disrupt, or even interdict the PLA's war effort. Such a strategy of enlarging the conflict area would allow Taiwan to create more political leverage while the economic activities in these regions would eventually be depressed due to concerns about the ongoing war, which would result in immediate economic and political pressure against China's invasion. Murray mistakenly believes that seeking offensive capabilities for Taiwan would mean engaging in warfare symmetrically (Murray, 2008, p. 17), but the fact is that offensive capabilities would offer Taiwan the ability to be active, as opposed to merely reactive, which would reduce the PLA's capacity to contain the conflict around Taiwan. Murray's porcupine strategy is stationary, and expected by China. As Sun Tzu pointed out: "the clever combatant imposes his will on the enemy, but does not allow the enemy's will to be imposed on him" (Sun Tzu, 2009, p. 21). The traditional advantage in Taiwan's operational environment is diminishing due to the PLA's advances in military technology and strength, but investing in offensive capability would offer Taiwan unexpected compensation for the disappearance of its geographic advantages.

In short, Sun Tzu stated: "Do not repeat the tactics which have gained you one victory, but let your methods be regulated by the infinite variety of circumstances" (Sun Tzu, 2009, p. 23). Hence, being offensive does not mean trying to engage with China symmetrically, because that would not stop Beijing from acting militarily. In fact, such a capability would ensure that Beijing considered Taiwan's offensive capability before the PLA acted with hostility. Beijing would question whether it was capable of ending the conflict quickly in the adjacent areas of the Taiwan Strait at a minimum military, political, and diplomatic cost. Failing to do so would damage any CCP leader's credibility by exposing them to the party's domestic critics and bringing massive risk and uncertainty to China's internal stability (Ignatius, 2018), which would taint Xi Jinping's political survival.

11.6 From Preventing War to Deterring Invasion

The above assessments echo Taiwan's national defense strategy of "resolute defense, multi-domain deterrence" (MND, 2023, p. 63). The objective of traditional deterrence is to prevent a war, not to win a war (Brodie *et al.*, 1946). This is achieved by threatening to retaliate against an adversary's attacks by imposing substantial costs, militarily, politically, and diplomatically. However, it seems that, at a certain point in time, deterrence in the Taiwan Strait is destined to fail as China has been promoting a historical determinist worldview along with its growing modernized military strength (Flournoy, 2020). It is not about whether China would want to use force against Taiwan, but when the CCP, under Xi Jinping's rule, will feel that the conditions are ready for him to do so. From this point on, once the conflict in the Taiwan Strait occurs, the ROC military would be better used to deter the PLA's amphibious/triphibious invasions, instead of being used to stop military attacks (MND, 2019, p. 48). China has three aircraft carriers and five military theater commands — the fruitful result of the 2016 military reform and enhancement. As witnessed by the strategic misstep of Russia's insufficient mobilization for its invasion on Ukraine in 2022, it could be expected that a PLA invasion of Taiwan would certainly be a conflict involving a sufficient amount of military assets from the Bohai Sea, Yellow Sea, East China Sea, and South China Sea (Liu, 2020). Hence, a porcupine strategy would be better used to complement, rather than to replace, Taiwan's improving offensive fighting capability. Standoff weapons for Taiwan are not intended to create overwhelming dominance over China, but are aimed at rejecting and disrupting an enemy invasion without being alleviated under the PLA's long-range air and naval missile defense, such as the S-400 and HQ-26. Also, an offensive capability does not aim to create a symmetrical advance or conduct a war of attrition; rather, it is a critical capacity that will enable Taiwan to exploit the PLA's vulnerabilities and deny its passage to China's triphibious landing craft. Only the combination of an offensive capability in tandem with a porcupine posture could offer Taiwan more bargaining power both politically and militarily in regard to a disparity in the cross-strait military balance.

11.7 Enhancing Asymmetric Capabilities Over the Taiwan Strait

Taiwan maintains a military strategy of "resolute defense, multi-domain deterrence" (MND, 2023, p. 63). It has been planning to "resist the enemy on the shore, attack the enemy on the sea, destroy the enemy in the littoral area, and annihilate the enemy on the beachhead" (Li, 2021). Under the gradual diminishment of the geographical barrier of the Taiwan Strait due to the advancements and technical modernizations in the PLA's operational capabilities along with its increasingly assertive behavior in the Taiwan Strait, Taiwan has been emphasizing the development of "asymmetric" capabilities to counter the PLA threat. However, Taiwan's definition of asymmetric is always questioned by Western observers (Hunzeker *et al.*, 2018; Murray, 2008), who argue that there is nothing asymmetric if Taiwan continues to counter China's conventional military threat with conventional military means. Nevertheless, such a debate may obfuscate Taiwan's original intention of highlighting the likely reality of a future imbalance in any cross-strait conflict, when Taiwan had to fight against a resource-rich and militarily advanced adversary in the region. A focus on asymmetric capabilities for Taiwan would dictate the need to plan meticulously and fight efficiently, targeting the PLA's military vulnerabilities.

Regarding the issue of "resisting the enemy on the shore," media and think tanks have indicated multiple times that Taiwan has made substantial investments in procurement and development of stand-off weapons, such as HF-2E, Wan-Chien, and Yun-Feng missiles, in order to interdict the PLA's military preparations within the coastline of China (Chen, 2016; Chung, 2020; Missile Defense Project, 2017). As for the ability to "attack the enemy on the sea, destroy the enemy in the littoral area," Taiwan has also employed anti-surface platforms, including anti-ship missiles, sea mines, unmanned platforms, and fast minelaying ships to delay and complicate the PLA's amphibious advancements (Lee & Lee, 2020). Another such example is that in 2023, Taiwan completed the Factory Acceptance Test and was moving toward the Harbor Acceptance Test of its indigenous submarine as another disruptive weapon to deny the PLA's naval power projection over the region (Chau, 2023). To "annihilate the enemy on the beachhead," not only has Taiwan procured and deployed coastal defense systems (Defense Security Cooperation Agency, 2020; Luo, 2021), the ROC government has also announced the establishment of the Defense Reserve Mobilization Agency, representing a determination to equip the public with a localized defense capacity and decentralized resistance capabilities (*Focus Taiwan*, 2021). All these operational platforms need to be lethal, mobile, resilient, deceptive, and affordable. Hence, in the long run, the success of the strategy is about not only the capabilities but also capacities. Eventually, Taiwan would need to make these capabilities sustainable, and manufacturing combat platforms indigenously and sufficiently would be one of the crucial elements to this end.

11.8 Policy Implications

Small powers follow rules, but great powers make rules. Since 1996, Taipei has refrained from scrambling ROCAF fighter jets to traverse the median line and into the west side of the Taiwan Strait, in order not to be seen internationally as a troublemaker, as well as to reduce military miscalculations in the region. Today, however, China has not only expanded its control of the Taiwan Strait, via the expansion of the M503 route, but it has relentlessly dispatched PLA military aircraft over the median line and even to the East China, the South China Sea, and the west Pacific Ocean to assert this "new normal." We must recognize that the chief characteristic created by the PLA over the Taiwan Strait is a permanent state of "violent peace," which is a unique strategic landscape that includes security challenges that are neither fully at war nor fully at peace. Just as China made Japan's Air Self-Defense Force increase its warning and emergency take-offs (scramble missions) against the PLA's air intrusions — up from 38 in 2009 to 675 in 2020 — it is naturally expected that the PLA's activities in the airspace zone adjacent to Taiwan will involve long-term and constant incursions. These actions are not only targeting specific events for political signaling, but they are also a stratagem: a salami-slicing tactic designed to erode Taiwan's defense capability and paralyze its quasi-security partners' vigilance in regard to the looming cross-strait conflict. China's motivation is evident, whether we name these behaviors "hybrid warfare" or "Gray Zone" tactics. China's renouncement of the very existence of the median line speaks to its strategy of reshaping past-accepted norms over the Taiwan Strait and intentionally sowing the seeds of conflict in the region. The stabilization of the region will not be successful if it relies on Taiwan's efforts alone. It will require the international community and regional actors to confine China's arbitrary interpretation of acceptable military behavior in the Indo-Pacific region.

Moreover, although Clausewitz believed that war is the continuation of politics by other means, for China, politics is also the continuation of war by other means. The old dichotomy between war and peace is ambiguous and disappearing in this region, and China's military activities, which implicitly contain the "use of force," have submerged the Taiwanese public into a continuous state of psychological and political pressure. The Taiwanese general public often has a short attention span when it comes to security developments around the remote islands administered by the ROC government, but at a certain point they may start to question the severity of PLA actions there. Hence, maintaining military pressure under the threshold of war is a kind of Gray Zone strategy, which grants China a better position from which to prepare for conflicts, but without creating immediate international resistance. Conversely, if the international community remains silent about the PLA's reckless behavior in the region, that will have an adverse effect, only fueling Xi's unconstrained ambitions. While the European powers wrongly believed that appeasement could maintain peace in Europe in the lead-up to WWII,

Hitler was determined to initiate a conflict right from the beginning of the negotiations over the Munich Agreement. When US Secretary of State Dean Acheson did not include South Korea in America's defense perimeter in the Pacific in 1950, it was criticized by some for giving the green light to North Korea's invasion. Likewise, the CCP's legitimacy in China comes from its self-imposed nationalist narrative, and this CCP dogma will naturally lead the country to engage with territorial issues not only with Taiwan, but also in the East China Sea, the South China Sea, and the Sino-India border. Taiwan must continue to harden its military investment in enhancing the internal balance with China. However, if the international community continues to send out mixed signals without creating any external balancing, China's assertive behavior will only be encouraged by its endogenous motivations and the lack of exogenous constraints.

11.9 Conclusion

To conclude, China under Xi Jinping's reign is increasing its military presence in the region either as the result of intentional posturing in the short term or contextual developments in the long run, and this development is continuing to cause regional security and stability to deteriorate. Although Taiwan is committed to defending itself, this goal is still very challenging to achieve by its efforts alone. Proper signaling from the international community is therefore an essential factor in maintaining regional peace.

In the past, international state actors used to restrain their security relationship with Taiwan due to the thorny issue of diplomatic recognition. However, diplomatic relations and security partners do not need to be in sync. Just as China maintains diplomatic relations with many countries, but is not a security partner with most of them, other regional actors could still enter into security partnerships with Taiwan for the purpose of maintaining global security, even without official bilateral diplomatic recognition.

Finally, it may be time for regional security actors to reassess their strategic posture in the region. A country's security policy needs to be revised regularly to reflect the dynamics of regional developments. In the past, the lack of security dialogues in the region only encouraged the PLA to gear-up its reckless military expansion, and continued to fuel China's voracious ambitions. An alternative way forward would be for regional actors to establish an all-inclusive security forum, or more stabilized security institutions, in order to mitigate such a "dilemma of responses."

References

Al Jazeera (2020, October 10). Taiwan to strengthen defenses as China tensions escalate. Retrieved from http://archive.today/Sf0sO.

Alert 5 (2018, May 15). Chinese Y-8 EW aircraft operating over Taiwan Strait. Retrieved from http://archive.today/L8wch.

Barnett, M. and Finnemore, M. (2004). *Rules for the World: International Organizations in Global Politics*. Ithaca, NY: Cornell University Press.

Booth, K. and Wheeler, N. (2007). *Security Dilemma: Fear, Cooperation, and Trust in World Politics*. Hampshire, UK: Palgrave Macmillan.

Brodie, B., Dunn, F. S., Wolfers, A., Corbett, P. E., and Fox, W. T. R. (1946). *The Absolute Weapon: Atomic Power and World Order*. New York: Harcourt.

Brunnstrom, D. (2020, October 8). US warns China against Taiwan attack, stresses U.S. 'ambiguity'. *Reuters*. Retrieved from https://www.reuters.com/article/us-usa-china-taiwan-idUSKBN26T01W.

Chan, M. (2020, October 22). South China Sea missile drills to blame for Taiwanese plane being turned back at Hong Kong, source says. South *China Morning Post*. Retrieved from http://archive.today/Dc5v8.

Chang, Y.-T. (2020, September 13). Countermeasures to PLA's air intrusion [gongji dijin yali yinying zhidao]. *Taiwan Daily*.

Chau, T. (2023, September 19). Taiwan submarine dream surfaces as China tensions rise. *Nikkei Asia*. Retrieved from https://asia.nikkei.com/Spotlight/Asia-Insight/Taiwan-submarine-dream-surfaces-as-China-tensions-rise.

Chen, S. (2016). Taiwan's security Dilemma in the face of a shifting cross-strait military balance. *The Korean Journal of Defense Analysis*, *28*(2), 299–315.

Cheng, J.-W. (2019, April 2). The median line is the US's restriction on Taiwan from retaking the mainland [haixia zhongxian moqi, dangchu jingshi meifang xianzhi guojun "fangong dalu"]. *United Daily News*. Retrieved from https://theme.udn.com/theme/story/6775/3732027.

Chinese Communist Party (2013). Collected work in Xi jinping's talks of the rejuvenation of the Chinese nation [Xi jin ping guanyu shixian zhonghua minzu weida fuxing de zhongguomeng lunshu zhaibian]. Beijing, China.

Chung, L. (2020, July 11). The Taiwan missile tech aimed at keeping a PLA attack at bay. *South China Morning Post*. Retrieved from https://www.scmp.com/news/china/military/article/3092791/taiwan-missile-tech-aimed-keeping-pla-attack-bay.

Copper, J. F. (2006). *Playing with Fire: The Looming War with China over Taiwan*. Connecticut, USA: Greenwood Publishing Group.

Defense Security Cooperation Agency (2020, October 21). Taipei Economic and Cultural Representative Office in the United States (TECRO) — HIMARS, Support, and Equipment | Defense Security Cooperation Agency. Retrieved from http://archive.today/rmePQ.

Detsch, J. (2021). The U.S. is getting Taiwan ready to fight on the beaches. *Foreign Policy*. Retrieved from http://archive.today/oFbCr.

Easton, I. (2020, November 2). Ian Easton on Taiwan: Think China's aggression is alarming now? Just wait. *Taipei Times*. Retrieved from https://www. taipeitimes.com/News/editorials/archives/2020/11/02/2003746192.

Easton, I., Stokes, M., Cooper, C. A., and Chan, A. (2017). *Transformation of Taiwan's Reserve Force*. Santa Monica, CA: RAND Corp.

Ellis, S. (2020, October 8). Here's what could happen if China invaded Taiwan. *The Japan Times*. Retrieved from https://www.japantimes.co.jp/news/2020/10/08/asia-pacific/china-taiwan-invasion-scenario/.

Flournoy, M. A. (2020, October 23). How to prevent a war in Asia — The Erosion of American deterrence raises the risk of Chinese miscalculation. Foreign affairs.

Focus Taiwan (2020, October 7). Chinese military aircraft make most median line crossings in 30 years. Retrieved from https://focustaiwan.tw/cross-strait/202010070008.

Focus Taiwan (2021, April 20). Taiwan to set up reserve mobilization agency, expand scope. Retrieved from https://focustaiwan.tw/politics/202104200014.

Focus Taiwan (2023a, March 21). 'Anti-war' scholars urge Taiwan to balance U.S., China ties. Retrieved from https://focustaiwan.tw/politics/202303210012.

Focus Taiwan (2023b, August 11). China announces military exercises ahead of Lai's visit to Paraguay. Retrieved from https://focustaiwan.tw/cross-strait/202308110019.

Global Times (2020, August 10). PLA fighter jets send clear message to Taiwan, US. Retrieved from https://www.globaltimes.cn/content/1197309.shtml.

howmuch.net (2020, January 28). Visualizing China's trading partners. Retrieved from http://archive.today/3juDII.

Hughes, C. R. (2006). *Chinese Nationalism in the Global Era*. Oxford, UK: Taylor & Francis.

Hunzeker, M. A., Lanoszka, A., Davis, B., Fay, M., Goepner, E., Petrucelli, J., and Seng-White, E. (2018). *A Question of Time: Enhancing Taiwan's Conventional Deterrence Posture: Center for Security Policy Studies*. ISBN is: 978-1-7329487-1-8.

Ignatius, D. (2018, December 14). China's hybrid warfare against Taiwan. *The Washington Post*. Retrieved from https://www.washingtonpost.com/opinions/2018/12/14/chinas-hybrid-warfare-against-taiwan/.

Jervis, R., Lebow, R. N., and Stein, J. G. (1989). *Psychology and Deterrence*. Baltimore, MD: Johns Hopkins University Press.

Kine, P. (2022, September 19). Biden leaves no doubt: 'Strategic ambiguity' toward Taiwan is dead. Politico. Retrieved from http://archive.today/0Fnd7.

Lee, H.-M., and Lee, E. (2020, November 3). Taiwan's overall defense concept, explained. *The Diplomat*.

Li, Z.-X. (2021, July 3). Chief of General Staff, General Chen, introduces the Executive Office, Admiral Mei [Chen zongzhang zhuchi Mei fuzongzhang zhixingguan xinzhi jieshao]. *Youth Daily News*. Retrieved from https://www.ydn.com.tw/news/newsInsidePage?chapterID=1420999&type=military.

Liberty Times (2020, September 3). Suspected PLA reconnaissance aircraft over the Taiwan Strait [yi gongjun zhenchaji you chumei zai taihai zhongxian nanbei paihuai].

Liu, X. (2020, September 14). PLA launches more than 30 sea drills amid US, Taiwan exercises. *Global Times*. Retrieved from https://www.globaltimes.cn/content/1200845.shtml.

Luo, T.-B. (2021, February 2). Military invested 1.2 billions to expand the range of Thunderbolt-2000 to 100 kms [Junfang 12 yi weichi leiting 2000 duoguan huojian zhanli zengchengxing yiyu 100 gongli]. *Liberty Times*. Retrieved from https://news.ltn.com.tw/news/politics/breaking news/3429411.

Madjar, K. (2020, October 30). NSB's work 'more crucial than ever'. *Taipei Times*. Retrieved from https://www.taipeitimes.com/News/taiwan/archives/2020/10/30/2003746046.

McDonald, P. J. (2004). Peace through trade or free trade? *Journal of Conflict Resolution, 48*(4), 547–572.

Mearsheimer, J. J. (2001). *The Tragedy of Great Power Politics*. New York, US: Norton.

Mearsheimer, J. J. (2018). RIP Taiwan? The National Interest. Retrieved from https://nationalinterest.org/blog/skeptics/rip-taiwan-26676.

Ministry of Foreign Affairs (2020a, September 3). Visit of Czech Senate President Miloš Vystrčil yields numerous tangible results; Taiwan and the Czech Republic working towards a comprehensive, democratic and cooperative partnership. Retrieved from https://www.mofa.gov.tw/en/News_Content.aspx?n=539A9A50A5F8AF9E&s=1826B69DB080C3C5.

Ministry of Foreign Affairs (China). (2020b, September 21). Regular News Conference on 21 September 2020 [2020 nian 9 yue 21 ri Waijiaobu fayanren Wang wenbin zhuchi lixin jizhehui].

Ministry of National Defense (2023, September 18). *Real Time Military News* [Jishi junshi dongtai].

Missile Defense Project (2017, July 13). "Yun Feng," Missile Threat. Retrieved from https://missilethreat.csis.org/missile/yun-feng/.

MND (2017). *2017 Quadrennial Defense Review (English Version)*. Taipei, Taiwan: Ministry of National Defense.

MND (2018). *2018 PLA Military Force Development* [107 nian zhonggong junli baogao shu]. Taipei, Taiwan: Ministry of National Defense.

MND (2019). *2019 National Defense Report*. Taipei, Taiwan: Ministry of National Defense.

MND (2023). *2023 National Defense Report*. Taipei, Taiwan: Ministry of National Defense.

Murray, W. S. (2008). Revisiting Taiwan's defense strategy. *Naval War College Review*, *61*(3), 12–39.

National People's Congress (1982). Constitution of the People's Republic of China. Retrieved from http://www.npc.gov.cn/englishnpc/Constitution/2007-11/15/content_1372962.htm.

Office of the President (2020, September 18). President Tsai holds a banquet for US under Secretary Keith Krach and accompanying delegation. Retrieved from https://english.president.gov.tw/News/6042.

Ou, S.-F. and Huang, C.-T. (2018). *2018 Annual Assessment of PRC's Political and Military Developments*. Taipei, Taiwan: Institute for National Defense and Security Research.

Pevehouse, J. C. (2005). *Democracy from Above: Regional Organizations and Democratization*. Cambridge, England: Cambridge University Press.

Qi, L.-Y. (2006). *Safeguarding Taiwan: 1996 Missile Crisis* [Hanwei xingdong: yi 1996 nian taihai feidan weiji fengyunlu]. Taipei, Taiwan: Liming Culture Enterprise [Liming wenhua].

ROCAF Facebook (2019, August 16). Schedule for the acquisition of new fighter jets [xin shi zhan ji chou huo li cheng bao ni zhi]. Retrieved from https://www.facebook.com/cafhq/posts/2358331441092679.

Russett, B. and Pevehouse, J. (2011). Democratic intergovernmental organizations promote peace. In: B. Russett (ed.), *Hegemony and Democracy* (pp. 161–185). New York, NY: Routledge.

Reuters (2022, August 2). U.S. house speaker Pelosi arrives in Taiwan. Reuters. Retrieved from http://archive.today/NmNDa.

Shepherd, C. and Chiang, V. (2023, April 8). Chinese military starts drills encircling Taiwan after Tsai's U.S. visit. *The Washington Post*. Retrieved from http://archive.today/RYBwT.

Shlapak, D. A., Orletsky, D. T., Reid, T. I., Tanner, M. S., and Wilson, B. (2009). *A Question of Balance*. Santa Monica, CA: RAND Corp.

Shlapak, D. A., Orletsky, D. T., and Wilson, B. A. (2000). *Dire Strait? Military Aspects of the China-Taiwan Confrontation and Options for US Policy.* Santa Monica, CA: RAND Corp.

Smith, Jr., M. E. (1977). The strategic bombing debate: The second World War and Vietnam. *Journal of Contemporary History, 12*(1), 175–191.

Stone, M. and Zengerle, P. (2020, September 16). Exclusive: U.S. pushes arms sales surge to Taiwan, needling China — Sources. Reuters. Retrieved from https://www.reuters.com/article/us-usa-taiwan-arms-exclusive-idUS KBN2671M4.

Sun Tzu (2009). *The Art of War* (L. Giles, Trans.). USA: Pax Librorum Publishing House.

Taiwan Affairs Office (China) (2019, January 2). Speech at the meeting marking the 40th anniversary of the issuance of the message to compatriots in Taiwan.

Taylor, A. (2020). Would the U.S. protect Taiwan from China? Taiwan's new envoy hopes for 'clarity'. *Washington Post.* Retrieved from https://www.washingtonpost.com/world/2020/10/15/taiwan-china-trump-tensions/.

The Central Commission for Discipline Inspection (2018, February 11). What are the purposes of ammending the party constitution to fufil the goals of "Two Centenaries" [dangzhang xiuzhengan diaozheng wanshan "liangge yibai nian" fendou mubiao de yiyi hezai]. Retrieved from http://www.ccdi.gov.cn/special/zmsjd/zm19da_zm19da/201802/t20180209_163794.html.

UN General Assembly, Definition of Aggression, 14 December 1974, A/RES/3314. Retrieved from https://www.refworld.org/docid/3b00f1c57c.html (accessed 30 November 2023).

US DoD (2020). *Annual Report to Congress, Military and Security Developments Involving the People's Republic of China 2020.* Washington, DC, US: Department of Defense.

Terrill, R. (ed.). (2016). *Xi Jinping's China Renaissance: Historical Mission and Great Power Strategy.* New York, NY: CN Times Books Inc.

Yang, S.-Y. (2009). Military? Politics? Reflections on the critiques of "porcupine strategy." *Prospect Quarterly, 10*(4), 85–123.

© 2025 World Scientific Publishing Company
https://doi.org/10.1142/9789811298301_0012

Chapter 12

Unmanned Aerial Vehicles: The Answer for Taiwan's Defense Capability Build-up

Takeuchi Toshitaka

The People's Republic of China (PRC) is not only resurgent economically but also militarily, and its policies reflect the confidence that China has in its military capabilities. This is especially true under the current regime of PRC President Xi Jinping, who in 2018 removed the term limits on his office to extend his reign beyond the traditional two terms. With Xi remaining at the helm of state beyond what would have been his retirement year in 2022, the current cross-Strait situation is expected to continue into the foreseeable future. Beijing has never ruled out the option of using military force to compel annexation of what the Chinese Communist Party (CCP) calls a "renegade province." Faced with this existential threat, the Republic of China (ROC) on Taiwan will have to beef-up its defense capabilities, and this chapter explores what investments Taiwan should focus on to achieve this end, especially in view of the threat from across the Taiwan Strait.

This chapter hypothetically assumes that there will be a PRC attempt to "unify" Taiwan by physical means, through a focus on an amphibious strike across the Taiwan Strait. It is not a detailed analysis based on specific scenarios as such, however, and is approached from a more generic perspective. The reason why the Strait crossing is chosen is that this is considered to be the most vulnerable phase during which Taiwan defenders plan to use, among other options, "unmanned vehicles" (MND, 2023, pp. 64–65).

First, we discuss Taiwan's general defense posture. This leads to an explanation of Taiwan's Overall Defense Concept, and its implications for Taiwan's arms procurement policy. Based on these examinations, the utility of drones is discussed. Finally, we suggest that Taipei must pay much more attention to the potential that Unmanned Combat Aerial Vehicles (UCAV) represent. The main rationale is, above all, the increasing gap between the ROC Armed Forces and the People's Liberation Army (PLA) in terms of traditional conventional weapons, such as naval vessels and fighter airplanes, which is acknowledged in Taiwan's 2021 Quadrennial Defense Review (MND, 2021, p. 26). China dwarfs Taiwan even now, and this imbalance is expected to become more pronounced in the future. The budgetary constraints are a big reason for this.

12.1 General Defense Postures Compared

12.1.1 *Taiwan's defense posture*

The guiding principle of Taiwan's defense policy is based on the Overall Defense Concept (ODC) to ensure that Taiwan possesses a resilient all-out defense system. The ODC was first unveiled in 2017, and it was aimed at "improving force preservation, prioritizing asymmetric, cyber and electronic warfare capabilities, as well as strengthening fundamental competences" (MND, 2019, p. 6). Taiwan's 2021 Quadrennial Defense Review is much clearer in its emphasis on a multidomain strategy, which is quite similar to Japan's prioritizing. China seems to have similar ideas as well, by emphasizing multidomain precision warfare.

According to an analysis of Chinese military strategy in the new era conducted by Japan's National Institute for Defense Studies, "The PLA's trend [is] toward active use of AI-equipped unmanned weapons amidst its preparations for intelligentized warfare" (NID, 2021, pp. 12–13). This appears to have been inspired by America's recent warfighting trends, which have seen a greater reliance on Unmanned Aerial Vehicles (UAVs), such as the Northrop Grumman RQ-4 Global Hawk and General Atomics MQ-1 Predator models, in actual combat. It is safe to say that the electromagnetic, cyberspace, and cognitive domains are almost universally perceived as being crucial today. In this sense, Taiwan is on track with other major countries in its basic defense strategy.

12.1.2 *Defense budgets compared*

There is one crucial difference between Taiwan's position and that of Japan and the United States: Taiwan faces a direct existential threat from China. Given this dire situation, Taipei has been implementing its ODC and increasing its defense budget recently in nominal terms, though not by much in real terms. China's official defense budget has been increasing rapidly and is now the second largest in the world, after the United States, dwarfing its neighboring countries. Furthermore, the official Chinese spending figures do not include certain expenditures that the standard budgeting and reporting methods used in Western countries would usually include. We can therefore assume that Beijing's official defense budget is underestimated to a not-insignificant degree. According to a new estimate of China's military spending conducted by the Stockholm International Peace Research Institute (SIPRI), a wide range of items are excluded from the PRC's budget accounting. These include "appropriations for arms imports; commercial earnings from military-owned businesses; additional funding for military research, development, testing and evaluation; para-military expenses for the People's Armed Police; military demobilization, retirement and pension payments; additional military-related construction spending; and subsidies to loss-making arms companies" (Tian and Su, 2021, p. vii).

The SIPRI report estimates that actual defense expenditures for 2019 reached US$240 billion (Tian and Su, 2021, p. vii). The gap with the official figure of around US$174 billion is quite significant. In contrast, India spent US$61.7 billion that year, Russia US$54.8 billion, and Japan US$53.9 billion. Taiwan devoted a mere US$10.9 billion to national defense in 2019 (Commission, 2020, p. 140). In a word, China is dwarfing Taiwan in terms of real defense spending to a much greater degree than previously thought. This imbalance is expected to become more pronounced in the coming years. The figures in 2022 in billions of US dollars, according to Statista, are as follows: The US ranks first at 877, China 292, Russia 86.4, India 81.4, Japan 46, and Taiwan 16.9. Taiwan is trying to increase its defense budget rapidly, given the heightened pressure coming from China (GlobalData, 2022). One might add that Japan's figure is misleading as it is rather higher in local currency terms and the Japanese government plans to raise it from 1 percent of Japan's GDP to 2 percent, a huge jump. The seeming decrease in terms of US dollars is due to a recently much weaker Japanese yen.

In most countries, including China, most of the line items in the defense budget are for non-procurement purposes. China has been spending around 40 percent of its budget on equipment, which is proportionally more than Taiwan spends on procurement. Taiwan devotes around a quarter of its defense budget to military equipment purchases (Tian and Su, 2021, p. 5; MND, 2019, p. 132). The National Defense Report of Taiwan (2019) clearly states that it gives priority to personnel costs: "Defense finances will be firstly used to satisfy personnel expenditures bound by legal obligations, then maintain operational readiness of main battle equipment, improve personnel living quarters, and realize the policy goal of a self-reliant defense" (MND, 2019, p. 130). Therefore, one can easily conclude that the difference in terms of arms procurement is much starker than the defense budgets themselves indicate.

12.2 Addressing the Widening Gap

Taipei cannot increase its defense budget sufficiently to keep pace with China's defense build-up. First, as a side-by-side comparison of the major naval assets of the two sides demonstrates, the gap in conventional military might is insurmountable, even in the Taiwan Strait theater. China has 32 destroyers to Taiwan's four, 49 frigates to Taiwan's 22, and 46 diesel attack submarines to Taiwan's two, to say nothing of China's four ballistic missile subs, two aircraft carriers, and one cruiser, all of which Taiwan has none (Commission, 2020, p. 165). Moreover, even compared to overall US Naval forces, China comes out on top. The Military and Security Developments Report on China (2022) states the following: "The PLAN is numerically the largest navy in the world with an overall battle force of appropriately 340 ships and submarines, including approximately 125 major surface combatants" (Commission, 2022, p. 50). The trend makes it abundantly clear that China is increasingly better equipped, at least numerically, than the US Navy. For example, comparing the total number of PLA naval vessels with the total number of US naval vessels; in 2000 it was China 210 to the US 318, in 2010, China 220 to the US 268, and in 2020, China 360 to the US 296. By 2030, estimates give China 425 to the US 290. One should keep in mind that these are the overall totals for both counties. Therefore, we can easily imagine the complete imbalance in China's favor in the Taiwan theater (O'Rourke, 2023, Table 2, p. 10).

Second, Taiwan is experiencing a budgetary squeeze and Taipei has no choice but to "select and concentrate" in terms of its arms spending. For example, Taiwan's National Defense Report (2019) reads, "Our nation has been using defense resources on prioritized items in force buildup and preparedness, and developing mobile, affordable, sizable, mass-producible, and expendable asymmetric capabilities" (MND, 2019, p. 52). This basic policy is maintained in the 2023 Defense Report. It states that "to compensate insufficient defense in-depth ... the Armed Forces have actively acquired 'mobile, small, portable, and AI-enabled' weapons, UAVs, and counter-UAV systems to rapidly improve deterrent asymmetric and critical capabilities" (MND, 2023, p. 65). The point is that Taiwan is consciously trying to develop small and expendable UAVs. As a matter of fact, "(T)he Overall Defense Concept emphasizes the development of asymmetric capabilities and tactics to capitalize on Taiwan's defensive advantages, enhance resilience, and exploit the PLA's weaknesses," the Commission's report reads (Commission, 2020, p. 446).

Therefore, it would appear that Taipei is prioritizing asymmetric capabilities and tactics, which implies that it is not big-ticket items such as expensive submarines and fighter airplanes that it prefers but rather an interest in acquiring weapons like drones (UAVs) that are both expendable and much cheaper. Despite this appearance and declared prioritizing, Taipei nonetheless seems to be engaged in something else. Recent indications are that there is still a desire for big-ticket weapons, such as indigenous made-in-Taiwan submarines, new, small, fast-attack missile boats, new missile defense systems, and mobile anti-ship missile platforms.

The common conception is that the significant advantage that drones have is their price tag. How much cheaper would drones be? The price of military drones varies, of course, depending on capabilities. The lowest comes in at around US$700,000, with larger and more sophisticated ones from US$1 million to US$25 million. For example, small tactical drones that a solider can carry would be around US$35,000. Medium-sized reconnaissance drones like Heron would be around US$140 million, including the ground station cost, which tends to be quite costly. "They are primarily used for Intelligence, Surveillance, Target Acquisition, and Reconnaissance (ISTAR) purposes. Heron is such a type of drone. It is used by the United States, Canada, Australia, Turkey, Morocco, and India, for reconnaissance use. One Heron and one ground station costs around US$140 million." Large surveillance and combat drones like Reapers cost around US$32 million. This would be the range that Taiwan would be interested in deploying in its fight in the Taiwan Strait. However, the RQ-4 Global Hawk that we quite often read about costs around US$220 million. To make a comparison with fighter jets, the most expensive is the most powerful Lockheed Martin's F-35, at US$177 million. The Eurofighter Typhoon is around US$124 million. China's Shenyang FC-31 (aka. J-35 or J-31) is estimated to cost around US$70 million, significantly less than US and European models. This type is assumed to be able to outperform the US's F-15 and F-16 (Bledsoe, 2023). It should be noted in this kind of comparison that the maintenance and operation costs of fighter jets are much higher than drones.

So-called Kamikaze drones, for expendable one-way strikes, are much cheaper, of course. For example, "Kamikaze drones cost around US$400 and can carry up to 3 pounds of explosives" (Schmidt, 2023). Their destructive power would not be enough to strike big naval ships. However, the point is that they can force the opponent to consume many of their anti-air missiles, and they can be effective in the shoring phase of amphibious operations. Moreover, the training for UCAV controllers costs significantly less than what it takes to train traditional combat aviators and is decreasing. The reason is that it is easy to utilize virtual reality to train drone pilots quickly and cheaply. One more advantage is that one controller can manage many drones, rather than being restricted to one single fighter jet. Training as well as manpower aspects are crucial given Taiwan's lack of volunteer servicemen. Even supposing that one adopts the draft system or extends the length of conscription, as Taiwan did, there is an insurmountable difference between China and Taiwan in terms of the pool of young eligible people for military service. It is easy to see why. China has a population of 1.4 billion people. The youth unemployment rate is more than 20 percent, a fertile ground for recruitment even if military service may not be popular. On the other hand, Taiwan has a mere 24 million people as a whole. Therefore, Taiwan has no choice but to prioritize an arms procurement policy that requires less manpower. UAVs, especially UCAVs, are a good candidate.

12.3 Review of Taiwan's Defense Concept

12.3.1 *The overall defense concept*

Given the widening gap in military might, force build-up is necessary even under tight budgetary constraints. Taiwan developed the ODC to cope with this situation. The concept rests upon three pillars (MND, 2019, pp. 75–76).

The first pillar supporting the ODC is Force Protection: This is the key to preventing initial destruction, to survive, and then to strike back against the advancing PLA assault. This is also supposed to maintain high morale. The second pillar is the mounting of a Decisive Battle in the Littoral Zone: This part states first to "develop long-range multi-functional and long-endurance UAVs to improve joint intelligence, surveillance, and reconnaissance (ISR) efficiency." Next, it aims to "acquire high-performance new fighter jets to strengthen capabilities for air dominance and sea control." The final pillar undergirding ODC is the Destruction of the Enemy at the Landing Beach: This is to "acquire unmanned combat aerial vehicles (UCAVs) with tactical and surveillance applications, to monitor adversarial moving targets and destroy them at (the) landing beach." The next area mentioned is to "procure new tanks to enhance ground defense and counterattack capabilities" (*Ibid.*).

12.3.2 *ODC's interest in drones*

The ODC is comprehensive, as the term "overall" would suggest, but it appears to be too all-embracing, too across-the-board. That is to say, it is not sufficiently selective and concentrated on future procurement. For example, it emphasizes high-quality, big-ticket items, especially in the second pillar. It also touts UAVs mainly for ISR, etc. in the third pillar described earlier. Given the budgetary constraints and the advancement of drone technology, including their accuracy as well as their destructive and ISR capabilities, it must be a better idea to focus more on UAVs than, for example, fighter jets.

Generally speaking, the ODC stresses an efficient, effective allocation and management of assets. The first pillar, Force Protection, is a matter of course. Given China's overwhelming number of conventional arms, Taiwan has to adopt passive defense measures, such as camouflage, concealment, and deception, among others. The second pillar, Decisive Battle in the Littoral Zone, in essence aims to beef-up traditional arms capabilities. It mentions that the UAVs for ISR are to help improve fighting capabilities. Traditional arms are to be deployed against China's gray-zone operations because they are highly visible. This "high visibility of traditional systems positively impacts Taiwanese morale and improves public confidence in the military." Thus, "the essence of Taiwan's traditional capabilities is a low quantity of large, high-quality platforms such as advanced fighters, destroyers and submarines, and tanks. They are strategic in nature: focused not only on defense but also achieving political effects" (Lee and Lee, 2020).

In terms of using high visibility as a deterrent, it would be effective as a demonstration to show that Taiwan has the capability to deal with a potential Chinese advance. On the other hand, UAVs are ideally suited to ISTAR, if not much better than traditional weapons, and also, importantly, they can be designed to be much less destructive, which should be effective against China's gray-zone operations. The reason is that their use would be better able to de-escalate an inadvertent incident and prevent it from flaring up than traditional arms would be. Nonetheless, one could argue that more usability might lead to a higher risk of confrontation.

In terms of the third pillar, the Destruction of the Enemy at a Landing Beach, by mentioning asymmetric capabilities, the MND (2019) shows some interest in drones. Referring to the report, Ian Easton *et al.* (2020) and his colleagues at the Project 2049 Institute write of the role of UAVs in Taiwan's Defense Strategy as follows:

"Taiwan's asymmetric systems are envisioned as small, mobile, lethal, numerous, and capable of being widely dispersed. They must be cost-effective and easy to develop and maintain, yet resilient and sustainable ... [The defense report] highlights the role of UAVs in the ODC's concept of operations. The ODC envisions fleets of future UAVs bolstering Taiwan's defense with strategic early-warning, tactical reconnaissance, target acquisition, and coastal fires."

"ROC military writings envision future UAVs with air-to-surface weapons, electronic warfare suites, and specialized explosives for one-way strike missions acquisition ... In addition to reconnaissance and target acquisition, the ROC Navy envisions UAVs providing electronic warfare and maritime interdiction capabilities" (Easton *et al.*, 2020, pp. 19–20).

The most recent National Defense Report of 2023 shows more emphasis on drones, but one could say that there is not much difference in overall procurement directions. Thus, one can say that planners in Taipei are more interested in the vast utility of drones, especially in their ISR capabilities. It seems, though, that there is much less interest being paid to the great potential of drones for strike purposes (UCAV), at least at the moment. This is understandable, as most of the current conceptualizations for the tactical deployment of UCAVs envision them serving as a complement to manned aircraft, rather than as a replacement. This limitation is largely due to technological obstacles at present, though future prospects are promising, and technological progress is seemingly quite rapid.

12.3.3 *The Washington factor*

There is little doubt that the United States will be of great help in any Taiwan Strait contingency. The overall trend in the future looks ominous, however. As discussed earlier, China outguns Taiwan in terms of naval hardware. It likewise has exceeded the US Navy in some areas, at least in terms of sheer numbers. Speaking at a Senate Armed Services Committee hearing on March 6, 2021, the (then) head of the US Indo-Pacific Command, Admiral Phil Davidson, made the following comment on this topic:

> "I worry that they're accelerating their ambitions to supplant the United States and our leadership role in the rules-based international order, which they've long said that they want to do that by 2050. I'm worried about them moving that target closer … and I think the threat is manifest during this decade, in fact in the next 6 years" (Shelbourne, 2021).

As if to underscore Davidson's prediction, it has been widely reported that, according to the results of a series of "eye-opening" war games conducted by the Pentagon, the United States would come out the loser in any sea war against China and would have a difficult time stopping a Chinese invasion of Taiwan (Evans, 2020). There is another comprehensive report on a recent wargaming simulation, however, which holds that, with help from the United States and Japan, Taiwan "defeated a conventional amphibious invasion by China and maintained an autonomous Taiwan. However, this defense came at high cost." This was the outcome in most of the 24 iterations of the wargame (CSIS, 2023). So, it is not certain. One thing is clear, however: It would be devastating for Taiwan and somewhat less so for China as well. This is also true for the United States and Japan. For its own sake, China should think twice before deciding to "unify" Taiwan by force.

12.4 Unmanned Combat Aerial Vehicles

12.4.1 *Merits and utility of drones*

What are the merits and utilities of drones? "The armed conflicts in Ukraine and elsewhere have demonstrated the growing reliance many militaries are placing on drones to conduct precise, lethal attacks, one that is likely to be sustained and replicated in the future" (Gettinger, 2023a). First of all, they are unmanned, and pilots or controllers do not have to be sacrificed. They do not get tired; do not need to sleep, eat, and so on. UAVs are also a cheap alternative to long-range, long-endurance warplanes. This is the case in terms of training time and cost, as well as necessary manpower. The manpower part is important in this age of recruiting difficulties and given the decreasing number of young people, as was mentioned above. Second, UAVs can be designed to be destructive if one so wishes. According to Paul Scharre (2015), "many of the innovations that enable swarming — low-cost uninhabited systems, autonomy, and networking — are driven by the commercial sector, and thus will be widely available."

For example, "fully autonomous GPS-programmable drones can be purchased online today for only a few hundred dollars … This is possible with today's commercially available technology. Cheap drones are proliferating worldwide, and they will incorporate increasing amounts of autonomy, enabling swarming with commercially available technology" (*Ibid.*). One might add that the Ukraine war is showing us that these commercially available drones can be fairly easily adapted by civilians to serve military ISTAR purposes. This is also true for strike purposes, by attaching small, improvised explosives, for example. These are, admittedly, crude instruments that can be easy targets. However, as has been pointed out before, the fact that they must be shot down means that one's adversary has no choice but to use and expend a large number of possibly high-priced missiles and other ordinance. Namely, UCAVs are quite cost-effective. Also, the most recent conflict between Israel and Hamas that started in October 2023 shows their potential as well. It was reported that the Hamas "sent drones to disable some of the Israeli military's cellar communications stations and surveillance towers, … The drones also destroyed remote-controlled machine guns," which "removed a key means of combatting a ground attack" (Bergman and Kingsley, 2023). This is how Hamas operatives could get into the heavily fortified southern Israel.

In its China Security Report, Japan's National Institute for Defense Studies nicely summarized the merits of drones as follows:

"UAVs are expected to be easier to design, have better stealth capabilities, have a smaller volume, and a lighter weight. Moreover, as UAVs can be produced at a lower price and in greater quantity than manned aircraft, UAV is a highly cost-effective weapon that can execute saturation attacks against the enemy's high-performance but high-cost targets. Furthermore, turning UAVs into AI will allow for instant parallelization of constantly changing battlefield information as well as selection of the most effective targets of attack and attack methods" (NID, 2021, p. 19).

There is a recent on-the-ground example that has been quite extensively analyzed as to the utility of UAVs. This is the Nagorno-Karabakh conflict between Armenia and Azerbaijan, in which UAVs are credited with playing a game-changing role. While this was a land war, not a naval one, it is still quite illuminating. Fighting flared up between the two countries in September 2020 and ended just six weeks later. Azerbaijan won a decisive military victory, and Armenia had to make a significant territorial concession as a result. "Azerbaijani drones provided significant advantages in ISR as well as long-range strike capabilities," Shaikh and Rumbaugh (2020) wrote, adding, "Their penetration of Nagorno-Karabakh's deep rear also weakened Armenian supply lines and logistics, facilitating later Azerbaijani success in battle."

"Azerbaijani drones effectively destroyed Armenia's tanks and ground defense facilities such as missile arsenals and rocket artillery. Armenia did have some home-made drones used for mainly ISR purposes, but not for strikes. This was no match because Azerbaijan had many more drones purchased from Turkey and Israel. The Israeli-made loitering munitions have been called 'suicide' or 'kamikaze' drones because they are designed to hover over the battlefield area until it is time for them to self-destruct into their targets." (*Ibid.*)

The most notable drone is the Harop (or IAI Harpy 2) that is manufactured by Israel Aerospace Industries, the capabilities of which are not precisely known. However, it is said to be multifunctional and use all-weather imaging sensors. It is of the semi-active laser homing type, which makes a very precise strike possible (the precision may be less than a square meter, whereas GPS-guided drones are only precise up to 10 m). It is somewhat expensive, with an estimated cost of around US$10 million, partly because of the cost of on-the-ground control facilities. It also has the reported capability to incapacitate and destroy an enemy's electromagnetic air defense systems (Hyodo, 2021, pp. 47–62, p. 68). This is a crucial capability for making full use of UAVs, especially for strike purposes, as demonstrated in the Nagorno-Karabakh conflict. This type of loitering munition that is capable of precision strikes with anti-electromagnetic devices would be ideal for Taiwan, as it could be deployed to prevent, if not fully incapacitate, the onslaught of PLAN assets from coming ashore.

UAVs are of course not omnipotent, and they have their share of vulnerabilities. These platforms tend to be easy prey for air-defense systems designed to counter them. In this sense, an air defense system (passive defense) is crucial for dealing with UAVs. Electronic warfare would be a very powerful countermeasure against swarms as well. Some examples are electromagnetic rail guns for shooting down drones and high-powered microwaves for wiping out an entire swarm by destroying or disrupting their electronics and jamming their communications (Scharre, 2015). The electro-magnetic capabilities and their counter-measures are an area of technological competition.

12.4.2 Swarming is key

The term "swarm" means exactly what it sounds like: many individual UAVs coordinating their actions and interacting as a group with a common goal, the way a swarm of flying insects move in concert. There are two methods of effecting a swarm: One is for the swarm to be preprogrammed by operators but not synchronized, and it shares one distributed brain for decision-making. The other is using AI in each drone to adapt to the movements of the others, autonomously making decisions based on shared information. This latter is closer to how the aforementioned insects swarm or how birds murmurate. For the time being, the current level of technology and computer control puts this latter mechanism of swarming out of reach, with the former being predominant.

"It is now possible to control multiple drones with a single application, sending commands to them all at once. However, the individual drones do not communicate and coordinate," writes Maaike Verbruggen (2021) in *the Bulletin of the Atomic Scientists*. "Swarms can be devilishly hard to target because they distribute combat capabilities across a wide number of dispersed assets and because they leverage mass to saturate and overwhelm defenses," according to Scharre (2015).

Swarming tactics can be applied to almost every theater, including the Taiwan Strait, and many other aspects of national defense. UCAVs can act like small bombers or fighter airplanes and can strike almost any target. That is, a theater commander with the ROC military can decide which PLAN vessel to strike almost instantaneously depending on his strategy, provided he has enough capable UCAVs loitering in the skies above. One can imagine a possibility where the ROC military can render a Chinese aircraft carrier effectively useless. Aircraft carriers are well protected, but they present a big target. With many loitering UCAVs, ROC forces can take out the carrier's command and control capabilities by surgically striking the combat information center or alternatively damaging the flight deck with relative ease. The point is that they could saturate the threat and overwhelm it with sheer numbers. Even supposing that the adversary's defenses include the capability of shooting down drones fairly easily, the sheer number in a swarm would be highly likely to overwhelm such a defense system. Numbers count here.

Major countries like the United States, Russia, China, the United Kingdom, and Turkey (and most likely Israel as well) have all conducted swarming experiments without any human control or direction. The UAVs themselves are cheap, but developing the appropriate software and other associated technological issues is not necessarily an easy problem to solve at present (Verbruggen, 2021). It seems, however, that almost all, if not all, of these countries are prioritizing R & D on this software and other aspects. So, we can assume that its technological progress might be quite quicker than we expect at the moment.

12.4.3 *Proliferation of UAVs*

Are UAVs proliferating in the world much too rapidly? According to Agnes Callamard and James Rogers (2020), writing in *The Bulletin of the Atomic Scientists*, "as of March 2020, at least 102 nations had acquired military drones, and around 40 possessed, or were in the process of purchasing, armed drones." They also point out that "some 35 states are now believed to own drones in the largest and deadliest class of these weapons, and at least 20 non-state actors have acquired weaponized drone technologies."

Gettinger points out one recent trend that should be noted is the following: "The development of one-way attack drones was an integral part of the transition of uncrewed aircraft from the era of high-speed target drones to that of remotely piloted vehicles, one that resulted in a burgeoning marketplace for armed and unarmed drones." Furthermore, "One-way attack drones are increasingly viewed as an alternative to the large, multirole uncrewed aircraft." It was the case that this one-way attack drone (aka. Kamikaze drones) market was dominated by the US and Israel just several years ago, with about a two-thirds market share. But "in the last 5 years, as manufacturers in countries like Turkey and China have risen in prominence, just 12 percent of new models of aircraft unveiled in this period originated from the United States and Israel. Between 2018 and 2022, producers in Asia accounted for more than one-third of new models of one-way attack drones" (Gettinger, 2023a). It is most likely that this trend will accelerate.

Given this rapidly increasing proliferation, it may sooner or later become necessary to have some kind of international regulations over drones. At the very least, some measures are needed to protect civilian lives, as well as some transparency in terms of the international transfer of armed drones. Not only do UCAVs lower the threshold for initiating a conflict, they also may make it easier to maintain one because they are usually much less destructive than traditional conventional weapons. This raises legitimate arms-control concerns, such as a possible arms race.

In any discussion about drones, there is the tendency to assume that they are being used against terrorist targets, and there is a concern about so-called collateral damage. In the case of a Taiwan Strait crossing, however, the only targets would be advancing Chinese forces, with no civilians expected to be in the theater. Thus, the ethical concerns that surround most drone usage do not apply in this case, or so we hope.

As far as the widespread use of UCAVs, and especially one-way attack drones, are concerned, there are abundant cases to point out in the Russian invasion of Ukraine that began in February 2022 and in the Israel–Hamas conflict that started in October 2023. One caution is that, once again, both these instances are land conflicts, and they involve smaller and less explosive munitions than would be necessary to defend against an amphibious attack. Nonetheless, they are quite indicative of the potency of drones. To mention just a few cases, it was reported that a drone called Saker Scout, developed by a civilian Ukraine firm, is now in operation "autonomously, making it immune to jamming." They are "operating in areas where radio jamming blocks communication and prevents other drones from working." This is the very first confirmed case of a drone being operational without a human operator. Another example is that "Ukrainian troops, and more recently Russian forces, have used off-the-shelf drones to improve the targeting of decades-old artillery." This is a nightmare for big and powerful countries with many expensive conventional arms, in particular, in that "defending against them requires expensive new equipment." The possible countermeasures would not be cost-effective, to say the least (Hambling, 2023). This is very suggestive in the case of China and Taiwan, wherein China analogous to Goliath, with Taiwan as David. In the case of the Hamas attack against Israel, as was mentioned, they "used pinpoint drone attacks in an effort to blind sophisticated surveillance systems and cripple local military command-and-control capabilities" (Michaels, 2023).

These (somewhat anecdotal) examples show the potency of drones, especially of UCAVs, as well as the important role that the civilian sector can play. The sector can contribute in terms of "spin on" technologies as well as commercially manufactured off-the-shelf products that are quite cheap.

12.5 Recommendations for Taiwan's Approach to UAVs

12.5.1 *China's interest in UAVs*

Before discussing Taiwan's interest in drones, let us take a look at what China has been doing in terms of this technology. As noted earlier, China has increased its drone production quite rapidly. This shows that Beijing is genuinely interested in, and is investing heavily in, UAV development. First, China showcased one of its newest drones by playing a video at a 2011 air show demonstrating a pilotless plane tracking a US aircraft carrier near Taiwan and relaying targeting information (Dowd, 2013, pp. 7–16). The National Defense Report (2019, p. 46) mentions that China has been developing new kinds of drones, such as UAVs that can be used on new, indigenous aircraft carriers and, one might add, shipboard electromagnetic guns as well. The China Security Report (2021) notes that one particular Chinese company showcased swarming technology, conducting "a successful test flight of 119 small fixed-wing UAVs, including catapult-assisted takeoff, aerial formation, group dispersion for multiple targets, and reassembly." Furthermore, the PLA National University of Defense Technology's College of Intelligence Science and Technology "carries out research and tests of UAVs and unmanned vehicles, and is anticipated to aspire to cooperate with entities like (China Electronics Technology Group Corp.) to enhance technologies through military-civil fusion" (NID, 2021, p. 19).

Writing in the Drone Databook, Dan Gettinger (2019) points out that "multiple PLA academies offer training courses for UAV personnel," adding that "since 2013, the East Sea Fleet has conducted periodic drone patrols over the Senkaku/Diaoyu Islands." This Databook lists the many types of drones that are under development, if not already deployed, such as a Class III (heavier than 600 kg in weight) fixed-wing system called Divine Eagle. This one has a 45-m wingspan, making it among the largest drones in the world. Another example is a Class II (150–600 kg) rotary-wing UAV called AV500W, which is China's first strike-capable unmanned rotary-wing aircraft (Gettinger, 2019, p. 14, p. 17).

China showed off its UCAVs that are currently in service at an air-show in September 2021. Writing in *Defense News*, Mike Yeo (2021) reported the following:

"China has put a number of operational and prototype unmanned aircraft designs on display at the ongoing Zhuhai Airshow, giving an insight to its increasingly wide range of unmanned systems in service. These include fast, air-launched reconnaissance systems and stealthy unmanned combat air vehicles, or UCAVs, that are already in service with the country's People's Liberation Army Air Force (PLAAF). The exhibit highlights the effort China's defense industry has made to broaden the types of drones the military has fielded."

So, we can safely assume that China has been steadily making progress in its drone technologies and capabilities.

12.5.2 *Taiwan's interest in UAVs*

Given this high level of interest and development of UAV technology undertaken by the PLA, it is imperative that Taipei follow suit. Indeed, to a degree, its military has also shown increasing interest in UAVs, mainly for ISR and, to a lesser extent, strike purposes. According to Gettinger (2019), the ROC military announced in September 2018 that it was planning to "establish an Air Force Reconnaissance Squadron equipped with long-range strike-capable drones." These drones "would be used to improve combat efficiency and precision-strike capabilities in Taiwan's littoral regions," he wrote, adding, "The Army is reportedly considering acquiring a Class I rotary-wing drone," which weighs less than 150 kg. The Army "has a requirement for 112 systems, or 224 aircrafts." Its Navy also activated the Maritime Tactical Reconnaissance Squadron in September 2017 and declared it operational in January 2019 (Gettinger, 2019, p. 50).

As cited above, the National Defense Report (2019) suggests that Taiwan planners think highly of drones. The 2021 Quadrennial Defense Review states that it prioritizes asymmetrical combat capabilities, especially those that are "small, numerous, smart, stealthy, mobile, and hard to be detected" as well as "multi-functional unmanned systems for surveillance and strike," in order to "avoid facing the enemy head-on." Furthermore, these capabilities are designed to "disrupt the enemy's operational tempo" (MND, 2021, pp. 26–28). The most recent National Defense Report (2023) mentions its intention to "merge defense technologies with civilian production capacities" (MND, 2023, p. 60). This is explained in more detail in a section titled "military UAVs":

> "the MND has … decided to delegate the R&D and production of 5 military-grade UAVs … to the National Chung-Shan Institute of Science and Technology (NCSIST), which will integrate domestic industries to accomplish the mission. … (M)ore than 700 military-grade UAVs are planned to be built from 2022 to 2028. … Development of 5 prototypes including the 'army-purpose UAVs' has been completed, with all 36 units delivered by 31st July 2023. More than 7,000 commercial grade UAVs are planned to be built from 2024 to 2028" (*Ibid.*, p. 137).

So, it is clear that Taiwan is much more focused on utilizing the civilian production capacity of UAVs than before. The report of 2023 mentioned that "the Armed Forces have actively acquired (the underline added by the author) mobile, small, portable, and AI-enabled weapons, UAVs, and counter-UAV systems to rapidly improve deterrent asymmetric and critical capabilities." (*Ibid.*, p. 65). Another report states that Taiwan has been "accelerating the production of drones for its military," especially its "consumer drone producers and electronics enterprises to the interests of national defense." Then ROC President Tsai Ing-wen announced in June 2022 "plans to establish the drone research center in Chiayi County." Soon afterward, in August 2022, Taiwan established the Asia UAV AI Innovation Application R&D Center "for helping its drone producers there." Moreover, NCSIST's newest drone offerings include various types of loitering munitions — expendable armed drones "designed to detonate upon impact with a target" (Gettinger, 2023b). So, Taipei is getting serious about developing and producing UCAVs, not merely for ISTAR purposes.

Nevertheless, the focus on UAVs has been mainly for ISTAR purposes, not yet for strikes. The Quadrennial Defense Review (2021) says that "asymmetric capabilities that are small, numerous, smart, stealthy, mobile, and hard to be detected and countered shall be built up." In addition, "new offensive and defensive technologies of EW and cyberwarfare, as well as multi-functional unmanned systems for surveillance and strike, continue to be acquired" (MND, 2021, p. 26). This policy is understandable, once again, given the current state of technology, but the need for investments in future technological developments should not be taken lightly. Taiwan is interested in drones, yes. However, the problem is that, first of all, its military decision makers are still interested in big-ticket items. Second, while there has been some mention of drones for ISTAR, not enough emphasis has been placed on the acquisition and development of strike drones, although it is focusing more and more in that direction, as mentioned earlier. One might say that it is going in the right direction, just not fast enough.

12.6 Recommendations

As discussed in this chapter, drones offer a number of advantages, dollar for dollar and in terms of manpower requirements, over the traditional big-ticket items that have been preferred in Taiwan's arms purchases. It is incumbent upon Taiwan's policymakers to adopt a more focused approach, as a general principle, to seek UAVs for strike purposes, in addition to the usual ISTAR purposes, instead of dispensing much-needed resources on procuring big-ticket items, no matter how high a capability they might have on paper. National defense is a giant system, and it must be a full-spectrum defense. Otherwise, one's opponent will take advantage of a specific deficiency or weak link to disrupt and destroy the whole system, hence the basic necessity of conventional weapons and facilities.

As far as active defense is concerned, one can afford to focus on one specific aspect and fashion it into an effective spear. In the case of a Taiwan Strait conflict, Taipei's goal must be to thwart an amphibious assault by the PLA. Drones offer Taipei a unique opportunity to overcome or at least ameliorate the double bind consisting of its budgetary woes on the one hand and the insurmountable conventional superiority of the PLA in the Taiwan Strait theater on the other.

As pointed out by Tanner Greer (2019), Taiwan's current defense strategy does not make much military sense. "Instead of allocating its limited defense budget on expensive equipment such as stealth fighters, tanks or submarines, the Taiwanese military should invest in cheap, expendable, mass-produced weapons systems that can be easily moved, disguised, and deployed against an amphibious invasion force," he urges. Greer continues that "Taiwanese leaders face what should be an easy choice: They can ensure their nation's survival through the mass production or procurement of low-cost, low-profile armaments. Or they can continue to waste their resources on … 'prestige' capabilities … with no tangible benefit in deterrence or war," concluding that "by building their military around expensive, high-tech military machines, the Taiwanese are committing themselves to an arms race they do not have the means to win."

It would seem that the main purpose of buying big-ticket items is for maintaining morale, not for military utility. Does the Taiwan government not believe in the people's will to resist a Chinese invasion? The trend is clear that the people of Taiwan increasingly identify more and more as Taiwanese and less and less as Chinese. For example, in the words of Margaret Lewis (2021, p. 35), "The long-term trend has been toward an increasing Taiwanese identity, with those expressing a dual Taiwanese-Chinese identity diminishing and a pure Chinese identity constituting just a sliver of the population." This shift in identity is accompanied by a growing preference for independence over unification, and given the way Beijing is using strong-arm police tactics to exert its will in Hong Kong, despite its promise to adhere to the concept of "One Country, Two Systems" — the same concept Xi wants to implement in Taiwan — it is little wonder that Taiwan is moving closer into the US orbit and seeking closer defense ties with Washington and Tokyo (Ihara, 2019). The ROC government should have more confidence in its citizens' will to maintain democracy.

12.7 Concluding Remarks

This chapter has argued the importance of focusing more on UAVs, especially UCAVs, as an investment policy for Taiwan's active defense. Taiwan has no choice but to focus on its defense, both passive and active, because of the existential threat that it faces from China and the increasingly huge gap in military might. Taipei has no chance of winning a conventional-weapons arms race against Beijing. Therefore, planners in Taipei must look for an alternative policy that would negate the PLA's overwhelming advantage in military resources, as well as its manpower potential. A focus on UAVs will ameliorate the problem with the budget squeeze and the seemingly insurmountable gap in conventional military might. Having numerous UAVs, especially UCAVs, would make it possible for Taiwan's Armed Forces to saturate the skies and the waters of the Taiwan Strait so that it could disrupt and halt advancing PLA forces.

Acknowledgments

This chapter is a result of the collaborative project "An Interdisciplinary Approach to Contemporary East Asia Studies" [21REN283] at St. Andrew's University Research Institute.

References

Bergman, Ronen and Kingsley, Patrick (2023, October 10). How Israel's Feared Security Services Failed to Stop Hamas's Attack. *New York Times*. Retrieved from http://archive.today/iEYGj.

Bledsoe, E. (2023, October 2). How much does a military drone cost? (The Answer You're Looking For). Retrieved from https://www.thesoldiers project.org/how-much-does-a-military-drone-cost/.

Callamard, A. and Rogers, J. (2020, December 1). We need a new international accord to control drone proliferation. *The Bulletin of the Atomic Scientists*. Retrieved from http://archive.today/OvScj.

Commission (2020, September 1). Military and security developments involving the People's Republic of China 2020: Annual report to congress. *US-China Economic and Security Review Commission*. p. 140, p. 165, p. 446. Retrieved from https://media.defense.gov/2020/Sep/01/2002488689/-1/-1/1/2020-DOD-CHINA-MILITARY-POWER-REPORT-FINAL.PDF.

Commission (2022, November 29). Military and security developments involving the People's Republic of China 2022: Annual report to congress. *US-China Economic and Security Review Commission*. p. 50. Retrieved from https://www.defense.gov/Spotlights/2022-China-Military-Power-Report/.

Center for Strategic and International Studies (CSIS) (2023, January). The first battle of the next war: Wargaming a Chinese invasion of Taiwan. p. 1. Retrieved from http://archive.today/n97NS.

Dowd, A. W. (2013). Drone Wars: Risks and Warnings. *Parameters, 43*(1), 7–16. Retrieved from https://press.armywarcollege.edu/parameters/vol43/iss1/3.

Easton, I., Stokes, M., Yang, K. S., Lee, E., and Ferland, C. (2020, June 30). Watching Over the Taiwan Strait: The Role of Unmanned Aerial Vehicles in Taiwan's Defense Strategy. *Project 2049 Institute* (pp. 19–20). Retrieved from http://archive.today/zz7u9.

Evans, M. (2020, May 16). US 'would lose any war' fought in the Pacific with China. *The Times*. Retrieved from https://www.thetimes.co.uk/article/us-would-lose-any-war-fought-in-the-pacific-with-china-7j90bjs5b.

Gettinger, D. (2019). The drone databook. *The Center for the Study of the Drone at Bard College* (p. 14, p. 17, p. 50). Retrieved from https://dronecenter.bard.edu/projects/drone-proliferation/databook/.

Gettinger, D. (2023a, June 5). One way attack: How loitering munitions are shaping conflicts, *The Bulletin of the Atomic Scientists*. Retrieved from http://archive.today/vnHZh.

Gettinger, D. (2023b, October 3). Taiwan's drone industry takes flight. *The Diplomat*. Retrieved from http://archive.today/5Iltl.

GlobalData (2022). Taiwan defense market highlights-2022. Retrieved from http://archive.today/6j4fx.

Greer, T. (2019, September 17). Taiwan's defense strategy doesn't make military sense. *Foreign Affairs*. Retrieved from http://archive.today/aEYb2.

Hambling, D. (2023, October 17) Ukraine's AI drones seek and attack Russian forces without human oversight. *Forbes*. Retrieved from http://archive.today/axbrn.

Hyodo, N. (2021). Senkakushoto wo Jieitai ha dou Boueisuruka [How does the SDF Defend the Senkakus?]. pp. 47–62, p. 68. Tokuma Shoten (Tokuma Bookstore).

Ihara, K. (2019, September 12). In Beijing rebuke, Taiwan signals closer defense ties with US and Japan. *Nikkei Asia*. Retrieved from https://asia.nikkei.com/Politics/International-relations/In-Beijing-rebuke-Taiwan-signals-closer-defense-ties-with-US-and-Japan.

Lee, H.-M. and Lee, E. (2020, November 3). Taiwan's overall defense concept, explained. *The Diplomat*. Retrieved from https://thediplomat.com/2020/11/taiwans-overall-defense-concept-explained/.

Lewis, M. K. (2021, March). What does Taiwan want? It wants to be Taiwan. *Global Asia 16*(1), 35. Retrieved from https://www.globalasia.org/v16no1/cover/what-does-taiwan-want-it-wants-to-be-taiwan_margaret-k-lewis.

Michaels, D. (2023, October 15). In Israel and Ukraine, mix of drones and brute force shows warfare's future. *The Wall Street Journal*. Retrieved from https://www.wsj.com/world/in-israel-and-ukraine-mix-of-drones-and-brute-force-shows-warfares-future-797946ed?st=h7tnsu26zlihbde&reflink=desktopwebshare_permalink.

MND (2019). ROC national defense report 2019. Ministry of National Defense of the Republic of China. p. 6, p. 52, pp. 75–76, p. 130, p. 132. Retrieved from https://www.ustaiwandefense.com/tdnswp/wp-content/uploads/2020/02/Taiwan-National-Defense-Report-2019.pdf.

MND (2021). 2021 quadrennial defense review. Ministry of National Defense of the Republic of China. p. 26. Retrieved from https://www.ustaiwandefense.com/tdnswp/wp-content/uploads/2021/03/2021-Taiwan-Quadrennial-Defense-Review-QDR.pdf.

MND (2023). ROC national defense report 2023. Ministry of National Defense of the Republic of China. p. 60, pp. 64–65, p. 137. Retrieved from https://www.ustaiwandefense.com/tdnswp/wp-content/uploads/2023/09/Taiwan-National-Defense-Report-2023.pdf.

NID (2021). China security report 2021: China's military strategy in the new era. *National Institute for Defense Studies, Japan*. p. 19. Retrieved from http://www.nids.mod.go.jp/publication/chinareport/pdf/china_report_EN_web_2021_A01.pdf.

O'Rourke, R. (2023, October 19). China naval modernization: Implications for U.S. Navy capabilities — Background and issues for congress. Updated October 19, 2023. *Congressional Research Service*, RL33153. p. 10 (Table 2). Retrieved from https://crsreports.congress.gov/product/details?prodcode=RL33153.

Scharre, P. (2015, March 31). Counter-swarm: A guide to defeating robotic swarms. *War on the Rocks*. Retrieved from http://archive.today/S2rU9.

Schmidt, E. (2023, July 7). The future of war has come in Ukraine: Drone swarms. *The Wall Street Journal*. Retrieved from http://archive.today/pgcpC.

Shaikh, S. and Rumbaugh, W. (2020, December 8). The air and missile war in Nagorno-Karabakh: Lessons for the future of strike and defense. *Center for Strategic and International Studies CSIS)*. Retrieved from http://archive.today/4AQIZ.

Shelbourne, M. (2021, March 9). Davidson: China could try to take control of Taiwan in 'next six years.' *USNI News*. Retrieved from http://archive.today/6Fm90.

Statista. Countries with the highest military spending worldwide in 2022. Retrieved from https://www.statista.com/statistics/262742/countries-with-the-highest-military-spending/.

Tian, N. and Su, F. (2021, January). A new estimate of China's military expenditure. *Stockholm International Peace Research Institute (SIPRI)*. p. vii, p. 5. Retrieved from https://www.sipri.org/sites/default/files/2021-01/2101_sipri_report_a_new_estimate_of_chinas_military_expenditure.pdf.

Verbruggen, M. (2021, February). Drone swarms: Coming (sometime) to a war near you. Just not today. *The Bulletin of the Atomic Scientists*. Retrieved from http://archive.today/FvCfe.

© 2025 World Scientific Publishing Company
https://doi.org/10.1142/9789811298301_0013

Chapter 13

Taiwan's All-Out Defense and Enhancement of Reserve Capability

Li-Chung Yuan

Given that the chances of China using force against Taiwan have increased, especially after then US Speaker of the House Nancy Pelosi's visit to Taiwan in August 2022, it is in the interests of the Republic of China (ROC) Armed Forces to strengthen its defensive capabilities and enhance its combat readiness at both the strategic and operational levels. In addition to its force of active-duty personnel, the ROC Armed Forces maintain a large reserve force which is subject to mobilization to support the regular force in the scenario of a Chinese invasion. Akin to Singapore's Total Defense concept, Taiwan's defense system integrates an all-out defense mobilization mechanism aimed at utilizing all available personnel and material resources to resist a foreign invasion. The foundation of Taiwan's all-out defense includes mobilization, all-out defense education, and the reserve force. This chapter investigates the current status of Taiwan's all-out defense and mobilization system and examines how Taiwan can enhance its reserve capabilities in terms of force structure, roles, and tasks based on publicly available research and expert discussions. Potential gaps and shortfalls are also identified to provide a comprehensive analysis of Taiwan's all-out defense capabilities and thus make feasible recommendations.

13.1 Taiwan's All-Out Defense

13.1.1 *Defense mobilization system*

Constantly facing military threats, small countries like Taiwan need to mobilize their people for national defense in the event of a worst-case scenario. Therefore, Taiwan must establish an appropriate all-out defense mobilization system to swiftly gather sufficient personnel and acquire the necessary resources during wartime. Enacted in 2001, the All-Out Defense Mobilization Readiness Act stipulates the preparation for mobilization. Article 1 of this act states that its purpose is to establish "an all-out national defense mobilization system and facilitate the concept of all-out national defense, to safeguard the rights and interests of the people" (Ministry of Justice, ROC, 2019). Abiding by the act, the ROC Ministry of National Defense (MND) has established a system to plan, prepare, and implement such a mobilization. The MND has been conducting various mobilization preparations and policy implementation efforts to integrate resources from all sectors to build up a comprehensive defense capability.

While the goal of all-out defense is driven by national security imperatives, during peacetime, such mobilization shall be called upon to participate in disaster prevention drills and assist in disaster relief efforts, according to the Disaster Prevention and Protection Act. In times of war, mobilized personnel and materials shall support military operations and contingency responses. Therefore, defense mobilization can be considered as the core of Taiwan's all-out defense, and it can be classified into two types: administrative and military mobilizations. Administrative mobilization integrates overall national strength to reinforce military operations, while military mobilization makes efficient economic use of the combat potential acquired through administrative mobilization to perform and achieve operational tasks.

The Executive Yuan (the executive branch of the ROC government) supervises the overall mobilization tasks and sets up mobilization systems at three levels: the conference for all-out defense mobilization preparation of the Executive Yuan (at the central government level), conferences of various mobilization preparation proposals, and mobilization preparation conferences of municipal governments (at the local government level). The MND acts as the secretarial agency of these administrative mobilization conferences, so it is tasked to investigate and utilize the essential combat capabilities and conduct various mobilization exercises and drills. It is a concrete practice of all-out defense and a display of the effectiveness of the annual mobilization preparation works. The mobilization system is mission-oriented and categorized into two phases: preparation and implementation. The preparation phase runs parallel to a normal state of readiness, while the implementation phase requires a recall of reservists. In addition to mobilizing reservists, the Executive Yuan is authorized to nationalize critical infrastructure and materials and assign the civilian workforce to civil defense units to support military missions. Mobilization plans also exist for public education and logistics-related materials.

The main goal of mobilization is to acquire material and human resources within the shortest period of time. Acquiring sufficient personnel to support military operations is the priority. It requires a well-planned military service system as well as an effective military mobilization system. The effectiveness of nationwide workforce utilization is to be verified by MND through a variety of mobilization exercises. As for gathering material resources, it aims to mobilize essential resources and fixed facilities (Armed Forces Reserve Command, 2021a). A well-coordinated intergovernmental effort has thus become essential for mobilization.

Regarding mobilization functions, Article 9 of the All-out Defense Mobilization Readiness Act stipulates that the mobilization readiness program is classified into eight functional areas; the duties of these areas are performed by eight ministries, accordingly (Armed Forces Reserve Command, 2021b):

1. Morale: Ministry of Education
2. Manpower resources: Ministry of the Interior
3. Material and economic resources: Ministry of Economic Affairs
4. Financial resources: Ministry of Finance
5. Transportation: Ministry of Transportation and Communications
6. Public hygiene: Ministry of Health and Welfare
7. Technology: Ministry of Science and Technology
8. Military: Ministry of National Defense

13.1.2 *All-out defense education*

Raising the public's awareness, understanding, and knowledge of all-out defense is essential if civilians are to be willing to engage in defense-related activities, especially in a small country like Taiwan. This requires reasonable efforts in education. Acquainting people with the importance of all-out defense has thus become the responsibility of the MND, with assistance from the Ministry of Education. Despite the fact that all-out defense demands comprehensive national power and the people's will to resist an enemy invasion, there has been skepticism about the extent to which the ROC military can defend the island against an invasion by the People's Liberation Army (PLA). For example, a public opinion survey conducted by National Chengchi University found that only about 20 percent of respondents believe the ROC Armed Forces can defend Taiwan. In contrast, over 70 percent of respondents doubted the military could successfully defend the island (Chen, 2019). This reflects that either the ROC Armed Forces are incompetent or that the Taiwanese people misunderstand their armed forces. To that end, the MND, over the past decade, has expended a tremendous effort to educate the general public, especially college and high school students, about national defense. It seeks to improve the military's public image, increase people's understanding of the ROC Armed Forces, and boost morale.

In order to coordinate and integrate relevant ministries, local authorities, schools at all levels, social groups, and even the private sector, there is a need to plan and carry out defense education. Hence, the ROC government legislated the All-Out Defense Education Act in 2005 (Ministry of Justice, ROC, 2005) with the purpose to "promote all-out defense education, advance national defense knowledge and awareness to defense, complete national defense development, and ensure national security."

Under the guidance of the All-Out Defense Education Act, the education curriculums and relevant promotions are planned and implemented by the MND, and it has become one of the nine major administrative targets for the year 2021 (MND, 2020a).

13.1.3 *Efforts for enhancing the capability of all-out defense*

To promote all-out defense education, the MND is continuously improving educational effectiveness through creative curriculum design, a variety of campaigns, and diverse supplementary activities to attract public attention and win support. Several measures have been taken by the ministry. First, they hold "All-out Defense Education Conferences" in collaboration with the Ministry of Education to encourage universities to organize defense and patriotic events. Second, they support the Ministry of Education's efforts to hold live-fire drills for high school students, to allow the students to experience and respect firearms. Third, they have implemented training for teaching faculty and other educational personnel to meet the need for all-out defense education in schools of all levels. Fourth, they produce supplementary teaching materials for children from elementary to junior high schools, to enlighten them and deepen their understanding of national security issues. Fifth, they provide informative content for promoting all-out defense so the public can access the latest news from various online sources managed by the ROC military. Sixth, with coordination and support from the Ministry of Education, the MND is paying frequent visits to schools and university campuses to promote national defense education. Seventh, the MND organizes summer camps for students to experience some of the physical challenges of military life. To enhance the efficiency of these "summer battle camps," the MND focuses on various activities aimed at raising students' awareness about national defense issues. Among those camps, the Nansha (Spratly Islands) Camp is the most popular and competitive, where university students can see and experience the real-life, pressing security hazards in the South China Sea. Eighth, the MND offers common defense-related courses to civil servants and provides qualified instructors for all-out defense education. Ninth, they have been expanding social education and increasing civil-military interactions through visits to military bases and barracks, local guided military tours, and cooperation with reserve force training institutes. Tenth, they are enriching online resources for all-out defense education on an official website dedicated to that project. Eleventh, they are marketing all-out defense educational networks to promote their work and improve military recruitment. Twelfth, they are electing and awarding institutions and individuals with outstanding achievement awards to encourage active engagement with the all-out defense educational networks (MND, 2020a, 2021a; Political Warfare Bureau, 2017).

The MND has been instilling patriotic awareness among the general public through institutional education and on-the-job training sessions to raise public awareness of all-out defense. Recall training sessions for reservists and disaster relief drills as well as air raid exercises are held to promote public awareness of the need for all-out defense and patriotism. Boosting morale and consolidating the fighting spirit is another focus of such education. It is implemented through patriotic education, political warfare training, resisting-stress training, and mental health education (MND, 2019). Through these efforts and the implementation of various courses, events, and activities, students and ordinary citizens can better understand the concepts of all-out defense and, in turn, participate and contribute to national security and defense.

13.1.4 *Efforts to enhance all-out defense education and exercises*

A positive and professional image of the armed forces can encourage people to participate and engage in defense affairs. Unfortunately, for a myriad of reasons, especially the burden of history, the public image of the military in Taiwan society has long been less than positive, and thus the MND has to work harder to gain support by organizing public events, opening military bases to the public, producing TV dramas, and conducting effective media marketing to improve its image (MND, 2021b). In addition to all these efforts, the MND continues to maintain well-coordinated Civil–Military relations and interactions. A significant effort is made to improve relations and promote communication with the media. Like all government agencies in the digital era, the MND has to respond to calls for clarification in a timely manner and broadly disseminate a positive discourse to gain support from society. The MND promptly responds to stop the spread of disinformation in order to prevent further public-relations damage. For example, unlike the MND's passive reaction to media inquiries in the past, nowadays the MND actively releases information to the media about Chinese military activities on a daily basis, such as the regular updates on PLA aircraft and warships that are operating in or near Taiwan's airspace and waters.

Another step forward is to widely utilize social media to create a positive image and promote all-out defense. To leverage the messaging effectiveness of the internet, the MND has set up pages on Facebook, Instagram, and X (formerly Twitter) for the MND spokesperson and service headquarters, to release information on defense policy implementation. In addition, the MND has adopted innovative advertising campaigns to enhance its marketing reach. Through the production of image-shaping advertisements and short films for the Armed Forces, and broadcasting these films through various domestic media channels, they offer a more accurate and positive message to the general public so society can better understand what the military does to protect the country (MND, 2019).

13.1.5 *Reserve force: Major pillar of all-out defense*

According to the 2023 National Defense Report, an all-out defense system is composed of four pillars: (1) main forces, (2) garrison forces, (3) reserve forces and reserve system, and (4) civil defense system. The key component of the overall all-out defense is the reserve force and reserve system (MND, 2023).

Operating as the last line of defense, the ROC reserve force will determine whether Taiwan's homeland defense force is capable of coping with a PLA invasion. Countries like Sweden, Finland, and Israel, which also face a constant threat from powerful neighbors, have already established territorial defense forces, such as Sweden's Home Guard and the Israel Defense Forces. In a worst-case scenario of the PLA breaking through the ROC Army's coastal defense line and establishing a beachhead in Taiwan, reservists will quickly need to augment their active-duty counterparts on the ground. In theory, Taiwan's reserve force is of critical importance to ROC war plans and cross-strait deterrence and would serve as Taiwan's last line of defense. The question that confronts analysts is whether Taiwan's reserve force is, at present, reliable and capable enough to shoulder such an important burden. Fulco (2021) discovered that, in Taiwan society, people frequently ask, "Are these people (reservists) trained and ready to defend Taiwan in the event of a major conflict?" Others note, "some of them do not have adequate training in the use of small arms. Is Taiwan going to provide the necessary equipment to train these people and to spend time training them?" This is an important question.

Given these concerns, it is imperative to enhance the capabilities and reliability of the reserve force because an all-out defense demands a competent reserve force to operate in line with the regular forces. In the past three decades, Taiwan has been carrying out several waves of large-scale military downsizing in an attempt to build a small but professional force. Nevertheless, a smaller regular force during peacetime requires a supplement of a large reserve force through effective and efficient mobilization in wartime. In contrast to the reserve forces in the West, Taiwan's reserve force merely contains ex-regular force personnel. Conscripts who have completed their compulsory service are automatically registered as reservists. This is still applied to all draft-age men after they have completed the 4-month basic training.[1]

---

[1] Taiwan's military has been transforming to an all-volunteer force, but all draft-age men still need to undergo four months of compulsory military training service.

In 2022, a huge U-Turn in defense policy was initiated due to changes in the international strategic posture (especially the Russia-Ukraine war), escalating military tensions over the Taiwan Strait, the actual demands of all-out defense, shifts in the nation's demographic structure, training and real combat experience of militaries in advanced countries, and conscription service terms in democratic countries. The ROC government has decided to shift the conscription service from 4 months back to 1 year. Starting in January 2024, all males born after 2005 are now required to serve 12 months of conscription service. For those born from 1994 to 2004, they continue to serve a 4-month conscription service for their military training (MND, 2023).

Regarding missions and tasks, the MND dictates that "main forces are deployed on the frontline to safeguard Taiwan's territories, territorial waters and airspace against enemy invasion, while the reservists conduct homeland defense in the rear and support the operations of the main forces." During peacetime, regular recalls are exercised to sharpen reservists' military skills and test personnel mobilization efficiency. As for mission content, disaster relief tasks have been designated as the responsibility of the reserves. In principle, young and junior reservists are mainly assigned to combat units while senior and more experienced personnel are deployed to technical and logistics units.

13.1.6 *Gaps and shortfalls of the ROC reserve force*

Although Taiwan's reserve force is large in number, its competence exists only on paper and has long been criticized as a symbolic force based on mass mobilization. Having adopted a rather traditional and conservative approach with only a focus on skin-deep structural changes, any radical overhaul in the conceptualization of the reserves would be limited, as the function, mission, and personnel type still largely remain unchanged. In other words, reservists are still treated as a symbolic backup force with on-paper competence. Hence, revamping Taiwan's reserve force to build a capable territorial force manned and operated by well-trained and equipped reservists who can resist an enemy invasion and protect the homeland is sensible. This means that Taiwan is seeking to reform its reserve force to prepare them to wage a protracted insurgency or guerrilla war.

Unlike the eye-catching active-duty units with their tanks, warships, and fighter jets that can easily draw public and international attention, the issue of reforming the reserves has long been neglected in Taiwan.

In theory, the reserve forces are supposed to resist an enemy invasion. In reality, as currently constituted, the reserve force has not yet achieved sufficient competence. One of the reasons is due to the transformation to an all-volunteer force (AVF). Ever since the transition from conscription to an AVF, Taiwan's reserve force has been gradually hollowed out: of the MND's listed 2.31 million reservists, approximately 760,000 were discharged from military service within the last 8 years (based on the military standard, they are the ideal group of people to be mobilized for reserve recalls) (MND, 2020b). They are mainly composed of three strata of personnel: (1) volunteer soldiers, non-commissioned officers (NCOs), and officers (most of whom served for a minimum of 4 years); (2) conscripts who served 1 year; and (3) conscripts who only served 4 months of military service.

The reason for there being three strata of reservists is that, after the AVF transformation, the original 1-year compulsory service was curtailed to 4 months of basic training, or boot camp, without deployment to an operational unit. Therefore, among the 760,000 discharged reservists, roughly 349,000 are former conscripts, and another 326,000 have only completed 4 months of basic military training. Only 84,000 reservists served as voluntary soldiers with a minimum of 4 years of service; they are also the better-trained and much more motivated group (Hille, 2020). These three figures call into question the quality of Taiwan's reserve force.

Owing to the ever-growing strength of the PLA, which is increasing not only in quantity but also in quality, the ROC military's current size of 185,000 active-duty personnel would likely be insufficient to deter a large-scale PLA invasion. They need to be paired with a reserve force capable of performing territorial defense tasks. Therefore, it is vital to review and re-assess how Taiwan's reserve force is constituted and how reservists should be mobilized, trained, equipped, and deployed to support regular-force units. By law, reservists are obliged to respond to call-ups and perform various reserve duties; the MND's Armed Forces Reserve Command manages this through the reserve mobilization system. The Reserve Command oversees three regional reserve commands: the North Area, Central Area, and South Area. Each area command has its own reserve training center and oversees several local- and county-level reserve commands (there are 18 city and county commands in total).

Additionally, Taiwan has nearly one million civil defense volunteers who can be mobilized to perform disaster response tasks. At a glance, the size of the reserve force and the mobilization system look ideal on paper;

nevertheless, many reservists have been called up for just a few days every 2 years, with the training quality judged by Ian Easton *et al.* (2017) to be "insufficient to meet the challenges posed by the increasing threat from the PLA." As such, it would be difficult for the current reserve force and mobilization system to contribute much to Taiwan's defense capability. A former senior ROC defense official even candidly called the reserves "a joke" (Brown, 2020).

Military experts and observers, especially from the United States, have discovered that in the absence of any significant reform, Taiwan's reserve force will prove ineffective against a large-scale invasion. Among the 2.2 million listed reservists that Taiwan can theoretically mobilize, only approximately 300,000 must participate in regular refresher training under current regulations (Stokes *et al.*, 2020). Not only are the periods of refresher training short, but the quality and strength of training are inadequate. Furthermore, during recall training, reservists spend a great deal of time attending in-classroom briefings and taking care of tedious administrative work rather than operating weapons and performing military drills (Minnick, 2019). Many reservists do not even know if they are subject to the training requirements, nor is it difficult to get a waiver on the rare occasion they find themselves called up. Hunzeker (2021) criticized the MND for not addressing reserve issues more seriously and questioned whether the reservists could prove combat-ready in the event of an invasion. No doubt, Taiwan needs to quickly and fundamentally reform its massive but gradually weakening reserve force. The question is how.

Fortunately, the reserve problem drew the attention of former ROC President Tsai Ing-wen. She visited the Reserve Command in June 2020 and announced that reserve force reform would be launched (Chao, 2020). Taiwan's closest military ally, the United States, has also noticed this problem and has urged Taipei to review and reform its reserve system. The most comprehensive overview can be found in the 2017 RAND report, compiled by Easton *et al.* (2017) and commissioned by the US government. This report addressed four important issues: assess Taiwan's current reserve force structure, missions, and roles; analyze needed future capabilities; identify necessary enablers; and recommend transitional needs in the context of Taiwan's future force requirements. It recommended that Taipei posture the competent reserve units alongside the active-duty regular units to fight on the front lines in the initial stages of a PLA invasion. In terms of structure, Taiwan was encouraged to develop more technically specialized units staffed by reservists, such as cyber warfare, air defense, and sea denial units. The MND should also consider the option to "employ the reserve force as an instrument of statecraft for deterring PRC use of force and other forms of coercion" through reserve mobilization exercises, to better signal their capabilities (Easton *et al.*, 2017). Another US report, written by Hunzeker *et al.* (2018), expressed doubts about whether Taiwan should try to replicate the American model of an operational reserve; rather, it suggested that Taipei restructure its bulky reserve force by transforming it into a territorial defense force capable of conducting a prolonged insurgency campaign and engaging in guerrilla warfare in urban, jungle, and mountain environments.

Perhaps the reform efforts are likely to fall short of America's anticipations. It was estimated that between 200,000 and 400,000 of the most capable reservists would be organized into units based in their hometowns and trained to fight with the same weapons as the regular forces. Due to the constraints of active-duty force training facilities, capacities, and personnel, not all mobilized reservists are able to receive good-quality training and equipment. Therefore, if war breaks out, reservists would be assigned auxiliary and support functions, such as cooking, guarding barracks, detaining prisoners of war, and performing humanitarian assistance and disaster relief (HA/DR) tasks (Hille, 2020). The MND has addressed this shortfall by assigning reservists to participate in Taiwan's biggest annual military exercise. During the 2020 Han-Kuang Exercise, the MND showcased its reform efforts by deploying two reserve battalions alongside regular-force units to defend a beach against a simulated PLA attack. These reservists were trained with the active-duty personnel for the first time, and they operated howitzer artillery to deter the enemy's amphibious landing forces. Their performance was judged by the media as the "toughest refresher training course ever" ("Concerns over combat-readiness," 2020). A similar drill was recently conducted during the 2023 Han-Kuang Exercise, where reservists were mobilized to defend the Taipei Harbor.

13.2 Reforming Mobilization of Reservists

13.2.1 *Revamping the reservist recall system*

The competence of the reserve force is but one of the many challenges and consequences of the shift from conscription to an AVF. Taipei has been committed to reforming its mobilization and reserve system by reviewing and refining the organizational structure, training, and equipment, and by holding mobilization exercises. According to the Enforcement Act of Military Service System, all reservists are subject to recall, with the most common reason being for education or to maintain their soldiering proficiency. Currently, these biennial recalls are to be implemented no more than four times, with an average of 5–7 days (maximum 20 days) each time, and made within 8 years of the individual's date of discharge from active duty. Nevertheless, due to limitations on training capacity, not all reservists will perform their duty these four times.

Since Taiwan's reserve quality and strength are widely viewed as being inadequate, the heightened tensions over the Taiwan Strait have led the MND to announce in February 2021 that it will increase the length and frequency of reserve recall periods and beef up the strength and toughness of the refresher recall training. The MND is also extending the period during which reservists can be recalled, from a maximum of four times (14 days each time) in 8 years to four recalls in 12 years after being discharged, to ensure that Taiwan has a larger pool of reservists. To cope with the upcoming significant increase in reserve recalls and training periods, the capacity of the existing eight reserve training facilities (five A-level infantry brigades and three reserve training centers) will be significantly expanded, from the current annual total of 125,000 reservists to 268,000, and the maximum capacity will reach 290,000 reservists (MND, 2020b). In terms of well-being, the daily pay for the reservists during recall sessions will be increased by 1.5 times, and medical treatment and travel reimbursement will also be increased.

Evaluating the effectiveness of reserve mobilization and the recall system will not be comprehensive if it is only judged by the numbers, i.e., the report rates.[2] The quality of reserve mobilization and training should also be taken into account. The Air Force and Navy have higher confidence that reservists could effectively perform non-combat missions, such as logistics, repair, and maintenance. On the other hand, it is questionable whether army reservists can receive sufficient training during mobilization recalls to prepare them for combat. Nevertheless, for dealing with non-traditional security issues, Taiwan has demonstrated the capacity to mobilize its military and society to respond to disasters, including during the COVID-19 pandemic. One good example is that, in 2020, reservists

---

[2] It would be violation of the law not to show up; therefore, the mobilization report rate has always been high.

were quickly mobilized to establish several production lines to make face masks.

13.2.2 *Restructuring the reserve force*

The MND is currently conducting large-scale reserve force organizational restructuring, both at the MND and Reserve Force levels. Under the previous structure, the Armed Forces Reserve Command was directly under the MND. Sharing similar characteristics with the Army and also following the principle of unifying active duty and reserve units, the MND has restructured the chain of command by placing the Reserve Command under the ROC Army Headquarters.

At the reserve force restructuring level, due to most of the reserve force comprising a large number of infantry brigades, they can be broken down into four categories based upon staffing, equipment, and readiness levels: A-level reserve infantry brigades are at the highest level of readiness and are manned by active-duty officers and NCOs. The Reserve Command currently operates seven A-level infantry brigades; they are supplemented with reserve personnel when mobilized and are supported by an organic artillery battalion. The B-level reserve brigades are composed of active-duty personnel not currently assigned to an operational unit due to professional military education. They are at a lower level of mobilization readiness than A-level brigades. The C-level reserve brigades are local defense brigades raised by municipal and county reserve commands. They consist of three to five battalions of infantry and one battalion of field artillery. They are at a lower readiness level than B-level brigades. The D-level reserve brigades are drawn from troops assigned to organizations directly subordinate to reserve command headquarters and constitute about two to three infantry battalions in strength. They are the least capable, have no artillery, and are only lightly armed; this brigade is tasked with replenishing the combat losses of workforce and equipment for both standing and reserve units.[3]

The MND noticed that some of these brigades can hardly demonstrate combat capability due to a manpower vacuum. These four types of reserve brigades have been restructured into three types: A Type One brigade is

---

[3] Information based on the author's interview with a senior active-duty official from the reserve force command on May 13, 2021.

responsible for "coastal defense;" a Type Two brigade is in charge of "operational depth and urban terrain," while a Type Three brigade protects High-Value Targets (HVTs) (MND, 2020b). Cutting down on the number of organizational levels is expected to facilitate the mobilization process and make it easier to deploy the reserve force.

In order for the Type Two brigades to be capable of defending urban terrain, the MND will increase the strength and toughness of its training, with a focus on combat skills and urban guerrilla warfare. The Type Three brigade for HVT protection will be integrated into each operational theater for garrison tasks such as harbors, air bases, and critical infrastructure. These brigades will also operate together with the civil defense teams and police to ensure the security of important key facilities. The characteristics of tasks for each type of brigade are explained in the following.

To beef up the capability of the A-level coastal defense brigades (Type One brigade after restructuring). The original seven infantry brigades are scheduled to be increased to 12 brigades. In December 2021, the MND announced that five additional Type One brigades for coastal defense were slated to be created by 2023 (Strong, 2020). Regarding combat power, each brigade will consist of five infantry battalions and one artillery battalion. This decision has been implemented quite quickly; starting in January 2021, one Type One infantry brigade has already been added in the north (the 109th brigade, established on March 3, 2021) as well as one in the south (the 117th brigade, established on January 20, 2021). Addressing the 109th brigade at its commissioning ceremony, then-Chief of General Staff Admiral Huang Shu-kuang predicted that the newly created brigades will beef up combat capability for frontline coastal defense. The 101st Infantry Brigade and the second reserve training center were established in 2022, the 137th Infantry Brigade was established in July 2023 and the 249th Infantry Brigade will be established in July 2024. These newly established brigades will be operating in line with active-duty units during wartime to defend the coastal areas (Wu, 2021).

To rapidly restore the combat skills of reserve soldiers and enhance the intensity of education and training, the training schedule has been adjusted from "2 years, 1 training, 5–7 days each time" to "annual training, 14 days each time," with field camping and other toughened training sessions. Combat coaching is implemented at tactical positions to familiarize reserve forces with the operational environment, ensuring readiness for future training and preparedness standards as a basis for subsequent policy research and troop training execution.

Taiwan is surrounded by the sea, being an island nation. The essence of Taiwan and Penghu's defense operations is primarily defensive in nature, with the first line of defense along the coast being particularly important. The mission characteristics of the Type One brigades make them responsible for restraining enemy forces from landing along the coastal areas. To preserve forces and unleash firepower in front of defensive positions, effective deployment using coastal terrain is essential. In addition to deploying troops and firepower, effective collaboration and coordination with regular forces are necessary to form a cohesive defense against the enemy's beach landing.

In terms of Type Two brigades, these are composed of reserve forces from various military academies, the Army's test and evaluation centers, and reserve forces affiliated with each county or city. To enhance the brigade's depth and urban defense capabilities, ongoing plans involve the integration of military training, recall training, and reserve force management. The Type Two brigade's mission is tailored to different defense areas, including terrain point defense, urban defense, and shallow mountain pass defense. Terrain point defense involves holding tactical positions in coastal areas to expand defense depth and hinder the enemy's advance after a beach landing. Urban defense is undertaken by reserve brigades assigned to specific areas, responsible for protecting localities, assets, and impeding and delaying the enemy's advancement. Shallow mountain pass defense is managed by reserve mountain companies, aiming to maintain the safety of traffic lines around shallow mountains and prevent enemy intrusion into core positions.

Type Three Brigades are responsible for defending important military targets such as air force bases, naval ports, radar stations, launch vehicles, and other critical military objectives that fall under the category of secure protection.

13.2.3 *Establishing the all-out defense mobilization agency*

As defense technology and challenges posed by modern warfare become more advanced, maintaining combat readiness must not solely rely on the regular forces, but also on the efforts of citizens. In order for the all-out defense and mobilization to be better implemented, the launch of a dedicated agency is crucial. To streamline and flatten the mobilization process, the All-Out Defense Mobilization Agency (ADMA) needs to be established that is responsible for the mobilization of reservists during wartime and for disaster relief during peacetime. It aims to resolutely safeguard Taiwan's national security.

The MND transformed and expanded the former "All-Out Defense Mobilization Office" into the "All-Out Defense Mobilization Agency" (ADMA); it was unveiled in January 2022. This organizational change is an important threshold for the reserve reform. A bill for creating this agency was passed on May 21, 2021, by the Legislative Yuan. The law aims to strengthen cooperation between the central government and local authorities. This newly established agency has more authority and a higher status in order to better coordinate and unify mobilization and reserve affairs among different governmental agencies. The director of this agency is a civil servant with an equivalent rank of lieutenant general.

With the consolidated authority to handle mobilization and reserve affairs, the ADMA also aims to improve the efficiency of mobilizing materials, resources, and most importantly, the reservists themselves, through cross-governmental coordination and negotiation. It performs several tasks, including planning, supervision, and implementation of mobilization policy; oversight of reserve forces; planning and implementing the mobilization information system; and planning and supervising military materials, transportation, and mobilization policies of defense contractors (Legislature Research Bureau of the Legislative Yuan, ROC, 2021). Preparing for war and raising people's awareness are essential responsibilities of the agency. The creation of the ADMA demonstrates the government's determination to effect reserve reform and is a significant step forward in enhancing Taiwan's all-out defense capability.

13.2.4 *Synchronizing weapons for active duty and reserve units*

The reserve forces are equipped with obsolete weapons. The MND is seeking to upgrade their weapons and equipment by arming them with the same modern weapons operated by frontline units.

The MND has been transferring the existing weapons and equipment in the inventory to the reserve forces. Furthermore, the MND has allocated a certain number of new weapons and equipment acquired from the annual procurement programs to reserve forces (MND, 2023). For example, current CM11 tanks, M113 armored vehicles, 105 mm-caliber howitzers, and mortars from standing units are to be transferred to reserve units yearly to enrich their strike capabilities. As for personal weapons, reserve units will be fully equipped with active-duty rifles, pistols, and combat outfits (MND, 2020b).

13.3 Recommendations

13.3.1 *Creating a territorial defense force*

With the creation of 12 Type One (currently called A-level) brigades aiming to conduct coastal defense, Taiwan should consider transforming other reserve forces with the purpose of traditional counter-invasion into a Territorial Defense Force designed to resist foreign occupation via a prolonged insurgency waged in the cities, towns, and mountain areas. This only makes sense, because despite Taiwan's island geography, 70 percent of the terrain is covered with rugged, densely forested mountains. Transforming Taiwan's reservists into something akin to Sweden's Home Guard to defend the homeland and local communities would be cheaper and more realistic than trying to turn a reserve force into a second army (Hunzeker and Davis, 2020). The ADMA of the MND is working closely with the Interior Ministry to amend the Civilian Defense Act to expand the pool of civilian forces and volunteers who can be mobilized. This act is the legal basis for the MND to recall civilians into active service. In case of war, it authorizes the MND to call up voluntary workers such as volunteer police and firefighters to assist in military operations. Moreover, the MND has even set its sights on extra manpower from among voluntary workers at Buddhist and Taoist temples and churches. There are a total of 12,279 Buddhist and Taoist temples with 938,099 voluntary workers on the books. According to the Legislative Yuan, it is likely that these people can be transformed into a territorial defense force (Legislative Yuan, 2021). Traditionally, with their high levels of enthusiasm, loyalty, and mobilization efficiency, temple and voluntary religious workers have long played an essential role in disaster relief efforts around the island (Everington, 2021). Apart from reservists, these voluntary civilian workers represent another ideal source of manpower with which to form a territorial defense force.

Former Chief of the General Staff Admiral (retired) Lee Hsi-min, a well-known and highly respected military strategist, endorses this proposal for transforming reservists to create a Territorial Defense Force (Lee and Wu, 2020). He believes that a better role for the reserve force in Taiwan's defense is to perform continuous all-out resistance; therefore, regardless of whether the enemy is still at sea or has landed on the beach, this territorial defense force can still survive, maneuver, and fight. The basic guideline is to correctly assign each territorial defense unit to garrison its responsible city, county, town, and even village. The main task during peacetime for these forces is to assist in disaster relief work, while during wartime, they would be tasked with launching counter-attacks against an invading enemy from their locally deployed communities. In the event of a successful PLA landing on Taiwan, the reservists and the civil defense force would then have a bigger role to play. Lee highlights three principles of the territorial defense force: mobility, decentralization, and survivability. Adopting the concept and tactics of guerrilla warfare associated with their home-team advantage, the territorial defense force should be able to harass and launch surprise attacks to impose attrition and sabotage upon the enemy. The territorial defense force should be composed of those who have been discharged from the voluntary military service, compulsory military service, alternative service, police, firefighters, coast guard, and similar organization of a paramilitary nature. In terms of training, the Army's Special Forces instructors who specialize in urban and mountain guerrilla warfare can assist in the training of this force's combatants, giving them the skills and tactics to survive and overcome.

As for tactics, the Territorial Defense Force could melt into urban populations and mountainous environments from which to conduct guerrilla strikes. The so-called starfish tactic should be adopted, wherein small tactical ground units operate autonomously within a communication-denied environment to sustain irregular resistance operations. Also, some unconventional Vietnamese tactics (developed during the Vietnam War) could be replicated by the territorial defense force to carry out a protracted resistance. It would also be helpful to embed small units of ROC Army special operations personnel to fight in line with the territorial defense force, in order to coordinate sabotage and resistance efforts, and maintain morale (Thomas et al., 2014).

13.3.2 *Integrating reserve force into the overall defense concept*

Having realized itself as a small military force and facing a much bigger and advanced military power, in recent years Taiwan has developed a new way of thinking: the Overall Defense Concept (ODC), aiming to re-orient defenses toward a genuinely asymmetric air and sea denial posture. The ODC was conceived and developed by Admiral Lee, mentioned above (Lee and Lee, 2020). The three tenets of ODC for force buildup are force preservation, traditional capabilities, and asymmetric capabilities; it envisions Taiwan adopting an asymmetric defense posture and fielding forces capable of overcoming a much stronger enemy.

In contrast to the conventional war-fighting concept, the reserve force can play a more significant role in the ODC. The 2019 National Defense Report explains that, in order to meet the objectives of the ODC, the reserve force needs to develop capabilities for "safeguarding littoral zone, protecting HVTs, and conducting anti-airborne operations" (MND, 2019). These are essential missions in the event of an invasion; in addition, given that the regular forces will be focusing on coastal defense, it is sensible to assign such tasks to reservists. The reserve force will become the last line of defense should the ROC Air Force, Navy, and Army fail to defend the nation, and the PLA succeed in putting boots on the ground. For such a worst-case scenario, the MND should plan to train and equip millions of reservists for a protracted war. Due to the nature of urban and guerrilla warfare, these reservists must be trained for localized operations with a decentralized organizational command.

Mobilization is key to the success of the ODC, as it will be validated to achieve the objectives of "prompt mobilization to support operations in time." To date, the MND has been following the principle of "smart mobilization, fast formation, and quick resilience" to conduct Tong-Hsin Exercise (manpower mobilization) and Zi-Chiang Exercise (material mobilization) to validate the formation of reserve forces, quick resilience of combat power, command-and-control mechanisms, backups of communications, expanded repair capacities of civilian construction companies, and integration of medical resources (MND, 2019). Regarding mobilization, under the guidance of "unifying regular and reserve units," individual mobilization offices will be merged to streamline the mobilizing process and thus save time. On the other hand, through inter-agency coordination to integrate mobilization efforts, the MND has set up individual mobilization offices in each service and operational theater to coordinate between regular and reserve forces (MND, 2021c).

13.3.3 *Recruiting part-time volunteer reservists*

Horowitz (2009) emphasized that a greater reliance on post-mobilization assets could reduce the need for active-duty recruits. His argument is backed by an ROC government research project that urged the MND to consider recruiting volunteer reserve soldiers as part of a complementary measure for the AVF (Executive Yuan, ROC, 2007). Recruiting volunteer reservists has long been practiced in many countries, such as the United States, the United Kingdom, and Sweden. The Singapore Armed Forces Volunteer Corps allows women, new citizens, and first-generation permanent residents to contribute to the national defense in non-combat roles (Easton *et al.*, 2017 p. 77). It is recommended that the government consider recruiting part-time volunteer reservists who can be drawn upon in an emergency on short notice to fill the rank and file.

Taiwan sits at the forefront of information and communications technology (ICT) research and development and is the most important link in the supply chain for the very microchips that enable the global proliferation of advanced, high-tech electronics. Therefore, the Reserve Command should create special units composed of ICT and cyber specialists (cyber reserves). In these reserve units, personnel would not be active-duty military staff but would serve on a part-time and voluntary basis, tasked with performing cybersecurity duties for the armed forces. They would possess the necessary ICT expertise and may already work in cybersecurity in their civilian jobs; hence they can use their civilian skills in the field for their military missions.

A six-country case study conducted by ETH Zurich compared why these countries were recruiting voluntary reservists and how they planned to use them in offensive and defensive cyber operations (Baezner, 2020). Their findings suggested that cyber reserve forces would have a positive impact in countering the workforce shortage in the armed forces. Cyber reserve force personnel employed part-time by the armed forces would no doubt be an appealing early-career option for young cybersecurity specialists. In Taiwan, Chen-Yi Tu (2020) identified that it is feasible to establish a cyber reserve force on a voluntary basis to promote integration between the military and civilians. Despite difficulties such as recruitment, the conflict of the part-time nature of the reserves, and the need for a security clearance due to the likelihood of contact with sensitive information, Yi-Suo Tzeng (2020) suggests that Taipei consider the approach of developing and using civilian cyber warriors. He identifies a relatively low level of risk to reserve cyber warriors, and if they are combined with civilian "white hat" hackers, Taiwan's combat power will be substantially enhanced. Thanks to Taiwan's advanced IT industry, the number of cyber reserve warriors can be significantly increased. This effort is ongoing but needs improvement: the MND's Information, Communication and Electronic Warfare Force Command recruited only seven reserve cyber warriors in 2020. Obviously this is insufficient, and a greater effort should be made (Su, 2018).

The other type of voluntary reservist is called the "reservist warrior." Starting in 2017, MND has been implementing this reservist warrior program as one of the most important measures taken by the MND to utilize the expertise of discharged personnel. These reservist warriors are required to serve 2 days per month (usually on weekends) and attend refresher training for 7 days per year, with regular service for a minimum of 29 days per year. These reservists are also known as "weekend warriors" and are qualified to act as backup soldiers to share the burden of combat readiness and assist active-duty personnel. Since recruiting voluntary reservist warriors was initiated, the results so far have been acceptable. For example, in 2018, except for the Air Force (which recruited only four out of a target of 28), the Army, Navy, reserve command, and military police command all achieved at least 90 percent of their recruitment goals. Overall, the recruitment numbers have shown a steady increase, from 100 in 2017 to 185 in 2020 (MND, 2017; Armed Forces Reserve Command, 2021).

13.4 Conclusion

Under both the current and previous US administrations, Taiwan has been purchasing more, and more significant, arms from the United States than ever before, which demonstrates a strong will to defend itself. However, the defense budget constraints and competition for resources have also caused planners in Taipei to seek more available and affordable ways to meet the growing threat from China. Among them, enhancing the All-Out Defense capabilities through reforming the mobilization system and reserve force and reserve system could be a more effective way of defending Taiwan. To enhance Taiwan's all-out defense capabilities and reserve force readiness and effectiveness, the MND has made a stride forward to revamp the reserve system. Although the outcome has yet to be seen, it is a positive sign that the issue of reserve capability is now being addressed. This chapter provides recommendations specifying what are believed to be the most promising fields in this regard. After the reform, Taiwan's reserve force will no longer be called a paper tiger, and all-out defense will be more reliable.

References

Armed Forces Reserve Command, Ministry of National Defense, ROC (2021a). Recall types. Retrieved from https://afrc.mnd.gov.tw/AFRCWeb/Unit_en.a spx?MenuID=6302&ListID=2304.

Armed Forces Reserve Command, Ministry of National Defense, ROC (2021b). [Hòubèi zhànshì] Reserve fighter. Retrieved from https://afrc.mnd.gov.tw/AFRCWeb/Content.aspx?MenuID=702.

Baezner, M. (2020). CSS Cyber Defense Report: Study on the use of reserve forces in military cybersecurity, April 2020, Center for Security Studies (CSS), ETH Zürich.

Brown, D. (2020, June). Reconceiving Taiwan's reserve forces. *Defense Security Brief*, 9(1). Institute for National Defense and Security Research, pp. 1–8.

Chao, P. (2020, September 29). Defense ministry to strengthen reserve forces. *Radio Taiwan International*. Retrieved from https://en.rti.org.tw/news/view/id/2004066.

Chen, L. (2019, January 18). Saving your country by yourself. *CommonWealth Magazine*. Retrieved from https://www.cw.com.tw/article/5093836.

Concerns over combat-readiness of four-month conscripts (2020, October 5). *Formosa News*. Retrieved from http://archive.today/zTw0b.

Easton, I., Stokes, M., Cooper, C. A., and Chan, A. (2017). *Transformation of Taiwan's Reserve Force*. Santa Monica, CA: RAND Corporation.

Everington, K. (2021, April 22). Taiwan to include 'spiritual warriors' in reserve force to fight off China invasion. *Taiwan News*. Retrieved from https://www.taiwannews.com.tw/en/news/4183778.

Executive Yuan, ROC (2007). The complementary measure of all-volunteer force. Research. Development and Evaluation Commission, pp. 148–167. Taipei, Taiwan.

Fulco, M. (2021, April 16). For Taiwan's defense, the focus is on asymmetric, indigenous capabilities. *Taiwan Business Topics*. Retrieved from https://topics.amcham.com.tw/2021/04/taiwan-defense-asymmetric-indigenous-capabilities/.

Hille, K. (2020, July 12), Taiwan strives to bolster forces in response to Beijing sabre-rattling. *Financial Times*. Retrieved from https://www.ft.com/content/92029f49-3e9a-47b7-b967-2af823f185cd.

Horowitz, S. (2009). *Implementing an All-Volunteer Force in Taiwan*. IDA, p. 4.

Hunzeker, M. A., Lanoszka, A., Davis, B., Fay, M., Goepner, E., Petrucelli, J., & Seng-White, E. (2018). A question of time: Enhancing Taiwan's conventional deterrence posture. *Center for Security Policy Studies*, George Mason University. Arlington, VA.

Hunzeker, M. and Davis, B. (2020, August 10). The defense reforms Taiwan needs. *Defense One*. Retrieved from https://www.defenseone.com/ideas/2020/08/defense-reforms-taiwan-needs/167558/.

Hunzeker, M. A. (2021, February 18). Hearing on "deterring PRC aggression toward taiwan" panel on "the cross-strait military balance." Statement Before the U.S.-China Economic & Security Review Commission, pp. 44–45.

Lee, H. and Wu, E. (2020, October 8). Transformation of the reserve force: Creating a territorial defense force. *Apple Daily*.

Lee, H. and Lee, E. (2020, November 3). Taiwan's overall defense concept, explained. *The Diplomat*. Retrieved from https://thediplomat.com/2020/11/taiwans-overall-defense-concept-explained/.

Legislature Research Bureau of the Legislative Yuan, Republic of China (April 2021). Assessment report for the organization bill of the defense reserve mobilization agency.

Legislative Yuan, Republic of China (2021, June). Assessment for incorporating temple volunteers into the reserve force. Issue Analysis Number 1323.

Ministry of Justice, ROC (2005). All-out defense education act. Laws and Regulations Database of the Republic of China. Retrieved from https://law.moj.gov.tw/ENG/LawClass/LawAll.aspx?pcode=F0080014.

Ministry of Justice, ROC (2019). All-out defense mobilization readiness act. Laws and Regulations Database of the Republic of China. Retrieved from https://law.moj.gov.tw/ENG/LawClass/LawAll.aspx?pcode=F0070013.

Ministry of National Defense, ROC (2017). 2017 Quadrennial Defense Review.

Ministry of National Defense, ROC (2019). 2019 national defense report.

Ministry of National Defense, ROC (2020a). The administrative plan of ministry of national defense for the fiscal year of 2021

Ministry of National Defense, ROC (2020b, October 22). Special report on promoting reserve force capability submitted to the legislative Yuan, Taiwan.

Ministry of National Defense, ROC (2021a). All-out defense education website. Retrieved from https://aode.mnd.gov.tw/.

Ministry of National Defense, ROC (2021b). 2021 work plan for promoting all-out defense education. Retrieved from https://aode.mnd.gov.tw/Unit/Content/1528?unitId=106.

Ministry of National Defense, ROC (2021c). 2021 quadrennial defense review.

Ministry of National Defense, ROC (2023). 2023 national defense report.

Minnick, W. (2019, March 19). How to save Taiwan from itself. *The National Interest*. Retrieved from https://nationalinterest.org/feature/how-save-taiwan-itself-48122.

Political Warfare Bureau (2017). Ministry of national defense, ROC. Retrieved from https://gpwd.mnd.gov.tw/english/Publish.aspx?cnid=267&p=4421.

Stokes, M., Yang, K., and Lee, E. (2020). Preparing for the nightmare: Readiness and *ad hoc* coalition operations in the Taiwan strait. Project 2049. Arlington, VA, p. 22.

Strong, M. (2020, December 24). Taiwan military to form 5 new coastal defense brigades. *Taiwan News*. Retrieved from https://www.taiwannews.com.tw/en/news/4085979.

Su, H. (2018, November 1). Measures and legal amendments for establishing the information, communications and electronic force command. The Legislative Yuan, ROC. Retrieved from https://www.ly.gov.tw/Pages/Detail.aspx?nodeid=6590&pid=176016.

Thomas, J., Stillion, J., and Rehman, I. (2014). *Hard ROC 2.0, Taiwan and Deterrence Through Protraction*. Center for Strategic and Budgetary Assessments, p. 60. Washington, DC.

Tu, C. (2020, September 30). *Cyber Reserve Force: Possibilities and Limitations. Reinforcing the Reserve Forces*. Defense Situation Special Edition, Vol. 5. Institute for National Defense and Security Research, pp. 27–35. Taipei, Taiwan.

Tzeng, Y. (2020, September 30). *Civil Cyber Warriors: A Path that Taiwan Can Take. Reinforcing the Reserve Forces*. Defense Situation Special Edition, Vol. 5. Institute for National Defense and Security Research, pp. 36–43. Taipei, Taiwan.

Wu, S. (2021, March 3). Qiánghuà hòubèi zhàn lì huáng shǔguāng zhǔchí lùjūn 109 lǚ biānchéng diǎnlǐ [Chief of General Staff Huang Shu-Kuang chaired the commissioning ceremony of the 109th brigade]. *Liberty Times*.

© 2025 World Scientific Publishing Company
https://doi.org/10.1142/9789811298301_bmatter

Index

Symbols
9/11, 63, 66

A
A2/AD, 84
Abaigatu, 64
Abrams tanks, 161
academic exchanges, 81
Acheson, Dean, 205
active denial military strategy, 166
active denial strategy (ADS), 154
Aerospace Industrial Development
  Cooperation (AIDC), 84
Afghanistan, 12
agile combat employment (ACE),
  28
AGM-84H, 195
Aigun, 60, 64
airborne warning and control systems
  (AWACS), 86
air defense identification zone
  (ADIZ), 39, 43, 69, 71, 98
air superiority, 158
air-to-surface missiles (ASMs), 158
all-out defense mobilization agency,
  249
Amami Ohshima Island, 108

American Institute (AIT) in Taiwan,
  7
amphibious, 45
amphibious attack, 197, 224
amphibious invasion, 219, 229
amphibious landing, 245
Amur region, 60, 64, 68
anti-access/area-denial (A2/AD), 28,
  154
anti-Americanism, 65
anticipated armed attack situations, 110
anticipatory self-defense, 11
anti-communist, 61
anti-submarine warfare (ASW), 176,
  182
arms buildup, 1, 14
Article 9, 82, 87, 109, 237
Asia Pacific Computer Emergency
  Response Team (APCERT), 85
Asia Reassurance Initiative Act, 82
Aso, Taro, 52, 101
Association of Southeast Asian
  Nations (ASEAN), 40, 98
asymmetric, 57, 69, 212, 215, 218,
  227, 253
asymmetry, 70
AUKUS, 192

260 *Index*

Australia, 45, 51, 82
Austronesian, 123
AV500W, 226
avenger air defense system, 159

B

back-to-back, 63, 65, 68
Baodiao protest movement, 130
Baoguang, Xu, 128
Bashi Channel, 24
Beijing Olympics, 64
Beijing Winter Olympics, 60
Ben-li, Luo, 200
Biden, Joe, 20, 27, 41, 52, 78–80, 100
Black Water Trench, 128
Blinken, Antony, 40
blockade, 6, 23, 45, 97, 104, 139
blue water, 182
Bohai Sea, 86
Bolotnaya Square protests, 65
Bolshoi Ussuriskiy, 64
Bucha, 67–68

C

2008 crisis, 64
C5ISR, 2
Cambodia, 40
Caroline test, 11
Carter, Jimmy, 5
casus belli, 3
CCP's propaganda, 89
censorship, 59
Chan, Eric, 43
Chengchi University, 99, 238
Chengdu J-20A, 157
Chicago Council on Global Affairs, 102
Chien, Wan, 158, 200
Chih-Cheng, Lo, 48
China–India border, 191
China Power project, 40

Chinese Civil War, 5, 20–21, 61
Chinese Communist Party (CCP), 5, 19, 23, 30, 40, 53, 61, 78, 84, 90, 99, 211
Chinese demographic threat, 63
Ching-te, Lai, 190
clarity, 106
Clausewitz, 204
coast guard, 252
cognitive warfare, 32
Cold War, 20, 77, 83, 89
collateral damage, 2, 224
collective self-defense, 2, 14, 109, 139
Communiqués, 88
Congress, 87–88, 96
constructive partnership, 63
constructivist, 90
counterinsurgency, 9
COVID-19 pandemic, 29, 66, 83, 246
Crimea, 58, 65
Critical Impact Situations, 110
cross-strait deterrence, 241
cross-strait relations, 3, 40
CSBC corporation, 180
cyberattacks, 84
cyber regime complex, 85
cyber reserve forces, 254
cybersecurity, 88, 254
cybersecurity intelligence, 84
cyberspace, 22, 212
cyber warfare, 244

D

Daewoo Shipbuilding & Marine Engineering Co., Ltd, 180
Davidson, Philip, 1, 19, 181, 219
declaration of independence, 26, 33
decoupling, 192
De-fa, Yen, 189
de facto sovereignty, 98

Index 261

defense attaché, 8, 43
Defense Buildup Program, 81
defense deployment, 113
defense mobilization, 115, 235–237, 250
Defense Reserve Mobilization Agency, 203
Defense Security Cooperation Agency (DSCA), 195
Definition of Aggression, 200
Democratic Progressive Party (DPP), 48
deployment order, 113
deterrence, 25, 33
Diaoyutai/Senkaku Islands, 122
diet, 101
Dilemma, Malacca, 162
disinformation, 99, 103, 240
Divine Eagle, 226
drills, 69

E
E-2Ts, 163
East, 71
East China Sea, 68, 85–86
Eastern Siberia–Pacific Ocean (ESPO) oil pipeline, 64
economic intelligence, 83
Eisenhower, Dwight, 107
Election Study Center, 98
electromagnetic, 212
electronic intelligence (ELINT), 86
emergency response situations, 110
energy geopolitics, 64
engagement, 20
Eurofighter Typhoon, 216
evacuation, 3
exclusive economic zone (EEZ), 24, 85, 40, 47, 95–96, 121
exercises, 96

F
F-5E, 158
F-15, 216
F-16, 158, 216
F-35, 216
Falklands, 149
Fan, Chen-kuo, 42
F-CK-1s, 158
Feng, Yun, 158, 200
Finlandized, 137
First Island Chain, 122, 154
First Sino-Japanese War, 124
First United Front, 61
force protection, 163, 217
Foreign Military Financing (FMF), 104
FORMOSAT-7R, 143
forward defense, 159
friendly fire, 2, 13
Fuchu Air Base, 143

G
G7, 79
game theory, 29
General Security of Military Information Agreement (GSOMIA), 86
geriatric peace, 177
Germany, 61, 63
Global Cooperation and Training Framework (GCTF), 88
Gorbachev, Mikhail, 62
gray-zone, 34, 114, 217 218
Ground Self-Defense Force (GSDF), 108
Guam, 161
guerrilla, 156, 242, 245, 248, 252–253

H
Han-Kuang exercise, 164, 245
Harop, 221

262 *Index*

Harpoon, 166, 195
Hateruma Island, 96
Hayashi, Yoshimasa, 98
Heilongjiang, 64
Heixiazi, 64
Heron, 215
HF-2E, 200
HIMARS, 195
Hofu Kita Air Base, 143
Hong Kong, 30, 100, 229
Hsiung Feng IIE, 158
Hsiung Feng III, 46, 158
hub-and-spokes, 89
human intelligence (HUMINT), 41,
    81, 86
humanitarian assistance and disaster
    relief (HADR), 9, 51, 85, 245
human rights, 25
hybrid conflict, 58
Hypersonic Cruise Missile (HCM),
    46
Hyper Velocity Gliding Projectile
    (HVGP), 46

I
Imagery Intelligence (IMINT), 81,
    86
independence, 50, 229
India, 46
Indigenous Defense Submarine (IDS)
    program, 145
Indonesia, 47, 180
Indo-Pacific Command, 28, 219
Indo-Pacific Strategy, 80
information and communications
    technology (ICT), 83, 254
information-sharing, 13
Ing-wen, Tsai, 26, 48, 78, 95, 98,
    228, 244
intelligence cooperation, 83, 86
intelligence exchanges, 49, 87

intelligence sharing, 41–42, 43, 81,
    87
intelligence, surveillance, and
    reconnaissance (ISR), 42, 85–87,
    163, 217, 227–228
intelligence, surveillance, target
    acquisition, and reconnaissance
    (ISTAR), 215
intermediate-range ballistic missiles
    (IRBMs), 157
international law, 6, 11
international values-based order, 57
invasion of Ukraine, 126, 224
Irpin, 67
Ishiba, Shigeru, 44
Ishigaki Island, 108
Ishihara, Shintaro, 132
Israel Defense Forces (IDF), 11,
    241
Itu Aba, 5

J
Japan Aerospace Exploration Agency
    (JAXA), 143
Japan Air Self-Defense Force
    (JASDF), 28
Japan–China Joint Statement of 1972,
    33, 131
Japanese Computer Emergency
    Response Team/Coordination
    Center (JPCERT/CC), 85
Japanese diet, 80
Japan Forum for Strategic Studies,
    114
Japan Maritime Self-Defense Force,
    178
Japan Self-Defense Force (JSDF), 9,
    27, 42, 80
Japan's Self-Defense Law, 14
Japan–Taiwan Co-Prosperity Chiefs
    Alliance, 49

Japan–Taiwan Exchange Association, 34, 42, 49
Japan–Taiwan Fishery agreement, 80
Japan–US security alliance, 2, 20–21, 23, 33
Japan–US security treaty, 31, 96
Jinping, Xi, 21, 23, 26–27, 29, 33, 39, 59, 64–67, 78–79, 84, 90, 96, 101, 211
Jintao, Hu, 64
Jinmen, 5
Joint Communiqués, 5
Joint Island Attack Campaign (JIAC), 155
Jōmon, 124
JS *Muroto*, 144

K

Kai-shek, Chiang, 4, 61
Kamikaze drones, 216, 221, 224
Kaohsiung, 180
Kavalan, 124
Kawasaki Heavy Industries (KHI), 180
Kennan, George F., 134
Khabarovsk Krai, 68
Khrushchev, 61
Kinmen, 155
Kishida, Fumio, 21, 35, 40, 79, 98, 100
Kishi, Nobuo, 89, 100
Kishi, Nobusuke, 107
Kono, Taro, 45
Korean War, 139
Krach, Keith, 190
Kremlin, 63
Kume-jima, 128
Kuomintang, 4, 21, 61
Kuo, Yu-jen, 43–44
Kurihara family, 132

Kuriyama, Takakazu, 31
Kyakhta, 60

L

land-attack cruise missiles (LACMs), 157
Leaf, Paul, 46
legal warfare, 3, 9, 14
Liberal Democratic Party (LDP), 48, 125
liberal international order, 21
Lithuania, 89
littoral regions, 227
littoral zone, 162, 217, 253

M

M47 Patton tanks, 177
M503, 194
Manchuria, 61
maritime disputes, 71
maritime domain awareness (MDA), 85
maritime militia, 147
maritime security, 122
Martin, Lockheed, 158, 216
martial law, 21
Matsu, 5, 155
Matsuda, Yasuhiro, 42
Matsuno, Hirokazu, 47
McCarthy, Kevin, 78, 98
median line, 77
medium-range ballistic missiles (MRBMs), 157
Medvedev, Dmitri, 60
midget submarines, 177
Mid-Term Defense Program, 21
military attachés, 82
military buildup, 19, 29
military cooperation, 51, 53
military drills, 1, 71, 78, 85
military exercises, 47, 77

264 *Index*

military industry exchange, 83
military operations other than war
  (MOOTW), 9–10
military relationship, 51
military-to-military contacts, 14
Minelaying, 183
Mirage 2000s, 158
Mitsubishi Heavy Industries, Ltd.,
  45
Miyako Island, 108
Miyamoto, Riku, 49
Mobilization of Reservists, 245
Monterey Talks, 4
morale, 146, 217, 237–239, 252
MS-110, 195
multi-domain deterrence, 201
multipolar world order, 67
Munich Agreement, 205
Mutual Defense Treaty, 193
mutually assured destruction, 148
mutual security treaty, 4–5

N

Nagashima, Akihisa, 53
Nansei Islands, 108
NASA, 144
National Chung-Shan Institute of
  Science and Technology (NCSIST),
  84, 227
National Defense Program
  Guidelines, 21
National Defense Strategy, 81
nationalism, 1
National Security Strategy (NSS),
  19–22, 35, 80–81
NATO, 26, 67, 84, 86
neo-colonialism, 174
Nerchinsk, 60
New Ocean Researcher, 121
Nixon, Richard, 52
no limits, 66

no limits friendship, 60
Noda, Yoshihiko, 132
non-combatant evacuation operation
  (NEO), 9–10, 34
nontraditional security, 51
Northeast Project, 128
North Korea, 22, 34, 47
nuclear, 33, 71
nuclear war, 20, 27
nuclear weapons, 25

O

O'Brien, Robert, 167
offensive defense, 196
Okinawa, 47, 52
One China, 32–34, 89
One Country, Two Systems, 20, 26,
  29–30, 99, 100, 229
Operation Entebbe, 11
opium war, 60
Out of Taiwan hypothesis, 123
overall defense concept, 212,
  215–216, 253

P

pacific deterrence initiative, 29
pacifist, 79
pacifist Japanese Constitution, 11
pacing threat, 20
Paraguay, 190
"passing exercise" (PASSEX), 85
Patriot Advanced Capability (PAC)-3,
  158
Pax Americana, 65
peacekeeping, 9
Peace Mission, 69
peace treaty, 5
Pearl River, 158
Peking, 60
Pelosi, Nancy, 1, 23, 30, 39, 50, 77,
  85, 95–96, 98, 123, 235

Penghu, 155, 249
Pentagon, 154, 219
People's Liberation Army Air Force (PLAAF), 6, 23, 40, 43–44, 68, 77, 84, 89, 97–98, 212, 226, 238, 241, 243–244, 252–253
People's Republic of China (PRC), 5, 21, 31, 39, 59, 95
Persian Gulf, 184
Philippines, 46
PLA attack, 245
PLA Navy (PLAN), 46, 156
policy coordination, 9
Policy Simulation of the Taiwan Strait Crisis, 30
porcupine strategy, 147
Potsdam Proclamation, 31
Pratas Island, 5
Priamure, 60
Primorsky Krai, 61
prior authorization, 111
prior consultation, 106–107
propaganda, 58, 65
psychological warfare, 3, 177
public opinion warfare, 3
Putin, Vladimir, 27, 41, 63, 65–67

Q
Qing dynasty, 128
QUAD, 79
Quadrilateral Security Dialogue, 192

R
Reaper drones, 166
Reapers, 215
Recent Defence White Papers, 23
renegade province, 95, 211
Republic of China Navy (ROCN), 173
Republic of China (ROC), 235
Republic of Korea, 142

resolute defense, 201
ROC Air Force, 253
ROC Coast Guard, 121
ROC military, 9, 14
RQ-4 Global Hawk, 216
rules-based international order, 60, 66–67, 71, 89, 219
rules-based (read: American) international global order, 59
Russo-Japanese war, 61
Russo-Ukraine war, 20, 41, 68, 81, 84, 86, 89, 242
Ryukyu Islands, 123

S
Saker Scout, 225
Sakishima Islands, 24, 124
salami-slicing, 129
Samarkand, 67
sanctions, 68, 89
San Francisco Peace Treaty, 5, 7–8, 12, 14
Satellite Intelligence (SATINT), 86
Satō, Eisaku, 52
Sato, Masahisa, 48, 132
Sato-Nixon Joint Statement, 31
Satoshi, Morimoto, 116
Sea Cooperation, 69
sea lines of communication (SLOC), 1, 137, 178
Second Island Chain, 122
Second Sino-Japanese War, 126
Second World War, 5
Security Consultative Committee's (SCC), 52
Security Council, 67, 70
Security Dilemma, 192
security guarantor, 5, 87
Self-Defense Forces (SDF), 14, 30, 49, 98, 101, 106

266 *Index*

Self-Defense Law, 3
semiconductor industry, 83
Senate Armed Services Committee, 181, 219
Senkaku/Diaoyu Islands, 226
Senkaku Islands, 22–24, 27, 34
Shaanxi Y-8, 194
Shaffer, Sabrina, 50
Shandong, 78
Shanghai Communiqué, 193
Shenyang FC-31, 216
Shenyang J-16, 157
Shih-Ying, Tsai, 48
Shinzo, Abe, 19, 21, 23, 39–40, 78, 101
Shōgun, 128
short-range ballistic missiles (SRBMs), 157
Shu-kuang, Huang, 248
Siberia, 63
signals intelligence (SIGINT), 41, 81, 86
Sinocentrism, 64
Sino-Soviet split, 58, 61
situational awareness, 43, 86
soft revisionists, 57
Soryu-class attack submarines, 146
South China Sea, 5, 68, 86, 71, 97, 239
Southern Theater Command (STC), 158
South Korea, 42, 46, 50, 64, 70, 106, 177
Southwest Islands, 24
sovereignty, 10
SpaceX, 86
Special Operation Forces (SOFs), 162
special operations personnel, 252
Stalin, 61
Starlink, 86

status quo, 21, 23, 26, 71, 80, 98–99
status quo ante, 21
strategic ambiguity, 20–21, 27, 106
strategic clarity, 103
strategic competition, 65
strategic competitor, 20, 27
strategic partnership, 63
strategic rears, 63
Suao Naval Base, 176
submarine cables, 138
submarines, 45–46, 84, 214–215, 218, 229
Suga-Biden Joint Statement, 31
Suga, Yoshihide, 52, 78, 100
supply chain, 50, 254
surface-to-surface missiles (SSMs), 158
surveillance, 217, 221, 225, 227–228
Survival-Threatening Situations, 110
Swanström, 50
Switzerland, 195

T
tabletop exercise (TTX), 96
tactical nuclear weapons, 146
Taigei, 45
Taiping Island, 160
Taiping rebellion, 60
Taiwan Allies International Protection and Enhancement Initiative Act, 82
Taiwan Assurance Act, 82
Taiwan Enhanced Resilience Act, 104
Taiwanese identity, 124, 229
Taiwan Foundation for Democracy, 26
Taiwan identity, 21
Taiwan independence, 21
Taiwan National Defense Industry Development Association (TW-DIDA), 84

Taiwan Relations Act (TRA), 2–7, 14, 21, 27, 49, 51–52, 87–88, 96
Taiwan Strait, 8, 23–24, 28, 31, 77, 82, 87, 89–90, 95, 216, 223–224, 229–230, 242, 246
Taiwan Strait Crisis Policy simulation, 20, 31, 85
Taiwan Travel Act, 4, 82
Taliban, 12
Tarabarov, 64
Tatsushirō, Koga, 129
Teng-hui, Lee, 131
Terminal High Altitude Area Defense (THAAD), 50
terra nullius, 129
territorial defense force, 251
Third Taiwan Strait Crisis, 20
Three Gorges Dam, 158
three warfares, 3, 9
Tianxia world order, 65
Tien Chien, 159
Tien Kung, 159, 161
Treaty of Shimonoseki, 124
trilateral, 2, 32, 52, 90
Triton, 143
Trump, Donald, 19, 65–66
Tzu, Sun, 41

U
Ukraine war, 30, 220
UN Charter, 67, 109
UN General Assembly, 67
unification, 1
United Kingdom, 82, 223, 254
United Nations Convention on the Law of the Sea (UNCLOS), 127
United Nations Security Council, 5
Unmanned Aerial Vehicle, 78, 159, 211

Unmanned Combat Aerial Vehicles (UCAV), 212
Unmanned Underwater Vehicles, 183
unsinkable aircraft carrier, 1, 138
US Indo-Pacific Command, 1
US–Japan alliance, 3
US–Japan Defense Cooperation, 86
US–Japan Mutual Security Agreement, 12
US–Japan security alliance, 51
US–Japan–Taiwan triangle, 14
US Navy Indo-Pacific Command, 181
USSR, 61

V
Vietnam, 61, 252
Vystrčil, Milos, 190

W
Wallace "Chip" Gregson, 43
war-gaming, 81, 219
war in Ukraine, 146
war of attrition, 147
Weston, John, 53
white group, 90
white paper, 39
Winter Olympics, 66
Wolf Warrior diplomacy, 29
World Chinese Alliance in Defense of the Diaoyu Islands, 129
World Health Assembly (WHA), 83
World Health Organization (WHO), 83
World Trade Organization (WTO), 80, 83
World War I, 198
World War II, 4, 14, 45, 87
Wuqiu Islands, 194

268   *Index*

X
Xiaoping, Deng, 62

Y
Yangtze River, 158
Yeltsin, Boris, 62
Yellow Sea, 86
Yi, Wang, 66–67, 89
Yilan, 124
Ying-jeou, Ma, 130

Yinlong, 64
Yonaguni Island, 24

Z
Zedong, Mao, 59, 61
Zhanshu, Li, 67
Zhenbao/Damanskiy Island, 61
Zhongnanhai, 61, 63–64, 67–68, 71,
    123
Zwaardvis-class, 181

Printed in the USA
CPSIA information can be obtained
at www.ICGtesting.com
JSHW010959140924
69724JS00003B/266